'Ann Bernstein has written the definitive answer to Naomi Klein's hugely influential and hugely overrated No Logo. *Drawing on her deep knowledge of the relevant literature and her personal experience of South Africa, the author argues that the great contribution business can make to development is to do what modern business alone can do on a sufficiently large scale to make a dent in entrenched poverty: create wealth. It is not by acting in accordance with the muddled agendas of well-intentioned proponents of "corporate social responsibility" that business makes a positive difference. It is by being productive and profitable. This book not only offers a new agenda for the role of business in development, but is also a call to arms. Business leaders should take from it the intellectual confidence they need to defend the irreplaceable role of business, qua business.'*

Martin Wolf
Chief Economics Commentator, Financial Times

'This book is a brilliant analysis of the role of business in economic and political development. It is also an original contribution from the Global South to a debate too often dominated by voices from the rich countries.'

Peter L Berger
Professor Emeritus, Sociology and Theology, Boston University
Senior Research Fellow, Institute on Culture, Religion and World Affairs,
Boston University

'Ann Bernstein is one of the most thoughtful writers today on development and the role of business in promoting it. She offers a penetrating analysis of the question in this exciting book whose importance also derives from the fact that hers is an authentic voice from the developing world itself. It is a book that policymakers in both rich and poor countries, NGOs and international aid agencies need to read if their good intentions are to translate into good results.'

Jagdish Bhagwati
University Professor, Economics & Law, Columbia University; and Author of
In Defense of Globalization (Oxford)

'In the great war of ideas there are few more important battles than the one over the role of business in economic development. In this powerful and provocative new book Ann Bernstein skewers the fashionable doctrine of corporate social responsibility — and shows, on the basis of her formidable command of the economic literature and unrivalled knowledge of South African business, that the best way to help the poor is also the simplest: let business be business.'

Adrian Wooldridge
Columnist for *The Economist*

'Few people seem to understand the role that responsible business plays in economic development. Not through acts of philanthropy or corporate social responsibility but through core business operations. In this book Ann Bernstein shows that instead of establishing investor and business friendly environments which enable and encourage economic growth, governments seek to dabble in areas outside of their competency often with disastrous consequences. An essential read for anyone involved in international development.'

Graham MacKay
Chief Executive, SABMiller

'In both developed and more especially developing societies, the business firm, ranging from multinational to micro enterprise, is one of societies best resourced, most flexible, and indeed vital resources. In this book Ann Bernstein reviews the role businesses, both individually and collectively, have played and can play in a society's social, political and economic development. This is an important contribution to what should be one of the critical debates of our times.'

Bobby Godsell
Chairman, Business Leadership South Africa

'Both activist NGO leaders who attack business for not contributing enough to society and business leaders who have gotten into the habit of apologizing for not doing enough should get ready to rethink their views when they see Ann Bernstein's penetrating and timely critique.

To her discerning ears, the current conversation about "corporate social responsibility" (CSR) is a captive of the interests and points of view of wealthy people in wealthy countries largely located in the northern part of the globe. This book is a provocative antidote to the feel-good orientation of most CSR efforts. Bernstein deals with the realities and complexities of development and growth in the low income countries where it is most needed – and emerges with a clear-eyed, bold, and unsentimental endorsement of the enormous value that businesses can and do contribute in the societies that operate free and competitive markets. Her perspective is fresh and candid and informed – and very much worth reading and reading again.'

Professor Herman (Dutch) Leonard
George F. Baker Jr. Professor of Public Management at the Kennedy School
and Eliot I. Snider and Family Professor of Business Administration at
Harvard Business School

'This is a really good book. Its thesis is incontestably right. The trouble with Africa, and the reason it continues to lag in terms of economic development is too little business, not too much, while the dramatic economic progress in Asia has been based one thousand times more on enterprise than on any form of aid.'

Lord Renwick of Clifton
Former UK ambassador to the United States and South Africa

'Ann Bernstein forcefully knocks down some of the debilitating shibboleths about business in developing countries. By challenging the "accepted wisdom" that all too easily creeps into the development debate she forces us to think much more constructively about the role that only business can and indeed must play in alleviating the plight of the world's poor.'

Ambassador Princeton Lyman (former US ambassador to
Nigeria and South Africa)

'A much needed developing country perspective on the notions of development, commerce and the powerful benefits of capitalism.

Bernstein's book reminds us that while many parts of our global financial system is in much need of reform, there are the other, larger elements which have been responsible for the greatest, most sustained social changes in our societies. It is a siren call for business to reclaim the debate on the profound good they achieve in society.'

Nicky Oppenheimer
Chairman of De Beers

'Capitalism has no myth and so no mythic potency, unlike communism or other dream-worlds. Its legitimacy derives not from people who preach it, but from what it does. This is more than enough. As this book argues, capitalism's delivery of societal advancement, even though untidy and not always pretty as a spectacle, leaves it without any need to apologize to the dreamers who cannot see that countries are not all on the same step of history's moving staircase. For critics to be that naïve dismisses their claim to attention anyway, but it is salutary to find a highly articulate spokesperson from the one place where their petulance can be answered with authority – the world of the poor looking for work.

'It is constantly surprising to read pious statements in corporate annual reports that treat the world as universally operating under the same conditions, with the piety transferable as easily as the money. This naïveté is mentally imperialist and speaks volumes on the ignorance in boardrooms about the world's realities of poverty and fear. But it allows executives to feel better, which is what it is for. They would do better to feel less pious. They would do better to help people by giving them what THEY most need, and being proud of doing so. They would do better by reading this book.'

Gordon Redding, Professor of Asian Business, INSEAD

'Ann Bernstein is one of Africa's leading students of development. The fresh and cogent ideas she presents in this book must be taken into account by anyone interested in African or global development.'

Walter Russell Mead
Henry A Kissinger Senior Fellow in Foreign Policy
Council on Foreign Relations, New York

THE CASE FOR BUSINESS IN DEVELOPING ECONOMIES

Ann Bernstein

PENGUIN BOOKS

PENGUIN BOOKS

Published by the Penguin Group
Penguin Books (South Africa) (Pty) Ltd, 24 Sturdee Avenue, Rosebank,
Johannesburg 2196, South Africa
Penguin Group (USA) Inc, 375 Hudson Street, New York, New York 10014, USA
Penguin Group (Canada), 90 Eglinton Avenue East, Suite 700, Toronto, Ontario,
Canada M4P 2Y3 (a division of Pearson Penguin Canada Inc)
Penguin Books Ltd, 80 Strand, London WC2R 0RL, England
Penguin Ireland, 25 St Stephen's Green, Dublin 2, Ireland (a division of Penguin
Books Ltd)
Penguin Group (Australia), 250 Camberwell Road, Camberwell, Victoria 3124,
Australia (a division of Pearson Australia Group Pty Ltd)
Penguin Books India Pvt Ltd, 11 Community Centre, Panchsheel Park, New
Delhi – 110 017, India
Penguin Group (NZ), 67 Apollo Drive, Mairangi Bay, Auckland 1310, New
Zealand (a division of Pearson New Zealand Ltd)

Penguin Books (South Africa) (Pty) Ltd, Registered Offices:
24 Sturdee Avenue, Rosebank, Johannesburg 2196, South Africa

www.penguinbooks.co.za

First published by Penguin Books (South Africa) (Pty) Ltd 2010

ISBN 9780143026525

Typeset by Nix Design in 12/17 pt Elegant Garamond
Cover: Flame Design
Printed and bound by CTP Book Printers, Cape Town

TABLE OF CONTENTS

PREFACE AND ACKNOWLEDGEMENTS

This is a book in praise of enterprise and corporations. In my view business leaders should stop apologising and stand up for business! They should recognise that the battle of ideas matters.

My professional life has been spent trying to improve conditions in my country, South Africa, so that more and more fellow citizens who happen to be black can enjoy the opportunities which I and many other white South Africans take for granted. I have done this mainly by working for business-funded public interest organisations, first the Urban Foundation, and then, for the past 14 years, as executive director of the Centre for Development and Enterprise, a think-tank focusing on vital national development issues and their relationship to economic growth and democratic consolidation. As a result I have had the unusual experience (for a social scientist, policy analyst, social activist) of getting to know many senior business executives and their companies.

From this base I could never understand – and came to resent – the almost automatic assumption by many people outside the business sector that there is something fundamentally wrong with enterprise and profit making. I became tired of having to explain and justify anything to do with business in a way that no other social sector I knew of was called upon to do. I also became all too familiar with the inability – and unwillingness – of many business leaders to appreciate and respond to the broader political dynamics that played such an important role in shaping the apartheid order as well as post-apartheid society.

In the mid-1980s I met the world-renowned sociologist Peter

Berger during his first visit to South Africa. Among many other titles, Peter is the author of *The Capitalist Revolution* (written at a time when it was very unfashionable to defend capitalism), and he and I started to talk about business and its role in society. Together with Bobby Godsell, then CEO of AngloGold Ashanti and now chairman of Business Leadership South Africa, we started to think about a series of projects aimed at placing the debate about business and the public good in its proper perspective.

In 2005 I received a generous fellowship from the National Endowment for Democracy in Washington, DC which enabled me to spend 6 months in that city. This gave me the opportunity to listen to contemporary debates about business and its role in the United States and other countries from the vantage point of one of the most important capitals in the world. I was stunned by the superficiality of much of the debate about global poverty and the challenges of development, and the almost automatic assumption that the only way companies could do any good in developing countries was if they followed a script devised by activists who lived in the wealthy developed world.

These experiences prompted me to start working on this book. Following my return to South Africa, the chairman of CDE's board of trustees, Elisabeth Bradley, immediately saw the relevance of this project for CDE's mission, and this ensured that I could complete the manuscript while continuing to run the organisation.

As invariably happens in the course of a project such as this, I have built up a long list of people I need to thank for their encouragement and assistance in one way or another.

I have learnt a great deal of what I know about business, its role in society, and the challenges this sector faces in trying to act beyond individual (often diverging) company interests from a large number of people. In particular I want to thank Bobby Godsell, Mike Spicer, Robin Lee, Elisabeth Bradley, Fred Phaswana and Laurie Dippenaar for everything I have learnt from them over the years.

Irene Menell, Lawrie Schlemmer, Jeff McCarthy, Soto Ndukwana and Charles Simkins – mentors, colleagues, and friends – have generously shared their knowledge with me in the course of many (some heated) discussions.

Riaan de Villiers, Robin Lee, and Sandy Johnston helped to distil this text from a much longer manuscript, and curbed my rhetorical flourishes. Stefan Schirmer helped with research, and in particular contributed substantially to Chapter 5. Megan McGarry diligently provided the references.

This book would not have been written without the support of Peter Berger, who – besides providing me with funding from his organisation – encouraged me to write it, sustained his faith in me over a long period, and has influenced my thinking in many areas.

Two people who were very important to me died while I wrote this book. My father Harold Bernstein was a model of how to live as a decent man in an unjust society and a difficult world. Throughout my life, he – and my mother, Jean – gave me the confidence and belief that I could set out to do anything I wanted to do, and succeed. These two remarkable and generous people have supported me in everything I have ever done, have provided guarantees of financial backing when required (personally and organisationally), and have been the best unpaid PR firm anyone could wish for.

Helen Suzman was my Member of Parliament, my employer for a short period, and subsequently a close friend. She profoundly influenced my life – from correcting my English to helping to shape the way in which I see South African politics, parliamentary leadership, and personal courage. She strongly believed in the power of market economies to undermine apartheid, and would have supported the central theses of this book – both the power of companies to do good, and the need for business leaders to be more aware of their own interests and to speak out with greater moral courage.

I hope this book will help to persuade at least some business leaders to stop apologising, stop appeasing their critics, stop saying one thing in the privacy of their homes and something else in public, and be proud of what they and the vast majority of successful companies are doing. And if they start to do that, they can have a significant impact on the most important question of how to increase and sustain economic growth, particularly for those people and countries that are not a part of the more developed richer world.

INTRODUCTION

'The 20th century could be regarded as the century of
the modern joint-stock company. It was also the most
economically successful century in human history – the
world's population rose fourfold, and world output per head
rose sixfold. This is no accident. The private limited liability
company has proved to be the world's most powerful engine
of innovation, large-scale organization and transmission of
know-how across frontiers. It is the responsibility of business
to make this case clearly and powerfully.'

Martin Wolf, 'Corporate Responsibility' (2004)

AN AGGRESSIVELY critical view of the role of business in society has gained ground in recent years. The book *No Logo* by the Canadian journalist Naomi Klein is a prominent recent example.

This rather strange work has been enormously popular and influential. Undeterred by its tenuous link with reality, and lack of serious analysis, newspapers and magazines, including *The New York Times*, *The Guardian*, *The Observer* and *Time* magazine, have lauded Klein and her book as 'a movement bible' (Brooke 2000), 'intelligently written, superbly reported', and 'the anti-corporate manifesto for Generation Why' (Knight 2000). While packaging these ideas in a distinctive way – and taking some of them to a new extreme – *No Logo* essentially repeats a set of criticisms of business in general and large corporations in particular adopted by many other critics and activists. These currently fashionable articles of faith have strongly influenced public views and perceptions, and have helped to fuel the 'corporate social responsibility' movement.

Klein takes anti-business rhetoric to new heights. Among other things, multinational corporations are accused of 'mining the planet's poorest back country for unimaginable profits'; carrying 'the torch of authoritarianism' around the globe; and 'stunting human development'. Free trade zones are described as 'miniature military states' with military-style management, abusive supervisors, and below-subsistence wages. In the Kleinian universe, entire countries are being turned into 'industrial slums and low wage labour ghettoes', where workers do not earn enough to 'adequately feed themselves, let alone stimulate the local economy'. The notion of 'industrialisation in the context of globalisation' is rejected as a 'myth'.

Besides these transgressions, corporations are committing a string of crimes against the natural environment, the food supply, indigenous people, and their cultures. Mass-produced corporate logos and slogans create a kind of 'cultural fascism', Klein declares, with little opportunity for criticism because 'our newspapers, television stations, internet services, streets and retail spaces are all controlled by corporate interests'.

As if they weren't busy enough already, corporations are also 'the most powerful political forces of our time'. She asserts that 'corporations like Shell and Wal-Mart bask in budgets bigger than the gross domestic product of most nations', and the top 100 economies consist of 51 multinationals and only 49 countries. 'Democracy is ineffective compared to corporate power,' she declares. What good is an open, accountable parliament 'if opaque corporations are setting so much of the global political agenda in the back rooms?'

As the ruling political bodies of our era, Klein believes that corporations set the agenda of globalisation. Citizens must go after companies because 'we have more influence on a brand name than we do with our own governments'.

Like all works informed more by emotion than reason, Klein's book has a certain heady appeal. The reader is carried along by a stream of rhetoric, which forms a closed discourse largely unrelated to the facts. Among other difficulties, Klein confuses media hype and advertising with the whole of social reality; fails to understand the nature of poverty in poor countries; confuses brand marketing with a lack of political or economic choices; defines a handful of street anarchists as a significant social movement; and presents evidence of criticism as mass support for a political cause.

The book displays little knowledge of or interest in accepted economic or political analysis, and fails to appreciate the difference between a 'factoid' and statistics. Like many activists, Klein assumes that her views represent those of millions of people – 'the citizens' of a country, and even the world.

Nonetheless, her views (and those of other corporate critics) are widely accepted by and reflected in the media and popular discussion, if in less exaggerated form. And if you think the reaction to *No Logo* was an aberration of pre-9/11 America, her latest book, *The Shock Doctrine*, which accuses companies of creating, causing, and profiting from political and natural disasters, from wars to hurricanes, is receiving similar popular respect and attention.

Books and views such as Klein's help to create a climate in which companies are painted as social outlaws who need fundamentally to change their ways. Instead of provoking vigorous reaction to what amounts to the moral delegitimation of business, this determined if ill-founded attack has been met for the most part by appeasement in corporate circles. This acquiescence has given rise to the burgeoning industry of 'corporate social responsibility'.

This book rebuts every one of Klein's emotional assertions about companies with facts, analysis, and experience, mainly drawn from developing country settings. I will argue that companies should not let such attacks stand unchallenged, and should certainly not repeat the 'factoids' that provide the shaky foundation for this body of ideas, which a number of corporate leaders have done.

The conviction driving this book is that, instead of appeasing their critics, corporations, business leaders, and business organisations should vigorously promote market economics and the role of companies as powerful instruments of progress, innovation, and development. It stems from an unusual source: South African business under apartheid.

BUSINESS AND APARTHEID

South Africa's Truth and Reconciliation Commission (TRC) was into the fourth day of a special week of hearings devoted to business and its role in the apartheid era. The doyens of South African business – captains of commerce and industry, and heads of English, Afrikaner, and African business organisations – had been called to account for their sins of omission and commission under the legally sanctioned system of racial discrimination and enforced segregation that comprised South Africa's notorious system of apartheid.

The commissioners were looking for contrition by business leaders and organisations. They wanted apologies from the tycoons representing the country's large and vibrant business sector. And, most of the time, they got what they wanted, especially from Afrikaner business people, who came to apologise for doing what the previous government had wanted them to do, and seeking to curry favour with the next government.

But not everyone stuck to this script. Eventually, Johann Rupert, son of one of the country's most successful Afrikaner entrepreneurs, who now runs the Rupert family's global empire, said in an exasperated tone: 'Would you have preferred Ernest Oppenheimer to have settled in Australia rather than in South Africa?'

Oppenheimer arrived in South Africa from Germany in 1902 and started working for a diamond brokerage for one pound a week. When he died in November 1957 the company he had founded in 1917, the Anglo American Corporation, controlled 40 per cent of South Africa's gold, half of its coal, and almost a sixth of the world's copper. Anglo had major stakes in South African paper production, platinum mining, fishing industries, and fruit farms, and a controlling stake in AE&CI, then the biggest explosives enterprise in the world. Oppenheimer also chaired De Beers, which controlled 80 per cent of the world's diamonds.

At the time of the TRC hearings on business in 1997, Anglo American was the dominant conglomerate in South Africa, and the largest corporation in Africa. By 2006 Anglo American plc was listed on the London and Johannesburg stock exchanges, and ranked as a Fortune 500 company. Its annual revenue amounted to US$38 637 million, and it employed 209 000 people around the world.

Anglo American helped to create and drive South Africa's industrialisation, from its mining base in gold, diamonds and other minerals into manufacturing and banking. South Africa's business community, led by Anglo and successive governments, helped to build the most urbanised, industrialised, and developed country on the continent.

The Oppenheimer family and the company they had built *did* oppose the apartheid state. They spoke out about the economic, political and moral consequences of apartheid, helped to fund the Progressive Party, the small liberal opposition party represented in the whites-only parliament by Helen Suzman, and supported many other anti-apartheid initiatives, people and ideas. Nonetheless, Anglo, like other companies, operated within the confines of the country's racially defined and racist laws, and paid taxes that helped to finance the apartheid state.

Despite this ambiguous legacy, the strength of South African business (even after operating under siege for most of the 1980s) meant that the African National Congress (ANC), elected to lead the first democratic government, inherited sub-Saharan Africa's strongest economy many times over when it won the first inclusive elections of 1994, and rose to power.

Rupert's question to the TRC was therefore a searching and challenging one. Would South Africa have been a better place without entrepreneurs such as (later Sir Ernest) Oppenheimer, Anglo American, and the rest of South African business? In asking this question, he effectively raised the issue of business and its role in developing countries in a way that challenged much of the conventional wisdom about business, globalisation and the developing world.

In that week of the TRC hearing, I was called as one of two independent expert witnesses on the role of business. On the morning of my presentation I was struck by a news item. Nelson Mandela, global human rights icon, leader of the South African political 'miracle', and president of the new democratic state, was visiting the People's Republic of China. From the steps of the Forbidden City, he called on South African business to invest in China – a repressive, semi-totalitarian state noted for various human rights violations, including the incarceration of hundreds of political prisoners.

The TRC hearings were not set up to deal with Mandela's call for business to invest in 'bad' countries, or how this chimed with the disinvestment campaign led by the ANC against apartheid South Africa. The formal agenda also did not allow for reflection on whether the founder of South Africa's largest business empire should rather have sailed on past South Africa, with its history of racial division and conflict, and gone to build up Australia or some other country instead.

But I was intrigued by the issues which the hearings had brought to life and, in some respects, avoided. The result is this book, and what it has to say about business, its broader social role, and the battle of ideas about corporations, development, and the public good. It is informed not only by the TRC experience but by many years of living, working, and championing the role of business in growth and development in a middle-income developing country.

If one looks at South Africa in relation to the rest of Africa, one sees a society with a sound infrastructure, world-class cities, a large number of civil society institutions, a stock exchange eleven times the size of its next African rival, and the largest airport and retail shopping centre on the continent. The telephones work, one can drink the water, drive on tarred roads lit by electricity, and bank, shop, work, and play in excellent facilities. Of course, one also sees a society that is still deeply divided and unequal, with too many communities living in poverty, largely because of the terrible policy of apartheid and the consequences of one of its greatest 'crimes': inferior education for black South Africans.

One nevertheless has to ask: 'Why does South Africa differ so markedly from the rest of Africa?' Certainly not because of apartheid. Nor are we different from the rest of Africa because of our gold, platinum, uranium and other minerals; many African countries are richly endowed with primary resources.

One of the key reasons we are different is because Ernest Oppenheimer and others like him came to South Africa and not to Australia; and because the South African business sector, and the black and white South Africans who have worked in it, have helped to build a strong, vibrant private sector with significant capacity in relative terms. That capacity not only makes us different from many other developing countries, but gives us hope that this new democracy will make it.

Although uncomfortable in some respects, the ability of companies to adapt to almost any political regime is in many ways a great asset. The durability of economic enterprise – often requiring steady nerves in the midst of turbulence – has given democratic South Africa one of its greatest strengths. We have emerged from decades of authoritarian and racist rule with a large, energetic, and reasonably competitive business sector which puts us at a considerable advantage compared with many other societies outside the industrialised world.

This positive legacy does not receive the acknowledgement it deserves. For various reasons, many South Africans deny the role of the business sector in South Africa's achievements, and when they praise it, they do so grudgingly. This is not really surprising, because business in many countries is treated with scepticism, suspicion, and downright hostility.

BUSINESS, APPEASEMENT, AND THE BATTLE OF IDEAS

This is a book about business, and the battle of ideas about capitalism, development, democracy, global civil society, poverty, and economic growth. This tale has its roots in southern Africa, but stretches from Brussels to Bangalore, from Washington to 'the wild west' of South Africa and many other emerging markets in the developing world.

A central message of this book is that the ongoing conversation about business and society is dominated by the perspectives and interests of those who live in rich countries. Most activists, analysts, and others in rich western countries – however well-meaning they may be – do not grasp the realities of poverty and the hard choices of development outside the rich industrialised world. As a result, the debate about business, 'responsibility', and corporate involvement in development is distorted, with few voices from developing countries being heard.

A second theme is how business leaders and their companies have responded to the attacks on profit-making as a respectable contribution to society. In almost all cases, business leaders have given in without a struggle, and accepted the general charge that companies need to 'do more' than 'just' business in order to contribute to society. Instead of boldly and persuasively making the case for business, we have seen a process of appeasement. Very few business leaders are proudly, loudly, and unapologetically making the case for business as an honourable activity that benefits society in numerous ways. Instead, companies are adopting the ideas, language, and framework of their critics and inviting activists into their midst to help them 'reform' their ways.

Many corporate social responsibility (CSR) advocates imply that capitalism is essentially rapacious, and must be transformed before it destroys all before it. Market fundamentalists argue that 'the business of business is business', and that anything else constitutes destructive socialism. Respected commentators tell business to 'do no harm', which is a misguided injunction when one thinks of the 'creative destruction' inherent in the innovative, efficiency-seeking processes of capitalism. None of these approaches captures the reality or complexity of business and society in general, and especially in developing countries.

A new approach and a new discourse are required to cut through an increasingly flawed conversation, with potentially dangerous consequences for the poor and for developing countries in particular. This is the challenge this book tries to address.

In the first third of the book, I argue that capitalism has won, but business is on the defensive. Business is not a separate vested interest operating outside of society. Its interests are not different from the rest of the general public. An expanding, inclusive business sector lies firmly at the heart of a 'good' society which will not work as well as it should if it regards this prime source of its wealth, jobs, innovation and taxes with distrust and suspicion. I critically unpack the assumptions that underpin conventional ideas about 'corporate responsibility', especially those that adversely affect developing countries. The CSR agenda does not help business or society to focus their attention on issues that encourage more entrepreneurs and greater business activity, improve the rules governing competitive market systems, or persuade the rest of society that the larger public interest is served by expanding corporate activity and not by curbing or continually attacking it.

In the rest of the book, I develop the case for business.

The myriad benefits conferred on numerous stakeholders across the globe by a large company's sustained economic performance is in sharp contrast to the devastation wrought by fraudsters like Bernie Madoff or short-term results from a company like Enron. Such sustained economic performance (rather than any other measure) should be the first dimension of good corporate citizenship.

Examining the remarkable contribution of successful companies to innovation, wealth creation, employment, training and numerous other societal benefits helps to underline the vital importance of private firms, which are at the heart of the development process. In addition to these visible and slightly better known – although much too little talked about – aspects of corporate social contribution, I introduce a further dimension, that of a company's indirect impact or 'invisible corporate citizenship'.

This phenomenon concerns the unintended, unexpected positive spin-offs from successful companies. Through their everyday activities, businesses have a revolutionary impact on people and places, inadvertently acting as 'beachheads' for democracy, human rights, the rule of law, greater opportunities for women and other disadvantaged sections of particular societies.

In its direct impact, then, business transforms individual lives and powers national development. Indirectly, companies act as transmission belts for modernisation and 'stalking horses' for democratisation.

In addition to both of these rich and complex contributions from normal profit making activity, there are actions that companies can and should take 'beyond the factory gate' that are in their own interests. I put forward a set of principles for guiding a more strategic approach to business social investments, particularly focused on developing countries.

Many important issues are missing in the current discourse about companies and society. The most important is the role of nation states, and how effective governments can create an enabling environment for economic development – driven by competitive domestic and international business activity – that could quickly result in phenomenal advances for the majority of the citizens.

It is time to recast the nature of the conversation about business, within business itself, in the media, academia, politics, and the wider world of public policy. What is required is a more comprehensive and therefore more accurate understanding of business and society. In so doing, we need to develop a new language for talking about business and its role in the 21st century.

And in case I am misunderstood, this is not a book that argues companies can do no wrong or that all that is required from business leaders is to run profitable enterprises. Far from it. The astute reader who goes through each chapter until the end will see that I am trying to carve out and define a new approach to business and society that is grounded in a more comprehensive accurate understanding of business and its many impacts; and that is also cognisant of the fallibility of all human institutions and individuals, including companies and business leaders. The book aims to create a new conversation about the roles and responsibilities of companies and their leaders that is based in their own interests as well as the wider society; and that recognises the difficult challenges and choices confronting companies in the complex realities of our modern world.

Business leaders should stop playing defence. They should stand up for competitive markets, business, freer trade, and globalisation. They should promote competition as a vital element for harnessing the maximum social benefits of corporate endeavour. They should publicly speak out about the misdeeds of companies that defraud the public or engage in corruption in developing countries.

The case for business has not been fundamentally undermined by the global economic crisis of 2008/9 and beyond. The complex causes and nature of this crisis do not affect the argument in this book.

Do we need to rethink capitalism? It's important to remember that the market-based system as a whole has not failed. Over the past three decades, market economics have lifted hundreds of millions of people out of poverty. The financial subsystem has failed. It now needs careful, thorough modification that avoids the dangers of under-regulated financial markets and the slower – but no less deadly – poison of excessive financial market regulation, which encourages rent-seeking, bad decisions, and curbs innovation.

Whatever the weaknesses of our current capitalist financial arrangements – and they have turned out to be considerable – the history of the world, particularly since World War Two, has demonstrated beyond dispute that every other system of economic organisation is far worse.

I argue throughout the book that corporate critics and 'responsibility' advocates are distracting attention away from the real issues facing business, market design, and development. This has been demonstrated in the financial meltdown that began in 2008. We have seen global economic imbalances, with China amassing enormous surpluses and the world's largest economy, the United States, living well beyond its means; the failure of government oversight and regulation; the creation of a global financial market with companies 'too big to fail', accompanied by a culture of greed, irresponsibility, and a lack of integrity among their managers.

The ironies of the crisis abound, and their consequences are severe.

While business critics have focused on multinational corporations and their supposed 'misdeeds', they have ignored the importance of the state as the key 'designer' of markets and enforcer of effective regulation – so clearly one cause of the global economic and financial crisis that began in early 2008.

While almost every large Wall Street bank and its equivalents in other mainly rich countries have signed on to onerous new global standards for disbursing project finance in developing countries, these same banks have been taking inordinate risks themselves, neglecting sound governance, and exhibiting levels of greed and fraudulent practice that have resulted in the global crisis that began in 2008.

And while the corporate critics have put more and more obstacles in the way of companies investing in countries outside the industrialised world, the results of the crisis, and measures to deal with it, are severely affecting many developing countries. Rich world protectionism could harm the prospects of certain poorer countries for years, and the global supply of capital will be monopolised by rich countries' debts, thus in all likelihood starving many developing countries of much-needed foreign investment.

None of these issues was front and centre of the global movement on corporate 'responsibility'. And as companies struggle for survival in a harsh downturn, unemployment rises, and numerous developing countries see foreign investment receding from their shores, the importance of freer global trade and the developing world's need for investment are underlined.

Whatever new form of capitalism emerges out of the ashes of the crash of 2008, it will be based on market economics, some new rules for finance capital and a new definition of the appropriate roles of and relationships between markets and states.

Competitive companies will continue to play a vital role.

They do not need social goals to contribute to the public good. Good intentions are not required for market forces to produce beneficial social results – enlightened self-interest operating within reasonably effective states ensuring domestic order and effective competition will suffice.

It's time business had the confidence and strategic vision to stop apologising, develop its own public agenda, and start propagating the phenomenal benefits of competitive capitalism for the less developed countries of the world.

PART
ONE

Capitalism won. Why is business so defensive?

Chapter One

MISCONCEPTIONS ABOUT BUSINESS AND GLOBALISATION

'A corporation in its normal activities is something good; something fantastic; something worth encouraging. And this directly contradicts the starting point for many advocates of CSR that a corporation is bad and irresponsible, and they have to compensate for their existence by doing something more than making a profit; by giving something back to the community. On the contrary – when a corporation makes a profit, it is an indication that they have already given something to the community.'

Johan Norberg, 'Why corporations shouldn't be socially responsible: a critical examination of CSR' (2003a)

IN 1997 I attended the launch of the Corporate Citizenship unit of the University of Warwick. Funded by BP, the unit was inaugurated with a three-day workshop on 'cutting edge' issues relating to corporate social responsibility. Coming from South Africa, this was my first exposure to what I came to understand was the growing international Corporate Social Responsibility (CSR) movement. A burgeoning set of interests – consultants, academics, business schools, managers within business, international NGOs, managers within multilateral organisations – had begun to develop around the expanding industry of 'telling business how to improve its behaviour'.

I was struck by a number of anomalies. There was a distinct lack of rigour about the topic at hand. What exactly was 'sustainable development', and what did this term mean for individual companies and their operations? Coming from a middle-income developing country, I knew how much we did not know about multiple issues, and the complexity of many of the issues we faced. And yet conference participants – representatives of international NGOs, corporate affairs managers, and a few senior executives, nearly all from rich industrialised countries – were quite prepared to expound on what was or wasn't good for developing countries around the globe.

The conference was infused by and built upon the assumption that business had a case to answer. I was taken aback by the way in which business representatives acquiesced in the attacks on corporate activity, and the surprisingly long list of areas in which they were being told to 'do more'.

I have subsequently attended two conferences presented by the world's largest CSR organisation, the United States-based Business for Social Responsibility, where all these impressions were confirmed.

I have spent my professional life working in business-funded organisations in South Africa, and together with others have thought a great deal about the role of the private sector in one rather unusual developing country. How best to promote social change in a deeply divided country? Could business help to get rid of apartheid, and did they do enough to oppose it? How can private corporations help to lift millions of South Africans out of poverty? How could companies and the organisations they fund help to consolidate a fragile new democracy? Could business leaders use their influence to improve state policies and programmes?

This book is a product of the growing disjuncture between my experience of working with companies in South Africa and wrestling with the hard realities of poverty in a developing country; and the global CSR movement, particularly its prescriptions for and impact on developing countries.

CSR — ITS SCOPE AND IDEAS

Some of the principles and practices of CSR date back more than a century, but interest in this area of corporate behaviour resurged in the United States and other industrialised countries in the 1960s and 1970s. Many current CSR strategies were developed in this period. These include voluntary codes of conduct; shareholder activism; the notion of 'socially responsible' investment; assessment by NGOs and others of corporate environmental performance; campaigns against individual companies or industrial sectors; the use of corporations as sites for political activity.

Since the early 1990s the CSR movement has expanded tremendously. It now encompasses hundreds of books, how-to manuals, websites, codes of conduct, university advocacy units, business schools, professional associations, multilateral organisations, and reports by companies around the world. Governments and international organisations are increasingly encouraging, prescribing or mandating various social, environmental and human rights practices to corporations. As *The Economist* has put it: 'CSR is thriving; it is now an industry in itself' (2004).

CSR is marked by its wide-ranging focus and rapid spread around the world. CSR advocates continue to address domestic corporate policies such as employment practices, investment priorities, and community engagement, but are increasingly concentrating on the conduct of multinational corporations, especially their operations in developing countries. Key issues are corporate responsibilities in respect of labour, human rights, and the environment.

The CSR movement

In this chapter I will unpack some of the key ideas and assumptions underpinning what could fairly be termed the CSR movement. I don't claim that every organisation or CSR advocate necessarily concurs with each of these ideas, but I do believe many would support most of the ideas which comprise the CSR view of the world.

Sometimes these ideas are stated openly, often they are taken for granted, and arguments for action built upon implicit assumptions. More and more companies are hiring activists and sympathisers from within the movement to help design their response to the issues raised.

The CSR 'literature' is a body of information whose size far outweighs its analytical precision. It consists overwhelmingly of corporate PR or advocacy material. Few objective academic studies can be found. When reading corporate material, it is difficult to distinguish between marketing and social investment. Corporate decisions are frequently made behind closed doors.

The impacts of CSR are inadequately analysed; commentators enumerate or extol projects undertaken or money spent, but seldom evaluate the impact of the programmes in question.

Defining CSR

There is no universally agreed definition of CSR. At its root, however, is the idea that the actions of companies and corporations are inherently tainted; that business activity is not only inadequate in some sense but actively harmful; and that CSR is required to ameliorate the inherently negative effects of entrepreneurial activity.

One critic has remarked that the core idea of CSR is the notion that companies have more stakeholders than shareholders! With the former including customers, employees, business partners, local and regional communities, environmental interest groups, and others. Companies are supposed to integrate the interests of all those 'stakeholders' in their everyday decisions. In other words, companies should no longer focus solely on making profits, but need to attend to a 'triple bottom line' consisting of social, environmental, and financial results.

Harvard University's Kennedy School of Government, which now has a special CSR unit, has defined CSR to encompass '… not only what companies do with their profits, but also how they make them. It goes beyond philanthropy and compliance to address the manner in which companies manage their economic, social and environmental impacts and their stakeholder relationships in all their key spheres of influence: the workplace, the marketplace, the supply chain, the community and the public policy realm' (Kyle & Ruggie 2005: 9).

Other definitions include:

Business for Social Responsibility: 'Operating a business in a way that meets or exceeds the ethical, legal, commercial and public expectations that society has of business. Social responsibility (should become) a guiding principle for every decision made, in every area of a business' (online).

European Commission: 'A concept whereby companies integrate social and environmental concerns in their business operations and in their interactions with their stakeholders on a voluntary basis' (online).

Institute of Business Ethics: 'The voluntary actions taken by a company to address the ethical, social and environmental impacts of its business operations and the concerns of its principal stakeholders' (online).

World Bank: 'The commitment of business to contribute to sustainable economic development – working with employees, their families, the local community and society at large to improve the quality of life in ways that are both good for business and good for development' (United States Government Accountability Office 2005: 6).

Not surprisingly, there is no consensus on what constitutes virtuous corporate behaviour. Are investments in non-democratic countries always immoral? Is it wrong to take advantage of lower labour and other costs in developing countries? Should companies pay market or 'living' wages? Should the interests of consumers or workers predominate?

However, when one delves into the huge (and growing) body of information on this topic, it is possible to unpack some of the key ideas, assumptions and misconceptions that underpin many people's approach to the relationship between business and society.

MISCONCEPTIONS ABOUT BUSINESS

One of the core ideas informing the CSR movement, and the world view of the NGOs, academics, and consultants who drive it, is their perception (explicit or implicit) that business is only interested in profits. Most of them know very few if any successful business people, and even fewer understand the nature of enterprise, risk-taking, and the demands of running organisations that produce competitive goods and services.

Business is motivated by more than profits

Anyone who has ever talked to a major entrepreneur or senior company executive will know that although profit is a key motivator, it is not the only factor driving participants in corporate endeavour. Great businessmen have generally been characterised by vision, hard work, stubbornness, perseverance, discipline, healthy egos, and a sense of personal satisfaction. Business is often a creative activity of mobilising people, resources, finance, and putting it all together at the right time at the right price to meet an identified need before someone else does. There is satisfaction and excitement in meeting new challenges, and coping with technical and organisational difficulties. Many business people derive satisfaction from providing a service that meets people's needs. Competition with other companies is also a factor, as is peer pressure.

Profit should not be equated with greed

Underlying much of the pressure on business is a misunderstanding of what companies are there for, and how their contribution to society can best be measured. This is the notion that making profits for shareholders is immoral, or at best amoral, and that a company can only meet its social responsibilities by doing other things beyond its profit-making role. This perspective fails to appreciate the role of profits in market-based activity.

The value people place on the goods and services they obtain from various companies is demonstrated by what they are willing to pay. The costs of producing those goods and services are a measure of what society has to surrender to consume some of those products. If what people pay exceeds the cost, society has gained, and the company has made a profit. 'So profits are a guide (by no means a perfect one but a guide nonetheless) to the value that companies create for society' (*The Economist* 2005). They perform a signalling function. If an enterprise does not make a profit its survival requires remedial action – change product or production process or location; pay less; or lobby for a change in laws, regulations or taxes. The permutations are endless, and keep business schools fully occupied, not to mention competing entrepreneurs. Without the profit motive the process of learning through market success or failure – one of the mainsprings of wealth and innovation – would not take place.

Many critics fail to appreciate another dimension of profit-making. They see a company's results for one year and assume that its declared profits are paid out to shareholders or owners. They do not allow for the investments that all companies need to make – in research and development, employee training, capital equipment, restructuring – to ensure that they remain competitive.

Those who see the pursuit of profits as a symptom of greed not only fail to understand their role in the market system, but ignore the 'moral benefits' of self-interested economic activity. Greed and profit are different concepts, as are greed and self-interest. The kind of self-interest that advances the public good is rational. The calculation of self-interest makes a firm or manager worry about its reputation for honesty, fair dealing, paying debts, and honouring agreements. Such companies look beyond the short term and plan ahead, sacrificing in the present for the sake of gains in the future. These are all important individual and civic attributes. Entrepreneurs make good neighbours because they protect their assets, look after their 'shop', want a crime-free neighbourhood for themselves, their employees and customers (Sternberg 2000).

Companies are often criticised for exploiting workers, and making excessive profits. Thus, if a designer jacket sells for $190 in New York while the worker abroad who sews it gets only 60 cents an hour, this is regarded as a prime example of exploitation. But, as Jagdish Bhagwati (2004b) has pointed out, there is no necessary relationship between the price of a specific product and the wages paid by a company in order to produce it. For every jacket that sells, nine may not, so the effective price of a jacket is $19, not $190. Moreover, duties and distribution costs almost double the price of a jacket between the time it arrives in the United States and finds its way to department stores.

Critics claim that multinational corporations earn huge 'monopoly profits' while paying their workers minimal wages, and should share those 'excess profits' with their workers. But, far from enjoying a monopoly, nearly all multinationals operate in increasingly competitive global environments.

Even though companies pursue profit, this should not be interpreted to mean that they profit at the public's expense. The magic of competition and markets are that they enable consumers and society as a whole to benefit from the self-interested activities of private enterprises. Consider what would happen if companies did not try to make a profit. They would soon go bankrupt, and the jobs and products they create would disappear.

A false choice

Adherents to the CSR world view frequently have a simplistic, unrealistic view of business. Even the most rational commentators believe that companies bribe, lie, and cheat as a matter of routine. Here again they misunderstand the nature of enterprise, and tend to equate non-CSR companies with either the worst imperialist companies in the 19th century, or the gross misbehaviour by a few American companies in Latin America in the 1950s and 1960s.

Actually, as Sternberg (2000) demonstrates in her excellent book on business ethics, companies that lie and cheat cannot expect to stay in business even if their actions are technically legal. Dishonest companies will be unable to borrow, obtain working capital, or establish the trust that marks ongoing relationships among partners, customers, suppliers, and consumers. Business requires respect for property rights – of all kinds.

Successful business is based on reciprocity and a network of relationships based on trust, reliability, and consistency. When people cannot be trusted, markets work badly. When a buyer pays cash for a recognisable item, trust is not needed. But most transactions are not as straightforward as that. In a well-run economy, business centres on the ability to make credible promises. Wholesale diamond dealers in New York exchange bags of diamonds worth millions of dollars without written contracts. A handshake with the words '*mazal u'brache*' (with luck and a blessing) creates a binding agreement. Anyone who breaches a contract loses the business not only of the person cheated, but also of all the other traders (McMillan 2002: 57).

Employers need employees to behave honourably and responsibly; workers need managers and owners to do the same; lenders need honest banks, and vice versa. In general it is reasonable to conclude that bad ethics is bad for business, and that good ethics facilitates successful long-term business activity. Some enterprises and executives behave badly, but, as in other spheres of life, these are individual actions, not a necessary feature of business itself.

For many business critics, what constitutes ethical conduct in business depends on how one defines the essential purpose of an enterprise. As we will see in the course of this book, many so-called business misdeeds turn out to be examples of misunderstandings – either of the purpose of business, or the nature of poverty in developing countries.

How responsible is the notion of the triple bottom line?

Measuring profits is a complex but reasonably straightforward activity. Assessing environmental protection or social justice is a different issue altogether. The notion of a triple bottom line – if taken seriously – is an incomprehensible one.

'Management has failed if it fails to produce financial results. It has failed if it does not supply goods and services desired by consumers at a price the latter are willing to pay and if it does not improve or at least maintain the wealth producing capacity of the economic resources entrusted to it' (Drucker 1954).

The notion of business needing to account for its performance financially, socially, and environmentally emerges from the stakeholder theory of capitalism. Business must certainly take stakeholders into account. However, there are a number of problems with this theory. It maintains that all stakeholders are equally important, and that companies should answer to each of them in a similar way. But, if one set of stakeholders – the company's owners – are not happy with its performance, this has far bigger implications than the views of any other stakeholder.

To think that companies are answerable in some way to 'the community' or 'society' assumes that communities or societies only encompass one point of view, which they rarely do. How can companies answer to the multiplicity of interests and concerns that exist even in smaller communities?

The second problem with stakeholder theory concerns accountability. Of course business is affected by and impacts upon various interests and groupings in the societies in which they operate, but to conclude from this that it is accountable to those interests makes no sense. Sternberg (2000) illustrates this brilliantly: the fact that business must take terrorists into account does not make companies accountable to them. Nor does the fact that terrorists are affected by businesses give them any right to control them.

The argument that business is accountable to so many extraneous entities actually undermines proper business accountability. Stakeholder theory argues that managers should take account of the interests of all stakeholders in their firm (including not only financial claimants but also employees, customers, communities, government officials, and – theoretically – environmentalists, terrorists and blackmailers). Because these advocates of stakeholder theory are unable or unwilling to specify how firms should balance these competing interests, they leave managers with a theory that makes it impossible for them to make purposeful decisions. According to Sternberg, this theory could be attractive to managers and directors. In substituting a notional accountability to all stakeholders for direct accountability to owners, the stakeholder approach makes it impossible to hold business properly to account. And a business that is accountable to all is effectively accountable to no one.

If stakeholder theory discards the objective traditional measure for evaluating business action – financial viability – how does it suggest performance should be evaluated? Should workers' wages be sacrificed for environmental reasons, for example? It is only if the economic bottom line is sound that any other issues can be tackled.

Why should shareholders be the least important stake-holders?

One of the fallacies of CSR concerns those who profit from business activity. Shareholder returns depend entirely on company profits: no profits, no dividends. If a company is liquidated, all the shareholders are entitled to is whatever remains of the company's wealth – if any – after it has met its liabilities to its creditors, be they employees, banks, suppliers, or other outside entities.

When managers bow to pressures from extra-business interests, they do so at the expense of the rights and interests of real stakeholders, namely its investors or creditors. As Milton Friedman once put it: 'Why is it that when [a company] gives money to a worthy cause it serves a high moral objective, while a company that provides a good return to small investors – who simply put their money into their own retirement funds or a children's college fund – is somehow selfish?' (*Reason* 2005).

Companies invested in social issues long before the CSR movement

Almost from the beginning shareholder companies have been involved in issues outside the factory gate. To many, this was simply an extension of the norms of 'basic decency' which they applied in their dealings with a wider world of social need and charity.

The multinational Procter & Gamble pioneered disability and retirement pensions in 1915; moved to an eight-hour working day in 1918; guaranteed work for at least 48 weeks a year in the 1920s; and, during the depression, kept lay-offs to a minimum. Henry Heinz paid for education in citizenship for his workers. Henry Ford became a global hero by paying workers $5 a day (Micklethwait & Wooldridge 2005: 111).

CSR as defined by activists or corporate critics is not the only way in which companies can play a role outside the factory gate.

CSR is built upon a static, selective understanding of business

The whole edifice of CSR seems to ignore the volatile nature of capitalism. Firms in a competitive environment are profoundly insecure. Corporations come and go; few members of the Fortune 500 remain there for long.

CSR focuses almost exclusively on big corporations, largely ignoring small and medium-sized enterprises, which dominate most economies. There are about 24,7 million small and medium-sized businesses in the United States, which generated 60 to 80 per cent of net new jobs and more than half of non-farm private gross domestic product during the past decade. They employ about half of all private sector employees, and pay nearly 45 per cent of the private American payroll (US Small Business Administration 2008). Despite this, there is not much interest in promoting CSR in this sector of the company spectrum. CSR advocates usually talk about it as an afterthought, or not at all. This raises important issues about what CSR really sets out to achieve, for how many people, and to what end.

Business doesn't owe society for the right to operate

This idea is a frequent refrain from CSR advocates, and increasingly from business leaders as well. The notion is that because of globalisation and society's largesse in letting businesses operate and make profits, they are in debt to society, which they need to pay back in the form of 'good behaviour'. Some go further, arguing that business has been given privileges which impose costs on communities, nations and the environment. Therefore business must pay something additional back to society for imposing those costs.

This is a very strange idea. This argument presupposes that companies are separate or distinct from the societies in which they operate; that, somehow, those societies stop outside the companies' door. But companies operating in any society are operating within a legal framework created by the national government and pay local and national taxes which an effective state should allocate for the benefit of citizens. Profits from these companies accrue to individuals, pension funds, sometimes governments who choose or are able to buy their shares.

Corporations and company law, including the principle of limited liability, should rather be viewed as a package of tools and arrangements that enable some people to take large risks, and by so doing enable lots of other people, sometimes everyone else, to benefit.

It is true that business operates in a political and social context that differs from country to country. How business engages with that political context plays a major role in how the politics around business within a particular society might play out. A 'licence to operate' is a part of the strategic reality with which business must contend, and yet another reason why business needs to engage more closely with the battle of ideas about capitalism, and develop a much more strategic arsenal of strategies with which to influence how different components of society see and think about business and its contribution to the public good.

Summary

The CSR world view contains a number of misconceived ideas about business, profits, and the nature of market relations.

Profits should not be confused with greed or selfishness. They play an important signalling function within the market economy and are essential for the reinvestments that enterprises continually make in order to survive and continue to produce goods and services that people need and want; and pay the taxes that fund most public goods.

A corporation that is profitable has by definition shown that it is already giving something to society. More and more people are able to share in the risk-taking of the entrepreneurial minority by buying shares in public companies and turning their savings into other productive investments that spread through society as a whole.

The triple bottom line is a concept that obfuscates and dilutes the one clear measure of business performance that we have. It is also a potentially dangerous idea in that it allows for a more fuzzy definition of management accountability which can very easily slide into increasingly bad governance practices in other areas of corporate life. Although companies must certainly understand the context within which they operate and the many diverse stakeholders with whom they are in contact, they are not accountable to these diverse interests. To assume that they are is to 'confuse companies with governments and stakeholders with citizens' (Sternberg 2000).

Many CSR ideas are built upon the notion of a static capitalism dominated by very large corporations when in fact the nature of markets is to continually renew business enterprises through destroying those that are least efficient and allowing new companies to start up. CSR has concentrated on large public companies, and tended to ignore privately owned companies and medium and smaller enterprises that comprise very large chunks of national economies.

As Norberg (2003a) has noted:

> Corporations are our means of guaranteeing an efficient use of society's resources. That is good for society. ... Corporations have created all the wealth that politicians and bureaucrats distribute in their socially responsible ways, they are the Atlases that carry the planet on their backs. To suggest that corporations acting as traditional profit seeking corporations are irresponsible is an insult.

MYTHS ABOUT GLOBALISATION

Many proponents of CSR regard globalisation as a negative phenomenon wreaking havoc in developing countries, on the poor, and the environment. They argue that multinational companies have become more dominant, and that, in the absence of some form of global governance, there are no existing sources of power that can restrain their negative, even destructive impact. States, on the other hand, have been emasculated, or have been so corrupted by business that they have no desire to 'rein in' giant corporations.

This perspective is accepted by a surprisingly large number of commentators. Remarkably, some leading business executives and managers have also bought into aspects of this argument.

Has globalisation transformed the environment in which business operates?

Critics often present globalisation as an economic tsunami, sweeping hapless individuals and governments before it, creating an anarchic, borderless world primarily serving the interests of large corporations.

This view is wholly misguided. Open economies and the liberalisation of trade have not been forced on countries but have resulted from political choice, often at considerable political risk, by the governments of different nation states consciously opening national borders to foreign influences. The explosion of cross-border links is as much a result of government decisions to remove restrictions on trade, foreign investment, and capital flows as it is of better transport and communications.

This process has not marginalised poor countries, nor made companies more powerful. It has made these companies more vulnerable to the increased competition resulting from opening up markets. Globalisation has expanded pre-existing tendencies towards greater economic freedom, particularly with respect to cross-border trade and investment flows. In so doing it has brought gains to most people in all those countries, rich and poor, where market economies are sufficiently developed for firms to operate and profit from the change.

Trade creates jobs as well as destroying them, and raises living standards in the process. Growing imports imply growing exports, and increased trade in goods, services and ideas will continue to produce long-term benefits. Movements in the opposite direction will undermine individual freedom, economic growth, and national prosperity. Now, as before, effective governments are playing a vital role in harnessing the positive effects of increased trade, and working to minimise any disruptions.

Has globalisation increased global poverty and inequality?

Supporters of markets, trade and individual freedom tend to focus on the removal of poverty, and whether opportunities are opening up for an ever expanding number of people. Critics of globalisation believe it benefits the rich, hurts the poor, and increases inequality. They hark back to the old dependency theorists who saw international trade as a means for the rich North to exploit the poor South.

On the contrary, globalisation has led to increased economic growth in less developed countries, thus reducing global inequality as well as poverty. China and India have been the largest (but not the only) success stories of globalisation since the 1970s. Both began to grow far more quickly and effectively when they opened their borders to trade and capital flows. In the early 1980s these countries were among the poorest in the world. Once they opened up to markets – both externally and internally – their per capita incomes rose rapidly. As a result, many millions of Indian and Chinese people have experienced a substantial improvement in their standard of living. Even if inequality has increased in these two countries in the process of economic liberalisation, global inequality would still have decreased as a result of millions of Chinese and Indians becoming less poor more quickly than the rich were becoming richer. Thus, despite the absolute gap between Chinese and American incomes between 1980 and 2000 rising from $20 600 to $30 200 a head, the relative gap improved dramatically: in 1980 Chinese incomes were only 3 per cent of American incomes, while by 2000 they were 12 per cent. The Chinese economy grew much faster than the American economy in this period (440 per cent to 60 per cent), and if this trend continues Chinese incomes will soon start to catch up to those of Americans (Wolf 2005: 149).

Xavier Sala-i-Martin, professor of economics at Columbia

University, has calculated that, in the 1970s, 11 per cent of the world's poor were in Africa, and 76 per cent in Asia. By 1998 Africa hosted 66 per cent of the poor, and Asia's share had declined to 15 per cent. Clearly, this reversal was caused by the very different aggregate growth performances. He has concluded that global inequality declined substantially during the same period. These findings are supported by other recent work. 'Between them,' notes Bhagwati, 'they raise a massive discordant note in the chorus singing from a libretto lamenting increasing inequality in the age of globalisation' (Bhagwati 2004a: 67).

Rapid economic growth in poor countries containing half the world's population has powerful effects on the only sort of inequality that matters – inequality among individuals – and similarly dramatic effects on world poverty. UN figures show that in 1990 some 28 per cent of the population of the developing world lived in extreme poverty. By 2002 this had decreased to 19 per cent (UN 2006).

Large-scale poverty is not caused by globalisation or the activities of international companies. It is the obstacles – such as ineffective governments, protectionism or bad ideas – preventing globalisation from spreading further and incorporating more countries and more people in effective market activity that accounts for the continued existence of poverty and inequality.

Has increased global trade been bad for developing countries?

Countries that have opened to trade have prospered. In 1970 – one generation ago – the average income in North and South Korea was roughly the same. Today the average South Korean is more than 19 times better off than his or her Northern counterpart – same people, resources, culture, and history. The only difference is that one country opened up its economy to free trade and global competition, while the other remained closed, and rejected integration (Fitzgerald 2003).

This does not mean that current global trade arrangements are either fair or good enough. Developed countries continue to protect many of their more labour-intensive producers against competition from those in less developed countries, while advocating increased liberalisation in those countries at the same time. According to a World Bank study, world income in 2015 would be $355 billion a year more with full trade liberalisation, and developing countries would gain $184 billion a year. Of this, $121 billion would be the benefits from their own liberalisation and thus increased trade between developing countries – an issue frequently ignored in the debates about European Union (EU) and American farm subsidies – while the rest would come from liberalisation by high-income countries (Wolf 2005).

During the past 50 years, an increasing number of previously poor countries have achieved unprecedented improvements in their material standards of living. Not all countries have shared in rising prosperity, but the disparities that have opened up or widened between more successful and less successful economies are neither the result of nor a manifestation of injustice. Many of the predicaments of most poor countries cannot be traced to globalisation, but to bad governments. What economically successful countries all share is a 'move towards a market economy, one in which private property rights, free enterprise, and competition increasingly take the place of state ownership, planning and protection. They choose, however haltingly, the path of economic liberalisation and international integration' (ibid).

Increased trade makes everyone richer. Foreign competition keeps companies efficient, close to their customers, and profitable; new technologies spread faster; and, as Legrain (2002) has remarked, 'countries specialise in what they do best and buy the rest for less from abroad. How else than through trade are poor countries going to get richer?' (ibid).

Are companies taking over the world?

Critics of globalisation maintain that corporations, not governments, now dominate societies. They force developing countries to compete for their investments, thus promoting a 'race to the bottom', and have an undue influence over national governments, thereby undermining democracy. All these accusations are either wildly exaggerated or completely false.

Myth: *Companies are bigger than countries*

Companies are far less powerful than it might seem. Although the influence of companies in general has never been more widespread, the clout of individual companies has probably declined. The much-vaunted idea that companies are now bigger than mere governments is not only factually incorrect but also misconceived (Wolf 2005: 223). Those critics who have tried to prove that corporations are bigger than most developing countries have made a serious error of measurement.

The much repeated 'fact' is that 51 of the world's 100 largest economies are now corporations, and only 49 are nation states. What the critics have done is to compare the total revenue of those companies with the GDP of developing countries. This is a serious mistake, as they are counting the input costs of those companies as part of their output, while counting only final goods and services in the case of countries. To obtain more comparable figures, one has to subtract companies' costs from their revenue. It then emerges that in 2000 only two corporations featured in the top 50 economies in the world: Exxon Mobil, at 45th, and General Motors, at 47th (ibid: 222). The economy of Sweden is more than twice as big as that of Exxon Mobil; the French economy is more than 15 times bigger, and the American economy more than 100 times bigger (Norberg 2003b).

Myth: *Expanding company size is always to be feared*

Many corporations have grown over the past two decades, but so has the global economy, and so have many other institutions. This is not a zero-sum game where, if corporations are growing, then governments have to be shrinking.

Company size needs to be placed in perspective. BP – the second largest oil company in the world – only encompasses a fraction of the world economy. As BP's CEO once argued: 'We don't control markets; however large we are, we produce less than 4 per cent of the world oil supply, and less than 4 per cent of world gas' (Browne 1998).

In 1982 the top 100 listed American companies accounted for 62 per cent of total stock market capitalisation; by 2000, the figure had dropped to 46 per cent (Legrain 2002: 139). In 1996 American corporations on the Fortune 500 list employed only 9 per cent of all employees in the country, whereas 20 years previously they employed nearly 19 per cent. This decline occurred because the American economy created some 37 million new jobs since 1975, but the largest corporations shed nearly 4,5 million jobs (Novak 1996a:5).

Inferring from a company's size that they are as powerful as countries is ridiculous. Companies and countries are very different entities. Companies have to attract capital and workers who are free to move elsewhere; they have to persuade customers to buy enough of what they produce to make sufficient profits to pay shareholders and workers an acceptable return. Companies that fail go bust or are taken over. States, on the other hand, can impose taxes, laws and regulations; declare war; conscript citizens; expropriate property, and nationalise companies, often without major repercussions.

What we should oppose is not size but monopoly. Companies in a liberal economy have no coercive power. One of the most dramatic results of globalisation is that companies which used to compete against other companies located in their city's Yellow Pages are now competing with companies anywhere in the world. Companies have not acquired more power; they used to be far more powerful in closed dictatorships, controlled economies, or when backed by colonial powers. The historical horror stories of companies' effectively running countries have always come from regions where there has been little competition, democracy, or free press. Freer trade has exposed large companies to enhanced competition and greater scrutiny.

Established businesses dislike competition, and are more likely to look for ways to reduce than expand it. Introducing a vibrant market economy and free trade is one way of taking legally protected monopolies and exclusive privileges away from companies and forcing them to offer the best possible goods and services, or be put out of business by another company. Nor do all companies necessarily favour privatisation, as this can disrupt lucrative government contracts for goods priced way above market rates.

Nothing forces people to buy a company's products. If companies gain market share, it is because customers want what they have to offer. Even the biggest companies survive at the whim of customers, and would have to close down tomorrow if they ceased providing what customers want: McDonalds sells mutton burgers in India, teriyaki burgers in Japan, and salmon burgers in Norway.

Those people concerned about the power of large corporations should favour globalisation and deeper liberalisation of national economies. For along with the increased scope for trade and investment comes amplified competition from other companies from all over the world. Who would have predicted that, in the early 21st century, an Indian steel mogul would aggressively acquire 'old steel' companies in Europe and elsewhere? Freeing trade curbs giant domestic companies by exposing them to foreign competition. Closed domestic markets where national champions can cosy up to government are much more likely to be monopolies or have special deals than global corporations. It is the absence of competition, not size, that gives companies extraordinary power and influence.

Myth: *Companies increasingly control societies and their governments*

Perhaps the most potent and most pernicious of the claims by activists is that companies and not governments now effectively control society.

The idea that big corporations control democratically elected governments, thereby undermining democracy across the world, is simplistic and greatly exaggerated. Contrary to the essentially Marxist idea that the power of money controls the world, big businesses have influence but not control, and ideas are frequently more important than interest groups.

Part of this myth is that big businesses inevitably collude with one another to advance their collective world domination. On the contrary, large companies generally compete ruthlessly with one another. Moreover, the interests of different sectors of business differ – what suits steel might not suit automobiles or computers. The interests of large, small and medium businesses might also differ on particular issues, and governments can play these differences off against each other.

Companies are probably the most regulated modern institutions – far more accountable to shareholders than governments are to citizens. They are constrained by competition law – the United States government almost broke up Microsoft, and the EU Commission prevented General Electric, one of the world's largest companies, from taking over Honeywell. Cartels are illegal, thus preventing companies from making excessive profits from collusion. Companies have to comply with an ever increasing battery of laws and regulations dealing with workers' rights; health and safety procedures; gender issues; environmental protection; product liability laws, that make companies accountable for any harm their products cause; and advertising standards. Listed companies have to comply with extensive additional requirements and disclosure rules.

Few people would argue that the courts in developed countries at least are under company control. Each year, people start almost two million lawsuits against American companies, winning damages of about $150 billion (Legrain 2002).

Myth: *Large companies are responsible for a 'race to the bottom'*

The argument that big corporations are causing a race to the bottom (with respect to social and environmental regulation) in less developed countries is also not supported by the evidence. Rather than big corporations being able to ensure that they pay particularly low wages and low taxes, and are subject to minimal regulations, the opposite is true.

A study by Edward Graham has shown that American corporations active in manufacturing pay 1,4 times more than those in high-income countries, 1,8 times more than those in middle-income developing countries, and twice as much as those in low-income developing countries (Wolf 2005).

Myth: *Multinational corporations are instruments of cultural domination*

There is no corporate cultural takeover, despite the ongoing chorus to this effect. In Asia, three quarters of music is locally produced, and Coca-Cola accounts for less than two of the 64 fluid ounces drunk by people every day. For every McDonalds in the United Kingdom, there are six Indian restaurants; in Chile, McDonalds are vastly outnumbered by Chinese restaurants (ICC 2004).

Globalisation is providing local cultures with new opportunities to develop and then export their own cultural attributes. A growing counter current is under way, with people in different parts of the world defending local cultures and simultaneously seeking to diffuse them globally. New technology and trade facilitates and encourages cultural exchange and mutual understanding.

The globalisation of communication is providing people with more personal freedom to choose the culture they want to be exposed to, rather than repressive governments dictating what citizens should dance to, wear, or hear.

Myth: *The state is declining, and has been sold out to corporations*

According to both critics and some of the more enthusiastic supporters of globalisation, the dominance of international markets and the role of multinational corporations are causing the state to become impotent or irrelevant. In fact, the state is now more omnipresent than ever before – dramatically illustrated by the expansion of the state in response to the global economic crisis.

In 1965 – the heyday of Keynesianism and government interference in economics – corporate taxes accounted for 8,8 per cent of total tax revenues in rich Organisation for Economic Co-operation and Development (OECD) countries. In 1999, in the age of globalisation, they still accounted for 8,8 per cent of the total tax take (Legrain 2002). Only Ireland had a lower ratio of public spending in 1996 than in

1980. The rate at which government spending expanded slowed down after 1980, but this had very little to do with globalisation.

Highly regulated social democracies have not shown any symptoms of either uncompetitiveness or of losing people and capital to less regulated countries. In fact, these countries have mostly had trade surpluses, and attracted both human and physical capital. The reasons for their success are that they are rich, stable, provide superb social services and great environments in which to live, work and play. Less developed and less attractive countries have been less successful at keeping skilled and wealthy people. Globalisation does not force governments to disappear; it forces them to take the interests of their most valuable assets – skilled and entrepreneurial people – into account.

The idea that globalisation means the end of democratically elected governments can be totally rejected, based on three crucial ideas that are strongly supported by the evidence. Governments do not merely interfere with markets; they are also an essential aspect of market-based systems, and have a vital role to play if countries want to take advantage of global market opportunities. Second, people and the networks of skills, trust, regulations, and ways of doing business that create value in most countries do not easily move across borders. Companies, people, and even money are still more or less tied to places, so governments still have some sway over them. Third, people are not opposed to all regulations; they frequently value and support them if governments provide them effectively and consistently. Therefore, people don't necessarily flee from regulations; instead, they flee from bad governments (Wolf 2005).

There are certain constraints on governments that wish to participate in the international economy. But these are positive constraints that tend to make policy more transparent, and governments more predictable. It may now be harder to run inflationary policies and to

impose predatory forms of taxation, but the only people who should
get upset about this are those who want to run predatory states (ibid).
What globalisation actually means is that states seeking to benefit
from this process have to become more democratic, more open, and
more effective. As long as they don't abuse their powers, they will have
a great deal of freedom to manoeuvre.

What about the environment?

Many of those opposed to what they see as the environmental damage
that globalisation inflicts are in fact opposed to growth per se. They
regard economic growth as inevitably leading to environmental
degradation, and therefore oppose the positive effects that globalisation
has on the growth prospects of poor countries. They then find
themselves in the difficult position of either opposing growth in poor
countries or of advocating massive redistribution from rich countries
to the poor.

Neither of these policies has any chance of being realised. Evidence
shows that, while higher levels of economic growth can increase
pollution, this is true only up to a point. Once countries pass a certain
level of per capita income, they invariably start to reduce the levels
of pollution. From that point onwards, growth is associated with a
reduction in local pollution.

It is also undeniable that market-based systems have inflicted far
less environmental damage than socialist ones. There is no 'race to
the bottom' in environmental regulations; on the contrary, they have
tended to tighten during the current era of globalisation.

CONCLUDING REMARKS

The ideas, assumptions, and world view underpinning the anti-globalisation movement reveal a profound hostility to business, trade, and markets. Proponents of CSR have been deeply influenced by these negative ideas about globalisation, and antagonistic attitudes towards multinational corporations.

The arguments about large corporations promoted by anti-globalisation activists are simply wrong. Companies are not taking over the world; global economic competition does not prevent government from taxing, spending and regulating; western and other democracies are not at risk from expanded trade; and economic integration and globalisation, far from harming the poor, offer new, unprecedented opportunities for improving economic growth, creating more jobs, and reducing poverty.

The corporate critics are also remarkably pessimistic about the prospects for growth, poverty or the environment. They greatly overstate international inequalities, deny or underplay all evidence of progress, and then blame western companies supposedly colluding with 'weak' governments for the injustices of an unequal world. Repeated calls on business to 'put a human face on globalisation' are dangerous, and make little sense. Globalisation *has* a human face. It consists of millions of people who are finally getting opportunities to work, get off the land, move off the most basic level of survival, and finding opportunities to improve their lives; millions of consumers who can now buy goods at low prices – what used to be luxuries affordable only by the very rich are now everyday items obtainable by almost everyone; it can be seen in the entrepreneurs, big and small, who are taking advantage of new opportunities to create wealth.

The attacks on business divert attention from more important issues, such as: how can more countries, regions, and individuals be involved in the markets that have served citizens of developed countries so well? How can the playing fields of global trade best be levelled? How can people who lose jobs in the process of increased global competition, technological innovation, and specialisation be assisted? How can the roles of states and markets best be balanced?

As the economic crisis that began in 2008 helped to illustrate, globalisation is not an irreversible process. Economic stagnation and protectionism are hurting everyone, especially the poorest of the poor, and with the least resources to survive a downturn. Whatever the challenges of increased global integration, the benefits far outweigh the negatives.

The CSR world view is not a convincing one. It is built on faulty ideas about business, profits, markets, and globalisation. It diverts attention from more important issues and challenges facing business, the difficult choices involved in operating in vastly diverse countries, and the inevitable trade-offs involved in creating profitable organisations. On the basis of misleading ideas, critics have significantly – and negatively – influenced popular thinking about the role of companies. Many CSR advocates downplay the primary role of business, and undermine the claim of profit-oriented enterprise to legitimacy and recognition. They have contributed to a set of attitudes that regard normal business activity as negative and destructive and therefore requiring ongoing 'reparations' to the 'rest of society'.

They focus the debate about business and society on 'what else' business should do rather than concentrating on its core function: to remain competitive, and make a profit. In so doing they ignore or totally understate the role of government in shaping markets and economic prospects.

The way in which the debate is structured sets up a 'them' and 'us' approach to business and society. In the process millions of shareholders who benefit from the operations of successful companies are ignored, despite the fact that the returns on their investments pay for children's education, or old age pensions. Similarly, consumers who benefit from the production of goods and services by corporate entities are deemed to receive no benefit, or to have no choice about how they spend their money.

In order to achieve the right accusatory tone, activists bemoan the level of world poverty and assert that it's getting worse and worse. This amounts to an extraordinary denial of the history of the past 50 years in the developing world, during which more people have been lifted out of poverty more rapidly than ever before.

Chapter Two

'SWEATSHOPS' AND OTHER IRRESPONSIBLE WESTERN CAMPAIGNS

'In the 2000s the "millennial collectivists" – red, green or communitarian – oppose a globalization that helps the poor but threatens trade union officials, crony capitalists, and the careers of people in western NGOs.'

Deirdre N McCloskey, *The Bourgeois Virtues*:
Ethics for an Age of Commerce (2006)

'Well-meaning American university students regularly campaign against sweatshops. But instead, anyone who cares about fighting poverty should campaign in favor of sweatshops, demanding that companies set up factories in Africa.'

Nicholas D Kristof, 'In praise of the maligned sweatshop' (2006)

SWEATSHOPS IN DEVELOPING COUNTRIES are the quintessential 'responsibility' issue; it seems to cry out for just the kind of intervention anti-business activists provide. But once one delves into the dynamics of labour markets, the scale of developing world poverty, the realities of incremental development (and there really is no other kind), it soon becomes clear that this 'simple moral issue' supposedly requiring greatly improved corporate behaviour is in fact a multifaceted development phenomenon occurring within an extremely complex set of market relationships. And, the 'anti-sweatshop' campaign is a part of a wider set of political agendas.

WESTERN 'COMPASSION'

In the last decade of the 20th century a number of reports appeared in the western media about workers in poor countries working long hours for low wages, often under very unpleasant conditions, to produce goods for western markets. These workers were abused, not paid on time, or treated in other ways which contradicted everything achieved in western places of work during the previous two centuries. Activists and trade unionists in industrialised countries organised campaigns aimed at exposing and then forcing individual companies to take remedial action. Targeted companies started to pay much more attention to conditions of work in developing countries and adopted codes of conduct and monitoring procedures. Activists in multilateral organisations, western governments, and even some in business are now calling for 'global labour standards'. As a result of these activities, conditions have improved in some factories in some countries for some workers.

However, the issues involved are a lot more complex than these campaigns suggest. And when explored, they reveal a great deal concerning the nature of the conversation about business and society, especially the limitations and distortions of this discourse.

The alternatives are worse

Although working conditions in factories in many developing countries seem terrible to westerners, for the workers these jobs represent a real step forward. The vast majority of people in developing countries work in subsistence agriculture, requiring hard physical toil, or the survivalist informal sector, which is unregulated, unprotected and insecure.

Only 1 to 5 per cent of the workforce in developing countries works in foreign-owned or operated factories. For most people in those countries, life is a fight for survival that is unimaginable for most inhabitants of industrialised countries. Jobs in factories manufacturing goods for export provide them with significant new levels of income as well as other opportunities.

It is absurd to blame the poor conditions in some of those factories on capitalism or global trade. They reflect the poverty and lack of development of the society concerned. If implemented, western calls for higher wages and better working conditions will result in investors and employers going elsewhere.

In 2000 the American academic Paul Glewwe analysed two major living standards surveys conducted in Vietnam in 1992-3 and 1997-8. The 1998 data showed that Vietnam had 37 per cent of its population defined as 'poor', and an additional 15 per cent as 'very poor' (Glewwe 2000). In 1998, average per capita consumption expenditures were $205 a year, and the average food intake per day barely enough to maintain adequate nutrition. The 1998 survey collected responses from 15 625 people who had worked in the seven days preceding the interview. Fifty-nine per cent of the workforce consisted of self-employed farmers. Of the remaining 41 per cent, half were self-employed outside agriculture, and the other half were wage and salary earners. About 8 per cent of the working population was employed by the government, either directly or by a state-owned enterprise; 8 per cent worked for wholly Vietnamese-owned enterprises (including small household businesses); and 1 per cent worked for foreign owned businesses (ibid).

Glewwe examined the status of workers in foreign-owned enterprises in terms of consumption expenditure, wages, and poverty. His conclusion is striking:

> Foreign investment in Vietnam provides better jobs for Vietnamese workers – jobs that would not exist in the absence of that investment. There is simply no possibility that wages could be raised to one or two dollars an hour in Vietnam because such wages would make foreign investment unprofitable and because they would be so high by Vietnamese standards that virtually everyone (working elsewhere) would quit their current jobs. While this might sound like a good thing, it could lead to economic chaos – something the Vietnamese government would never permit (ibid: 4).

Many factories are in countries undergoing rapid industrialisation with a policy of export processing zones where government regulations are relaxed in order to attract foreign investment. This approach – harsh as it might seem to outsiders – has resulted in dramatic declines in poverty. According to World Bank figures the number of people in the east Asian region, excluding China, living on less than $1 per day fell from 114 million in 1987 to 54 million in 1998 (Litvin 2003: 235).

Take the example of Samyang, a Nike factory in Vietnam, as described by Philip Legrain in his book on globalisation (2002). Here, as elsewhere in the developing world, one dollar can buy a lot more than it can in a rich country, so comparing dollar-based wages is often misleading – a point frequently missed in sensational reports about people living on less than a dollar a day. According to the World Bank, the comparative purchasing power of a dollar in Vietnam is about five times as much as in the west, so the 'shock wages' reported in western media need to be placed in this context. Samyang pays twice the average local wage of $27 a month, and much more than the legal minimum monthly wage in foreign factories of $35 in rural areas, $40 in suburbs, and $45 in cities. In state-owned factories the minimum wage is $15 a month. Not surprisingly, Samyang's workers are not desperate to leave, and two thirds have been with the company for more than three years (ibid: 56).

Western critics like to compare what workers are paid and how much the company charges for its products. The implication is always that the gap between the costs of labour and the retail price is pure profit. In Nike's case, what are the facts? According to Nike it pays its contractors an average of $18 per shoe, comprising $11 for materials, $2 for labour, $4 for other costs, and $1 for profits. It then marks up the shoe by 100 per cent and sells it to retailers for $36, which covers product and design costs, R&D, marketing, advertising, shipping, production management, other sales and business costs, taxes, plus a profit. The retailer marks the shoes up by another 100 per cent and sells them to consumers for $72: these retail costs include product costs, rent, staff wages, shrinkage, insurance, advertising, supplies and services, depreciation, taxes, risks, and profit. Higher-end shoes costing more than $100 make up only a small portion of overall sales (ibid).

A favourite argument by campaigners, that Samyang's workers could not afford the shoes they make, is specious. Italians who work at the Ferrari factory can scarcely afford the cars. 'People do not work in order to consume what they produce; they do so to earn money to spend on other things' (ibid).

The impact of that spending power can be felt for miles around. Since Samyang opened in November 1995, the share of local people earning less than $10 per month has fallen from 20 to 8 per cent. One in five local people now earn more than $30, twice as many as in 1995. More than three quarters have a television set, compared with only a third in 1995. Eight per cent have phones, four times more than before. Two in three have a motorbike, up from one in three. Samyang's workers and their neighbours are no longer just subsisting, they have resources for extras; the new bike repair shops, mini markets, and food outlets testify to that (ibid).

The experience and status of workers in these types of factories defy simple characterisation: they often find work hard, and are poorly paid, but almost all regard their status as better than any other available option. Young workers in export factories want to make money as quickly as possible so that they can return to their rural homes and families, or use the money to start their own business, pay for a dowry, or send their children to school.

The example of Samyang is supported by other cross-national evidence. According to Theodore Moran, ILO surveys regularly find that while workers in export processing zones in developing countries earn far less than workers in developed countries, they still earn far more than other people in their villages (Moran 2002: 11). Other surveys have found that foreign-owned export-oriented factories offer higher pay and better working conditions than domestic companies or agriculture.

Survey evidence from three footwear and two apparel factories in Thailand shows that 72 per cent of workers regarded their overall income from factory work as fair, with 60 per cent stating that their wages allowed them to accumulate savings, 71 per cent characterised the relationship between workers and supervisors as good, and three quarters stating that they were recognised by factory management, and had received pay increases (ibid).

> Of workers surveyed at seven apparel and footwear plants in Vietnam, more than 71 per cent stated that their work gave them a feeling of personal satisfaction, they were treated with respect, they would recommend their factory as a good place to work, and they were provided with an opportunity to improve their skills (78 per cent). No comparable survey data is available for Bangladesh, which, along with China and India, pays unskilled workers the least. But while garment workers in Bangladesh take home an average wage of only $35 to $40 a month, these meagre earnings are nevertheless 25 per cent higher than the country's average monthly per capita income. Wages and working conditions in foreign-owned or controlled factories in Mauritius, Madagascar, Philippines, the Dominican Republic, and Costa Rica also compare favourably with those of alternative occupations (ibid: 14).

Raising new barriers against imports from developing countries would displace these workers back to domestic inward-oriented sectors where wages and working conditions are generally far worse. It would also reduce these countries' overall economic growth, the most decisive factor in raising standards.

Former Mexican president Ernesto Zedillo has pointed out that workers in trade-related activities often found that their new job was a significant improvement over their prior occupation (agriculture or the informal economy). '... these jobs are a step toward better opportunities. ... It is progress that matters the most when considering the standards of a given country' (ICC: 2004: 16).

IN PRAISE OF CHEAP LABOUR

Nobel Prize winning economist Paul Krugman has commented as follows on the issue of 'sweatshops' in developing countries:

'In a substantial number of industries, low wages allowed developing countries to break into world markets. And so countries that had previously made a living selling jute or coffee started producing shirts and sneakers instead. Workers in those shirt and sneaker factories are, inevitably, paid very little and expected to endure terrible working conditions. I say "inevitably" because their employers are not in business for their (or their workers') health; they pay as little as possible, and that minimum is determined by the other opportunities available to workers. And these are still extremely poor countries, where living on a garbage heap is attractive compared with the alternatives.

'And yet, wherever the new export industries have grown, there has been measurable improvement in the lives of ordinary people. Partly this is because a growing industry must offer a somewhat higher wage than workers could get elsewhere in order to get them to move. More importantly, however, the growth of manufacturing – and of the penumbra of other jobs that the new export sector creates – has a ripple effect throughout the economy. The pressure on the land becomes less intense, so rural wages rise; the pool of unemployed urban dwellers always anxious for work shrinks, so factories start to compete with each other for workers, and urban wages also begin to rise.

'Where the process has gone on long enough – say, in South Korea or Taiwan – average wages start to approach what an American teen-ager can earn at McDonald's. And eventually people are no longer eager to live on garbage dumps' (Krugman 1997).

Save us from western 'concern'

A former Mexican ambassador to the United States, Jesus Reyes-Heroles, has remarked: 'In a poor country like ours the alternative to low paying jobs isn't high paying jobs – it's no jobs at all' (quoted in Norberg 2003b: 194).

Child labour has been a core focus of western campaigns. The thought of young children being robbed of their childhood, opportunities for schooling and possibly their health is depressing. Sentiment aside, the question we need to examine is whether those children are helped if developed countries stop trading with the countries in which they live, or consumers decide not to buy products made in those countries.

The absurdity of these moralistic sentiments and 'fair trade or no trade' policies becomes clear when we discover that the great majority of children in poor countries are employed in sectors that have nothing to do with global trade. At most, 5 per cent of children are employed in export industries (ibid: 5). The rest are doing back-breaking work on farms, working as domestic servants or in hazardous local industries. All the available evidence shows that children employed in export industries work under better conditions and do less dangerous work than those in other sectors.

A number of harmful campaigns have been documented. In 1992 it was revealed that Wal-Mart was buying garments manufactured by child workers in Bangladesh. The United States Congress threatened to prohibit imports from countries using child labour. In response, Bangladeshi employers dismissed an estimated 50 000 children (Bhagwati 2004a: 71). Follow-up work by international organisations showed that many of these children then moved to more dangerous, less well paid jobs, including scavenging on rubbish dumps, street hawking, brute physical work, and prostitution (Norberg 2003b: 199).

Sialkot in Pakistan is the world centre for making cheap, hand-stitched soccer balls. Contractors farm out production to hundreds of small workshops and homes. In one highly publicised case, manufacturers moved production from private homes to a manufacturing facility in order to facilitate monitoring the ban on child labour. The main effect was to eliminate employment for women, who were unable to work outside their homes (Litvin 2003: 98). The campaigners had not thought through the impact of their actions. As Litvin puts it:

> It was not just that western attention was focused on just one small aspect of a broader problem: Pakistan's entire football production industry employed roughly 6 000 child labourers in 1996 compared with 3,3 million working children in the country as a whole. It is that even dealing with these 6 000 or so children proved to be a moral quagmire, for these children are enmeshed ... in a social context which was neither amenable to a quick fix nor had been sufficiently understood at first by either the western companies or their critics (ibid: 243).

A study conducted in Sialkot in 1999 found that women's levels of employment as well as earnings had dropped since the child labour controversy, and that many households involved in the football industry were eating fewer meals a day (ibid: 244). As a result, more children were dropping out of school in order to earn some kind of wage.

Sue Lloyd Roberts, a BBC journalist, was one of the western journalists who originally drew attention to the issue of child labour. When she visited Sialkot in 1998, she discovered that children were working in far worse conditions. The experience of the campaign changed her mind. Children had been 'liberated' from high-profile companies which had embarrassed western consumers, but were now working in indigenous industries. The west wasn't interested in these kinds of industries, and that's where they would stay. 'The problem is more fundamental than the headline-grabbing campaigns I and other journalists have been guilty of in the past' (quoted in ibid: 245).

Traditional values

The activist Malini Mehra says the problem with child labour in many countries is that laws against it are in place, but are not being enforced because of a lack of political will, institutional weakness, and lack of capacity. In her view, public habits and values are not aligned with the basic social goals of these regulations. 'In India, generations of lower to middle-class families continue to rely on servants who are often below the legal age. Even civil servants, the very people who should be out to prevent this, are employing child labour in their homes. Nothing will change unless there is value shift' (openDemocracy 2003).

The question of child labour and rights for women outside the home is a complex one in many developing countries. One of the key instruments for bringing about the required value shift is in fact employment by large foreign companies, which introduce different values around work and work practices.

People living outside a country need to think very hard about the impact of boycotts, sanctions, a single global standard, and other international trade-related measures against the employment of children. The only viable solution to large-scale child labour is not to ban it, which would make families poorer and children worse off, but to help families get richer so that children don't have to work. This requires more trade, more factories, more investment, and more consumers buying the products of developing countries.

It is misguided to try to standardise labour laws and regulations throughout the world. This could only have harmful consequences, and the measures would not be enforced. Standards will improve over time as countries get richer. A mandatory global minimum wage for export workers as called for by the ILO would hit poorest countries the hardest by depriving them of the opportunity to use their cheaper labour as a comparative advantage. In Moran's view, a mandatory minimum wage of $2,31 an hour (in 2000 dollars) – the average wage in export zones in Costa Rica – would prompt investors to abandon the Dominican Republic, where the average wage is less than $2 per hour, in favour of Costa Rica's more productive labour, and never even consider pools of previously cheaper but also less productive labour in El Salvador, Haiti, Nicaragua, Bangladesh, or Indonesia. In this way, a uniform minimum wage would penalise the very countries for which foreign investors with labour-intensive operations constitute the greatest relative opportunity (Moran 2002: 53). And, within poor countries, a mandatory minimum wage leads to mechanisation and fewer jobs.

Monitoring: who is kidding whom?

The Ethical Trading initiative estimates that in 2000 as many as 85 per cent of all large American companies operated under social responsibility guidelines of some kind. In the United Kingdom, more than 60 per cent of the largest 500 companies had established codes of conduct, up from 18 per cent a decade previously. A key component of almost all these codes concerns labour, social and environmental standards, and their application to developing countries.

In November 2004, in response to a report entitled 'Clean up your computer' that criticised labour conditions in factories manufacturing computers for the big brand names, Cisco Systems, HP, Microsoft, Dell, IBM, and Intel announced the formation of a supply chain working group to implement an electronics industry code of conduct, and committed themselves to auditing compliance. Twenty European companies have signed framework agreements with international trade unions, covering their own employees as well as those of their contractors; the agreements are intended to 'create a framework within which all workers are guaranteed established international minimum standards of work' anywhere in the world (Vogel 2005: 108).

In order to unpack the implications of these agreements, we need to appreciate the complexity and scale of modern production systems involving global supply chains. When researching his book on globalisation in the 21st century, Tom Friedman, author and *New York Times* columnist, asked Dell to trace the global supply chain that supplied the components for his laptop computer (Friedman 2006). The results are revealing:

Dell has six factories around the world, and sells 140 000 to 150 000 computers on an average day. One notebook contains about 30 different major components, and Dell uses multiple suppliers for most of these.

- The Intel microprocessor comes from an Intel factory in the Philippines, Costa Rica, Malaysia, or China.
- The memory comes from Samsung in Korea, Nanya in Taiwan, Infineon in Germany, or Elpida in Japan.
- The graphics card comes from MSI, a Taiwanese-owned factory in China, or the Chinese factory Foxconn.
- The cooling fan comes from CCI or Auras in Taiwan.
- The motherboard comes either from a Korean-owned Samsung factory in Shanghai, a Taiwanese-owned Quanta factory in Shanghai, or Compal or Wistron in Taiwan.

And so on through the keyboard, the LCD, the wireless card, the modem, the battery, the hard disk drive, the CD/DVD drive, the carrying bag, the power adapter, the power cord, the removable memory stick involving many more different companies. From Malaysia the computers are flown to Nashville, Tennessee, using China Airlines. On six days a week, a China Airlines 747 flies from Penang to Nashville with 25 000 notebooks. We won't go into the number of companies and suppliers one would have to monitor in the airline production business, including maintenance, airport security, and so on. Another large multinational was responsible for getting Friedman's laptop from Nashville to Washington DC.

Ultimately, the total supply chain for Friedman's computer, including suppliers of suppliers, involved about 400 companies in North America, Europe, and Asia (Friedman 2006: 517-8).

How could this huge, intricate, and far-flung supply chain conceivably be monitored? And what would it cost? This single example begins to illustrate the extent of the issues and problems involved in any serious monitoring of social, labour, environmental, and other codes of conduct.

Uneven implementation

Nike, which has probably been studied more than any other company, is run in a similar way to Dell. According to one account, in 2000 a Nike team of more than 30 labour compliance staff together with a large array of consultants and local charities were faced with the overwhelming task of monitoring some 700 factories, employing some 500 000 people (Litvin 2003: 245). Checking on fire extinguishers is easy enough, provided factories don't put such equipment on display only for the inspector's visit. Less easily ascertainable are

issues involving day-to-day human interactions, when managers
and employees often tell inspectors different stories. Are workers
being harassed, for example? Are managers hiring thugs to rough up
potential union organisers?

Even monitoring the age of workers is difficult, as birth certificates
are not necessarily accurate or reliable. And if the main factories
manufacturing Nike goods are obeying its code of conduct, what about
their suppliers? Or the suppliers of their suppliers? The typical Nike
shoe has about 50 components manufactured in anything between six
and ten countries. It is not uncommon for more hazardous jobs to be
shifted further down the supply chain or into the informal sector to
avoid international scrutiny.

Monitoring a large company and its many contractors with any level
of accuracy is in fact impossible. Thus it is not surprising that the vast
majority of codes of conduct do not mention monitoring. The OECD
has found that some two thirds of corporate and industry codes in the
garment industry do not address the issue of monitoring. For those
that do, compliance presents a number of very difficult challenges.
Sourcing networks may involve tens of thousands of factories spread
across dozens of countries; a range of buying agents, suppliers and
subcontractors all operating under different national systems, values
and cultures.

Disney, for example, sources its products from more than 30 000
factories, and Wal-Mart from an estimated 50 000 to 100 000. According
to one study, a Hong Kong-based supplier to major European and
American clothing brands uses factories in almost 40 countries, with
scores involved in producing a single garment. It took the European
clothing retailer C and A four years just to identify the factories
that were producing its clothes (Vogel 2005: 89). And this inventory
excluded the agricultural producers of raw materials, a dimension
beyond the scope of every manufacturing code.

The costs of monitoring

How much money could a company be expected to spend on auditing its code? Who should do the audits; which issues should they focus on; and how often should a given factory be audited?

According to a World Bank study, buyers for western firms generally believe the costs of monitoring are growing constantly, and are not sustainable in the long term. This is especially true when monitors start to look beyond the first tier of suppliers to the far greater numbers of contractors supplying the suppliers. The report concluded that while the present system of monitoring implementation had resulted in some improvements, it might have reached its limits, and might not bring about further improvements in workplace standards in developing countries (ibid: 93).

Not surprisingly, monitors often miss key issues. Most of the time, the lead players are large international accounting firms. It seems incongruous to send accountants to assess complex human rights, cultural and managerial issues.

In 2000 a BBC documentary team found children working in a Nike contract factory in Cambodia whom they thought to be under age, and which Nike's monitors might have missed. Nike then interviewed all the suspected workers, but the problem of unreliable birth certificates emerged. The company admitted that even at the end of the process 'there was no absolute assurance that we had got it right' (Litvin 2003: 246-7).

The media also drew attention to a Nike contract factory in Puebla, Mexico, owned by Koreans, where a strike had erupted and two unions were competing with each other to represent workers. Employees alleged that labour leaders had been fired, a charge denied by management. 'Clearly our monitoring had missed key elements of the factory labour situation,' Nike later confessed (ibid: 247). At the same time, Global Alliance, a partnership organisation of companies and NGOs, recorded allegations of sexual harassment and physical and verbal abuse in Nike contract factories in Indonesia. Again, these issues had eluded Nike's monitoring system.

Socially responsible politics?

The western coalitions that have spearheaded the 'sweatshops' campaign comprise a mix of trade unions, environmental campaigners, church groups, student organisations, human rights activists, and feminists. Many are fuelled by a general hostility to large corporations, globalisation, and its assumed American imperialism.

Trade unions in developed countries have played a particularly active role. Their domestic bargaining power has diminished steadily in recent years as jobs have moved to Asian and Latin American countries, and they are mostly motivated more by a desire to protect remaining jobs in their own countries than a genuine concern with workers in the developing world. They have camouflaged these protectionist interests by putting money and muscle behind broader campaigns and alliances.

For example, some of the most damaging reports on conditions in Nike factories during the 1990s were produced by a Jakarta-based activist funded by American labour federation, the AFL-CIO. 'We don't give a damn about workers in the third world; we just want to protect our members' interests,' one trade union leader has confessed (Legrain 2002: 64).

These broad coalitions have brought disgruntled factory workers from developing countries to appear before legislative committees, and to visit American or European superstores to tell shoppers how badly they are paid. Conspicuously, they have not invited representatives of developing country governments or trade unions opposed to this new form of protectionism to air their views.

When, in 2000, the American president Bill Clinton raised the issue of boycotting countries with inadequate labour standards at the WTO talks in Seattle, the Egyptian trade minister, Youssef Boutros-Ghali, remarked: 'The question is why, when third world labour has proved to be competitive, industrial countries suddenly start feeling concerned about our workers' (quoted in Norberg 2003b: 193). Dr Amit Mitra, secretary-general of the Federation of Indian Chambers of Commerce and Industry, believes the pressure on Asian countries to uphold first world working standards is holding back their development. One example was the United States telling Bangladesh to introduce western trade union rights in a very successful special economic zone (personal communication 2003).

The former Mexican president Ernesto Zedillo has stated:

> Paradoxically, those opposed to globalization proclaim purportedly altruistic reasons. They point for example to the fact that wages and standards of living in poorer countries are inferior to those of developed countries. They then conclude that homogenous core labour standards should be imposed and enforced through trade sanctions – clearly a protectionist proposal. Trade mostly occurs because there are differences among countries, including their labour situations. If labour standards were dictated by mere bureaucratic will and enforced through trade sanctions, developing countries would be further marginalized (2005).

One of the problems with the call for global standards is that activists want developing countries to conform to western standards that have evolved over centuries, with different countries allowed to proceed at their own pace.

Norberg, a Swede, has illustrated this as follows:

> Suppose this idea had been in vogue at the end of the 19th century.
> Britain and France would have noted that Swedish wages were only
> a fraction of theirs, that Sweden has a 12-13 hour working day, and
> six-day week, and that Swedes were chronically undernourished.
> Child labour was widespread in spinning mills, glassworks, match,
> and tobacco factories. One factory worker out of 20 was under 14
> years old. Accordingly, Britain and France would have refused to
> trade with Sweden and closed their frontiers to Swedish cereals,
> timber, and iron ore. Would Swedes have benefited? Hardly. Such
> a decision would have robbed them of earnings, and blocked
> their industrial development. They would have been left with
> intolerable living conditions. Children would have stayed in the
> factories. … Instead, trade with Sweden was allowed to grow
> uninterrupted, industrialization got under way, and the Swedish
> economy revolutionized. This didn't just help Sweden, it also gave
> Britain and France a new peer for prosperous exchange (2004).

If today, as a condition for trading with developing countries,
westerners require the mining industries in those countries to be as
safe as their own, they are making demands that western countries
did not meet when their own mining industries were developing. It
was only after incomes improved that richer countries were able to
develop the technology and safety equipment taken for granted today.
If westerners require developing countries to adopt those practices
and equipment before they can afford them, they will make it harder
for those industries to survive, never mind compete globally.

Two distinctions in the debate about 'sweatshops' need to be
emphasised. Support for greatly enhanced global trade should not be
confused with a vote of confidence in many of the governments of
developing countries, which range from repressive authoritarian states
to vibrant democracies.

Second, it is dangerous to blur the distinction between genuine slave labour – an evil that should be unambiguously condemned – and providing lower-paid jobs for individuals who can choose to take them up and use them as stepping stones to a better life.

Summary

There is an enormous difference between running an effective campaign designed for a first world audience, sitting in heated homes with hot and cold water and every modern convenience, and making a sustained difference to the lives of millions in countries that are either very poor or only starting to take off industrially.

At no stage has this debate focused on how to achieve large-scale development for millions of workers in those countries; or determining what is best for developing countries and their citizens. For some campaigners, lower working standards in developing countries provide a convenient stick with which to beat their favourite villains, large multinational corporations. The issue of 'sweatshops' is a convenient tool to undermine or forcibly refashion global enterprise. For others, the 'sweatshop' issue is one way of mobilising against globalisation through using industrial world workers' fears of losing their jobs to countries where standards and pay are so much lower. For what is probably the majority of people sympathetic to the attack on sweatshops, this is often an emotional reaction to the hard realities of life and work in poor countries that fails to see beyond the immediate symptoms to appreciate the wider context of third world poverty.

Previously poor countries such as Hong Kong, Taiwan, and Singapore show clearly what the issues of development really are. In all those places industrialisation started with sweatshops and worse;

standards then rose rapidly and dramatically through a combination of forces within those countries. We know from experience that the more foreign investment a country gets, the more this spurs domestic companies to expand and prosper, the more pressures there are on developing country governments to liberalise, and the tighter domestic labour markets become. This has two effects: it provides workers with greater bargaining power, as their skills grow and the demand increases, and also generates greater pressure on employers to find ways of attracting labour, which then leads to improvements in working conditions.

This process has a lot more chance of sustainability than the strange charade going on about codes of conduct. Many companies actively participate in this game on the terms and conditions set by their opponents and by those who do not appreciate the mechanisms whereby companies can play such an important role in helping poor countries develop.

'The impact of transparency, social reporting and consumer and investor pressure in the west can be a virtuous circle raising standards and income for producers rather than a race to the bottom,' says Robert Davies, CEO of the international business leaders forum (quoted in Hilton & Gibbons 2005). He is correct in asserting that this is not a race to the bottom as many anti-trade, anti-globalisation critics maintain, but completely wrong in his advocacy of consumer and investor pressure in the west, social codes and so on. This is the wrong terrain for business leaders.

If you are interested in the alleviation of poverty in a country, it is hard to understand why improving conditions of work for a tiny minority of workers employed in foreign-owned or contracted factories is seen as the key to development. And especially when these workers are the best paid and have the best conditions in the country already.

South Africa's recent history is an instructive example of a developing country that prematurely adopted first world standards – a consequence of the battle against apartheid and the complex politics of business and unions in an undemocratic state. There can be little doubt that the chillingly high unemployment rate of the country – estimated to be just under 40 per cent of the working population in 2009 – is due in no small consequence to these totally inappropriate standards that have encouraged companies to mechanise in urban and rural sectors and created a powerful urban labour aristocracy that uses its political power to block reforms that would increase the labour absorbing capacity of the South African economy.

No one with any understanding of the increasingly sophisticated, complex, multi-country global supply chain approach to production can really want, afford or believe that this can be effectively monitored for compliance. It is a reflection of the world power balance that developing country governments, especially democratic ones and other organisations in those societies (business, trade unions) are not heard or listened to in the western debate about global standards. It is also an indication of the weakness of business – individual companies, collective organisations, associations of leaders – that all the signals are moving towards more and more voices calling for government regulation and increasing intervention in how business is conducted.

We have given so much attention to the story of so-called sweatshops and the many misunderstandings of reality in developing countries that it represents, because it is a bedrock issue for almost everyone involved in talking to, working in and around western multinationals on any aspect of corporate responsibility or citizenship. It is now so taken for granted that it is just assumed as a given in almost all discussion on this topic.

In order to fully appreciate the irresponsible and highly charged political nature of many, not all CSR campaigns, it is important to add two other cases to our analysis of the 'sweatshop' campaign.

BRENT SPAR — THE COLLAPSE OF REASON

The story of Greenpeace and Shell's Brent Spar oil platform is an example of a company based on engineering and scientific expertise capitulating to a well-orchestrated and unscrupulous activist campaign. The Brent Spar was an oil storage and tanker loading buoy in the Brent oilfield in the North Sea, operated by Shell UK. In the early 1990s it became redundant, and Shell applied to the British government for permission to sink it in the deep Atlantic Ocean, about 250 kilometres from the coast of Scotland (Vogel 2005: 112).

Shell had concluded that this was the best solution after commissioning more than 30 studies to assess the technical, safety, and environmental implications of various disposal options for the 14 500-ton platform. All these studies recommended deep-sea disposal as the safest, most environmentally responsible course of action. Furthermore, they stated that the second option – disposing of the platform on land – posed a six-fold higher risk for workers as well as the threat of onshore water pollution should the platform break up during transit.

Land disposal would require Shell to find a deep-harbour port whose local government would agree to accept the environmental hazards of dismantling and recycling the platform. Deep-sea disposal was also more than four times less expensive than disposal on land: 11 million pounds compared to 46 million. In February 1995 Shell received approval from the British Department of Energy to tow the platform out to sea (ibid: 112-113).

Greenpeace, an international environmental NGO, decided to challenge Shell's disposal decision. It claimed that it was irresponsible and dangerous to use the deep sea as a 'rubbish bin'. Brent Spar was the first of 90 deep-sea platforms in the north-east Atlantic scheduled to be decommissioned, and Greenpeace wanted to prevent all of them from being disposed at sea. It allocated close to a million dollars to its campaign against Shell, and designed a series of media-savvy stunts aimed at attracting maximum coverage of its views. The campaign against Shell gained momentum, and consumers began to boycott some Shell petrol stations in Europe and the United Kingdom.

The highly organised campaign was endorsed by a coalition of politicians, businesses, labour unions, and environmental and religious organisations and was unusually effective. Some individual station owners reported an up to 50 per cent decline in sales, although the average drop in Germany – the centre of the campaign – was estimated at 20 per cent. At one point consumer protests were costing Shell an estimated 5 million pounds a day, and nearly 50 Shell service stations in Europe were vandalised (ibid: 113).

Shell continued to insist that sea disposal was the soundest environmental option; however, the negative publicity proved too much for management, and on 20 June 1995 Shell announced that it had decided to abandon its plans to sink the rig at sea. The platform was dismantled on land and subsequently became part of a ferry terminal in Norway at the cost of $40 million, a process that took five years.

Buoyed by this victory, Greenpeace later succeeded in a larger goal, thanks in part to a rule passed by the Oslo-Paris Commission in 1998, and all similar platforms will now be disposed of on land. The additional costs of land disposal for the 90 platforms involved are estimated to be at least $5 billion. It subsequently turned out that the oil sludge remaining in the Brent Spar tanks was not more than 5 000 tons, as claimed by Greenpeace, but some 100 tons. (It later apologised for this error, but by then it was too late) (ibid: 113).

According to Vogel there is no scientific evidence that deep-sea disposal is environmentally hazardous. The respected independent journal *Nature* carried an article which concluded that Shell's original studies were sound and had been conducted using 'rigorous scientific standards'. The guidelines of the International Maritime Organisation also permit deep-sea disposal.

As one Shell executive said, this controversy showed how easily pressure groups could use 'mischievous methods' to challenge a decision that had been made on a 'factual scientific basis'. Shell executives indicated then and subsequently that the group had been taken unawares. They had failed to see the changes in society, and how these affected the political climate with respect to large corporations. Another Shell executive put it differently: 'Just relying on the scientific results does not cut it. At the end of the day, the feeling of the public was, Shell should not ... dump the Brent Spar' (ibid: 114).

This experience, coupled with its Nigerian troubles, led Shell to become the cheerleader and for a period most vocal advocate of CSR, adopting the slogan 'people and profits', and running an extensive global campaign to 'listen' to activists and NGOs. In many ways it symbolised what one might call corporate appeasement. Here was a situation where loud and effective protesters were conflated with 'the public', their views were taken to represent the public interest, and the principles of science, objective enquiry and ultimately reason were forgone by a large corporation, founded on the application of accurate scientific knowledge to energy supply.

This corporate collapse did much to start the general trend of small, well-financed, media-savvy interest groups arrogating the right to speak for the 'people', both nationally and internationally, and attempting – often with remarkable success – to impose their views and beliefs on large multinational companies, governments, multilateral organisations, and others.

THE WORLD BANK PLAYED THIS GAME

In 1995 James Wolfensohn succeeded Jim Preston as president of the World Bank. At the time, the Bank was under pressure from many quarters about global trade and other issues. Sebastian Mallaby's book on Wolfensohn, the Bank, and NGOs (2004) provides instructive reading. It is in part a case study of what happens when a global organisation gets too close to campaigning special interests, in this case international advocacy NGOs.

When Wolfensohn took office, he knew that the Bank's size and intellectual dominance had made it remote and arrogant, provoking the resentment of many groupings and individuals around the globe, as well as influential NGOs based in the capitals of the developed world.

He spent a lot of time trying to bridge the gap between the Bank and NGOs, making 'dialogue' with them one of the Bank's central priorities. More than 70 NGO specialists worked in field offices around the globe, and more than half of Bank projects involved NGOs as implementing partners (Mallaby 2004).

Wolfensohn also changed Bank policies in ways the NGOs wanted. He announced that all recipients of aid should prepare participatory Poverty Reduction Strategy Papers, effectively giving NGOs a say in the Bank's choice of projects; invited some NGOs to help formulate Bank strategy; and set up various commissions to consider its record on issues such as structural adjustment. But this outreach campaign failed to protect the Bank against continued assaults by anti-globalisers and their allies. In fact, the NGOs were more interested in sustaining their general anti-globalisation campaign – with the Bank cast in a central role – than the specific issues raised by the Bank.

Prompted by NGO lobbying, the Bank introduced operational guidelines to protect the rights of indigenous people, the environment, and so on. However, as a condition for World Bank assistance, they required poor nations to meet environmental and social standards they could ill afford, and developing countries regarded them as a burden. According to one Bank study, safeguard policies of one kind or another inflated the institution's project preparation costs by $83 million a year. Moreover, the Bank's borrowers, namely developing countries, spent anywhere from $118 million to $215 million a year on complying with these safeguards, so that the direct and indirect costs to developing countries totalled as much as $300 million. The red tape surrounding these conditionalities also alienated developing country officials from the Bank, and some of its better policies (ibid).

The result of the rules and guidelines aimed at placating the concerns of the loudest, most organised NGOs was a development bank that lost touch with developing countries – one that reflected the agenda of northern activists and not the hard realities and preferred choices for action of its poor clients.

In 2001, Larry Summers, former chief economist of the Bank, and Clinton's last treasury secretary (current senior adviser to President Obama) attacked the Bank's rhetoric of 'empowerment', arguing that inviting the participation of NGOs would not improve decision-making. He pointed out that NGOs had no special claim to speak for the poor, and that they could claim far less legitimacy than the elected governments of many developing countries. Rather than deferring to these unelected groups, the Bank should defer to its own technical experts. 'The best route to successful development lay in rigorous analysis and not participatory waffle.' The Bank should, for example, promote environmental standards when hard-headed cost-benefit analysis suggested that this made sense, and not in the blanket NGO-appeasing way embodied in the organisation's new safeguards (ibid: 297).

From Berkeley with love

One consequence of the enormous influence of the international NGO movement was that the Bank moved away from funding certain types of infrastructure – including large dams. In fact, the controversy surrounding dams vividly illustrates the consequences of the Bank's attempts to placate the NGO community.

During Wolfensohn's first five-year tenure, infrastructure investment project lending declined from 36 to 29 per cent. Social sector lending grew from less than 20 per cent of the Bank's portfolio to 25 per cent. Wolfensohn's Bank wanted to 'focus directly' on poor people. 'It did not want to be guilty of harming the environment, and it wanted to make peace with NGOs' (ibid). Everything pushed it to stay out of controversial infrastructure projects, and during Wolfensohn's first five years in office, no big new dam projects got off the ground. The Bank was 'encircled ... by NGO critics who filed dams under the same heading as structural adjustment and torture' (ibid).

A key player in this process was International Rivers, then the International Rivers Network (IRN), based in Berkeley, California. Its mission statement says: 'International Rivers protects rivers, and defends the rights of communities that depend on them. It opposes destructive dams and the development model they advance, and encourages better ways of meeting people's needs for water, energy, and protection from damaging floods' (International Rivers online).

Given this point of departure, all dams are necessarily bad, regardless of whether or not they could benefit poor people or entire regions.

The World Bank's first efforts to placate critics of dams came in the mid-1990s when it reviewed 50 Bank-funded dams. Organisations such as IRN were informed of this review, in an attempt to elicit their support. The review found that some dams had caused environmental damage and displaced some communities, but concluded that the construction of most large dams was justified. Rather than producing the hoped-for appreciation from the campaigning NGO world, the report was vigorously attacked. The IRN claimed it 'exaggerated the benefits of the dams under review, underplayed their impacts, and displayed a deep ignorance of the social and ecological effects of dams' (ibid). To the surprise of even the NGOs involved, rather than dismissing such attacks as the work of cranks or fanatics, the Bank invited them to a workshop in Switzerland.

Organised by the Bank and the World Conservation Union, one third of participants were representatives of NGOs, and the rest of public sector dam building agencies, private sector dam companies, the Bank, and academia. Representatives of developing country governments were excluded. Participants formed a reference group to oversee the establishment of a World Commission on Dams (WCD), agree on a mandate and a list of commissioners.

IRN director Patrick McCully has written a revealing article on the formation and outcomes of the WCD (McCully 2001). He provides an insight into the process in which he coordinated efforts by dam critics to lobby for an independent international review committee of dam building. He also participated in decisions regarding the committee's composition and mandate. In his view, the workshop established dam critics as central to the legitimacy of the review. It also enabled 'the exclusion of governments from substantive power in the process. ... Had the governments of leading dam building nations like Brazil, China, India, Japan or Turkey formed an organised bloc within the reference group, it is almost certain that their coalition would have destroyed the commission's potential to issue a progressive report' (ibid).

The WCD was tasked with researching the impact of dam construction and recommending a framework for future dam financing. Despite being chaired by Professor Kader Asmal, then a cabinet minister in newly democratic South Africa, the commission was dominated by experts and environmentalists from the North. The consultative WCD Forum did include representatives of dam construction companies and a few relevant government officials from Lesotho, China, Mexico, Sri Lanka and India. But its membership was biased in favour of Northern environmental groups and 'affected people's groups' funded by Northern agencies.

Published in 2000, the report reflected this orientation. According to Rodney Bridle of the British Dams Association (BDA), 'the social aspects of the report were most revealing, particularly the poor record on resettlement, the impacts on livelihoods downstream, and poor performance on social, technical and economic criteria', but he also noted that the 'benefits of dams to humanity were barely mentioned' (WWF-UK 2003: 9).

The report reflected the bias of the NGOs that initiated the process. Based in developed countries, or funded by agencies from such countries, they can afford to focus on preservation, and toy with notions of romantic populism, in which any dislocation or hardship induced by processes of change is regarded as unacceptable. Predictably, the criteria for funding dams proposed by the commission allow for dams to be funded only if this would cause no environmental damage or social dislocation at all, and also seek to impose a process where everybody has been consulted. Such unrealistic notions of 'consultation' and 'participation' ensure that dam construction effectively becomes a thing of the past.

The commission settled on seven strategic priorities, starting with gaining public acceptance and ending with the equitable and sustainable development of water and energy resources (WCD 2000: 211). The first priority requires dam constructors to obtain 'permission' from indigenous groups in countries such as Argentina,

Bolivia, Brazil, Chile, Colombia and Ecuador, Australia, Canada, India, New Zealand, and the Philippines (ibid: chapter 8). The last requires that, 'in addition to having ratified international agreements, individual states should specifically address shared river basins in their water policy or legislation, providing clarity on their intention to co-operate in water resources management'. National governments were also encouraged to set up 'an independent, multi-stakeholder committee to address the unresolved legacy of past dams'. NGOs were asked to help establish forums of stakeholders 'to enable them to identify, articulate and represent their legitimate rights'. Professional associations and agencies were urged to 'extend national committees to include a consultative group of NGOs, environmental scientists, and affected peoples' groups' (ibid).

According to the IRN, the commission's main recommendations include the following:

- No dam should be built without the 'demonstrable acceptance' of affected people, and without the free, prior and informed consent of affected indigenous and tribal peoples;
- Comprehensive and participatory assessments of people's water and energy needs, and different options for meeting these needs, should be developed before proceeding with any project;
- Priority should be given to maximising the efficiency of existing water and energy systems before building new projects;
- Mechanisms should be developed to provide reparations, or retroactive compensation, for those who are suffering from existing dams, and to restore damaged ecosystems (International Rivers online).

The IRN clearly believed that the commission had achieved the organisation's ultimate goal of ending dam construction in the 'third world'. As McCully commented, a report written by anti-dam activists would not have exhibited the optimism of the commission that 'the planning criteria set by the WCD could be met, and a dam still be built' (McCully 2001).

Luckily, the World Bank regained some of its sanity. The assault on the WCD came from a World Bank staffer, John Briscoe, who had been involved with the commission. Personal experience in Bangladesh had taught him the value of large infrastructure investments, and extensive consultation with representatives of large developing country governments had reinforced this conviction. In 2002 Briscoe presented the first draft of a new World Bank water strategy. It pointed out that 13 billion people lacked access to clean drinking water, and that some of the world's poorest people were farmers whose lives would be transformed by irrigation. On this basis, Briscoe argued that the Bank should revitalise its commitment to funding large infrastructure projects such as dams, and, while remaining committed to 'sensible environmental and social standards', it should jettison the restrictive approach proposed by the WCD (Mallaby 2004). Briscoe's proposals were supported by many governments and other organisations, but loudly opposed by the NGOs that had formed the backbone of the WCD.

By this time both Bank and government officials in richer countries increasingly realised that, although these NGOs were skilled at taking what seemed like the moral high ground and at launching highly visible email campaigns, they did not speak for governments or for people in poor countries. Government officials in countries such as Brazil, India and China were much more likely to have the best interests of the country and its citizens at heart, and they vigorously supported Briscoe's initiative. Besides this, Chinese and Indian Bank directors began to advocate a bolder infrastructure policy. As Mallaby describes it, these board members criticised the Bank for merely tinkering at the margins, pointing out the contrast with the bold water strategy, and noting that between the two of them they spoke for more than 2 billion people, or one in three members of the human race. The Chinese and Indians e-mailed the joint rebuke of the Bank's managers to all staff members who worked on infrastructure. Soon the people in the trenches were replying to the board members, heartily agreeing that their sector needed to respond more energetically to their poor clients (ibid: 361-2).

CONCLUDING REMARKS

The interests and ambitions of western activists should not be confused with the interests of society as a whole and particularly not with the interests of developing country populations on whose behalf they so frequently claim to speak. The best representatives of the interests and wishes of developing countries are their governments (preferably democratically elected).

The story of Brent Spar, Greenpeace and Shell is a stunning example of the appeasement of a sectional interest at the expense of society. The two other examples – sweatshops and dams – illustrate how the concerns and interests of outsiders act against what is clearly in the best interests of developing countries and their citizens. They demonstrate the danger of many western campaigns.

Business should think again about how it responds to the increasing chorus of demands in rich societies for so-called 'responsible' action in developing countries.

Chapter Three

THE POLITICS OF CSR

'Nobody would wish to defend corporate irresponsibility, or suggest that business should behave antisocially. It is little wonder therefore that CSR is a popular notion. To attack it is like assailing motherhood. Yet the idea is not merely problematic but in some respects dangerous. ... The collapse of communism destroyed the illusion that the abolition of private property would create a paradise. However, this failure barely touched the enemies of the market. What has changed is their means. Today's aim is not to eliminate private business but to transform the way it behaves.'

Martin Wolf, 'Corporate Responsibility' (2004)

WHO CAN POSSIBLY be opposed to aid? Rich countries helping poor countries sounds like such a good idea. It is only when one delves a little deeper that the complexities and ironies of this phenomenon become clear. It frequently involves taxing the masses in industrialised countries to enrich the elites of developing countries; the money is generally spent on industrialised country professionals and companies providing the 'aid' deemed suitable by the 'donor' country; it is built on a paternalistic notion that consultants, experts, officials and politicians in rich countries know what is best for other countries; and it puts a nice moral glow on what is essentially foreign policy – that is, the promotion of the rich country's own interests by other means.

Similarly, who could possibly oppose CSR? Like 'aid' and 'motherhood', it seems as if all right-thinking people should support this injunction. But, like aid, the reality of CSR is very different.

CAPITALISM WON, BUT BUSINESS IS ON THE DEFENSIVE

When the Cold War ended, capitalism gained the ascendance over communism and socialism. But this did not mean that all those with socialist inclinations changed their minds, or disappeared (see Novak 1996a). In the euphoria about markets following the collapse of the Soviet Union, few people thought about where all the anti-capitalists had gone.

While markets were now 'the only game in town', and the swing to increased international trade and investment greatly boosted large companies, leftists had the brilliant insight that individual corporations were vulnerable to attack on their brands and corporate reputations; that, in tandem with its growing importance, the entire business sector was vulnerable to pressure. The hard slog of political organisation, mobilisation, constituency building, elections, and the compromises that characterise democratic politics looked like a long, thankless, probably hopeless task, whereas large corporations appeared to offer a far more promising target.

As a result, many on the left have morphed into anti-corporate campaigners, anti-sweatshop activists, global human rights activists, CSR campaigners, environmentalists – all working on many different fronts to engage with and hopefully 'transform' corporations. Instead of socialism, one could have a 'softer', less 'selfish', 'more accountable' kind of capitalism.

It's important to bear in mind that practically every demand made on business concerning its impact on society (reducing carbon emissions, protecting forests, labour standards, poverty) could all in principle be addressed by government action – in other words, through national democratic debate and policy-making. But many activists have seen that getting large corporations to change their policies and approaches is often much easier than changing public policy. When this is coupled with an exaggerated notion of the importance and power of corporations, the assumed impact of working with and through companies is seen to be tremendously significant. It is this set of dynamics that lies behind many of the demands for CSR.

Disdain for and antagonism to business has a long history

Markets have provoked hostility from the time of Plato and Aristotle. Aristotle not only regarded well-to-do land-owning Greek males as the only persons fit to take part in public life, he also regarded being a gentleman farmer as the only respectable way to live. Honest toil was bad for the character; trading was dubious, because it encouraged people to profit from other people's needs; and lending money at interest was a crime against nature.

This long-standing set of beliefs can be added to the tradition of aristocratic contempt for those who engaged in the grubby business of making a living by serving other people's needs in the marketplace. In Britain and elsewhere money was to be inherited, mainly through land, not 'made', and aristocratic disdain for 'mere merchants' and the demeaning business of trade has long been a feature of British culture.

Today, it is difficult to find positive attitudes in public to business, capitalism, and the people who work in large corporations. In a detailed study of prime time television in the United States, Medved has found that prior to 1965 most business people portrayed on television were good guys, but in the 1970s this trend had been reversed, with villains outnumbering 'good guys' more than twice over. By 1980 most CEOs portrayed in soap operas were felons, and seemingly respectable business people were committing 40 per cent of murders and 44 per cent of serious crimes such as drug trafficking and pimping (Medved 1992).

Many mainstream religious leaders, in developed countries and elsewhere, are opposed to business. It is hard to recall any religious leader saying anything good about business per se, as opposed to corporate charity or disaster relief. (Many of the new rapidly growing evangelical churches strongly favour private enterprise, but – outside the United States at least – their views are not heard very loudly in public debates.)

Universities are not immune to this general hostility; in fact, many are centres of anti-capitalist thought. The social sciences in particular are almost universally influenced by a range of anti-business ideas and attitudes. Prominent academics talk of the dominant discourse whose goal is to fashion 'the merciless logic of corporate profit-making and political power into a normal state of affairs' (Edward Said, quoted in Bhagwati 2004a); or dismissively of the 'policies of increasingly rapacious global corporations' (Alan Wolfe, quoted in ibid: 20-21). And comments by academics such as these are usually accepted at face value.

To many members of the 'chattering classes', capitalism and profit are evil, the American (or western) soul has been corrupted by markets and materialism, and the enrichment of the west depends on exploiting the poor in the 'third world'.

Politicians, planners, academics, and many non-financial journalists tend to view business almost exclusively through the prism of whether corporations are being socially responsible. Making money isn't good enough; providing goods and services at historically low prices is taken for granted; funding large R&D departments that develop important innovations or products isn't what counts; and running a large and successful organisation isn't sufficient, and could in fact be harmful. Business has to redeem its inherently bad nature; it has to become a good corporate citizen; it must – in effect – pay 'reparations' if it is to be regarded as acceptable.

A NEW INTERNATIONAL PLAYER

Organisations involved in anti-corporate campaigns are part of a large, growing international NGO sector. The forces aligned against companies or lining up to 'transform' them are often well-funded international NGOs with large staff complements, media directors, and global impact strategies operating from imposing buildings in Washington DC, London, New York, and Europe.

These enterprising organisations came into their own in the 1980s and especially the 1990s with the innovative use of the internet. They muscle their way into international and national public policy debate. The great diversity of these organisations makes it hard to generalise about them. Some – such as Oxfam or the World Wildlife Fund – are surprisingly large, with headquarters as imposing as those of many large corporations. Others are smaller, but can quickly mobilise a large number of like-minded organisations to support their campaigns.

The category NGO encompasses research organisations, service organisations, small local groups, citizens' organisations trying to improve conditions in a city or around a particular social theme, and advocacy organisations. There are analytical and information-gathering NGOs; some provide important services, such as training officials of developing countries in WTO laws and regulations.

Advocacy organisations themselves assume a number of forms, but in many respects the most important divide is that between national or local organisations and cross-border or international NGOs; this does not necessarily mean that they are active in several countries, but that they concern themselves with international issues.

NGOs active in non-democratic or authoritarian countries play a distinctive role: they help to expose repressive conditions in those countries, and give citizens some sort of voice which they do not have at the ballot box. These NGOs sometimes claim to be more influential and representative than they actually are; this will differ from country to country, and the different issues on the table.

International NGOs, especially advocacy organisations (as opposed to service NGOs), play a different role. They frequently pursue selected issues, often acting as umbrella bodies for smaller organisations with a similar interest.

In the 1990s the number of international NGOs headquartered in rich industrialised countries grew dramatically. Some analysts put their number at well over 11 000; according to another estimate, their numbers have leapt from 6 000 in 1990 to 26 000 in 1999, with the environmental movement growing especially quickly (Legrain 2002: 262). In 2001 the number of NGOs operating internationally was estimated at about 40 000 (Wikipedia). Some are financed by members and member organisations in different countries, mainly rich industrialised countries. Some are national in orientation, funded locally. Others have some members, but also receive government subsidies.

Over the past 15 years, international NGOs have taken political commentators and corporations by surprise. Whether mobilising protests at global events such as WTO and World Bank meetings, or generating publicity about events in remote areas, these organisations have hugely magnified their influence. In the current climate, it is often far easier for journalists and members of the public to believe an NGO that claims to represent the public interest or the rights of indigenous people, workers, women, 'the landless' and can issue statements without consulting anyone, than large companies, which generally have to consider various public and private interests and agencies before they can make public statements on any social issue. Many companies have been slow to respond to external challenges, and slower to appreciate the new world of global media, and public issue management.

Michael Moore, former director-general of the WTO, has characterised these kinds of NGOs as 'selfish observers and self-appointed critics who need to maintain the rage of their supporters to raise funds to stay in business and on the front pages' (Moore 2003: 134). It is far from clear why the WTO should answer to Greenpeace, which is scarcely accountable to 2,5 million members, rather than the Indian parliament, which is elected by 600 million voters. 'And if to Greenpeace, why not to the Road Haulage Association or the National Front as well?' (Legrain 2002: 204)

Sebastian Mallaby has explored the impact of NGOs on the World Bank (2004: chapter 2). He and others have identified a number of instances when international NGOs have used false information or actually lied in order to create a furore about a particular issue.

CALLING THE KETTLE BLACK — THE LIMITATIONS OF SOME NGOS

Hypocrisy about transparency

Advocacy NGOs have led numerous campaigns to pressurise private sector companies into revealing exactly how they make and spend their money, in the hope that this will give them an opportunity to change corporate behaviour. However, when pressure is exerted on NGOs to become more transparent, many of the activists who have led the charge against 'corporate corruption' become extremely defensive.

Famously, Ralph Nader and Naomi Klein, at the forefront of efforts demanding accountability from corporations and governments, have lashed out at calls for holding NGOs similarly responsible. Nader, for example, objected to a new NGO Watch website created by the American Enterprise Institute, calling it 'a politically motivated effort to go after liberal or progressive NGOs'. Klein compared it to a 'McCarthyite blacklist' (Christensen 2004).

Many NGOs and activists have cultivated a self-righteous attitude based on the idea that because they do good works, they need not be accountable to anyone, including donors (Eisenberg 2000:45). Some NGOs also oppose transparency because of what this reveals about their funding sources. Bhagwati cites the example of Lori Wallach, head of Global Trade Watch, refusing to answer questions about contributions received from Roger Milliken, an ultra-right-wing textile magnate based in South Carolina (Bhagwati 2004a: 44).

Exaggerating, even lying about problems

To mobilise supporters and forment outrage, it is in the interests of campaigning NGOs to exaggerate the injustice or issue being publicised. Sometimes they lie about the facts.

In response to a World Bank proposal to build a dam in Uganda, the IRN claimed that 'the Ugandan environmental movement was outraged' and 'poor people near the site would be uprooted from their land and livelihood'. When Sebastian Mallaby checked on these facts on a trip to Uganda, he found that 'Ugandan environmentalists' consisted of one Swedish-funded organisation with 25 members; and that 'the only people who objected to the dam were the ones living just outside the perimeter. They were angry because the project was not going to affect them. They had been offered no generous payout, and were jealous of their neighbors' (2004a: 8).

Bhagwati mentions cases where NGOs lied about and/ or exaggerated the use of child labour by suppliers to large multinationals. In one, a German NGO released a video depicting child workers for companies supplying the Swedish manufacturer IKEA. When the allegations were investigated, it turned out the video had been faked (Bhagwati 2004a: 45).

Ignorance about complex local situations

Some NGOs often speak out on behalf of poor people located in less developed countries while understanding neither local problems and opportunities nor the preferences of local people. This emerged clearly from the NGO campaign against the mining company Placer Dome, led by Earthworks, Oxfam America, and MiningWatch Canada.

'People all over the world have concerns with this company,' said Catherine Coumans, research coordinator at MiningWatch Canada. 'There is a huge discrepancy between what they say and what they do.' The NGOs unveiled a consumer education campaign aimed at the gold mining industry called No Dirty Gold, in which Placer Dome was condemned for its 'environmental policies and its treatment of native Americans'. Placer Dome's Porgera gold mine in Papua New Guinea was specifically identified as a problem (Taylor 2004).

Papua New Guinea is one of the poorest, most remote countries in the world; the Porgera valley, inhabited by the Ipili people, is its most remote region. In 1990, after lengthy negotiations with the Ipili, the mine poured its first gold bar. By 1992 it was one of the richest gold mines in the world, accounting for more than a quarter of Papua New Guinea's exports (ibid: 3).

According to University of Chicago anthropologist Alex Golub, the Ipili told Placer they would agree to the mine as long as the company provided them with various amenities and long-term economic development. An agreement was reached on that basis.

Through agreements with the local community and national and provincial governments, Placer has spent US $48 million building roads, schools, sports clubs, and other amenities – priorities identified by elected governments. The local land owners' association shares a 5 per cent equity stake in the mine with the two levels of government. They also receive compensation for the use of the land. During the construction phase, Placer built new homes for every displaced resident, with free electricity and the first electrical appliances the Ipili had ever owned.

In response to demands from local politicians that Porgera generate more local economic benefits, the mine scaled back its fly-in/fly-out labour policy and agreed to build a town, called Paiam. It forms the centrepiece of the firm's plans for leaving behind a viable economy when the mine closes in 10 years or so (Taylor 2004).

Placer also funds community health patrols that visit isolated villages along the Porgera river system. All told, Placer has returned US$863 million to Papua New Guinea and the local community through taxes, royalties, compensation payments, provision of social services and development activities since 1990.

If CSR is supposed to require corporations to accept broader responsibilities in the community and act more like governments, then Porgera sounds like a feather in Placer Dome's cap, rather than the liability portrayed in the No Dirty Gold literature (ibid).

Important projects that could provide jobs and help lift many people out of poverty are being held up all over the world for fear of activist resistance, most often organised by tiny and unrepresentative groups. The media quickly latch onto their distorted or exaggerated claims, and spread them around the world.

No 'off' switch

Some NGOs cannot be reasoned with; in fact, their whole reason for existence is to be unyielding. As Mallaby puts it, 'campaigning NGOs as distinct from those with programs in the field almost have to be radical. If they stop denouncing big organisations, nobody will send them cash, or quote them in newspapers. Partly for this reason and partly out of the conviction that the status quo is never good enough, most NGOs do not have an off switch' (2004: 277). Their targets could accede to their demands, or disprove their allegations, but they will still not stop maligning them.

Many advocacy NGOs operate on a 'gotcha' mentality. They portray any misdeed by corporations or other targeted institutions as though that single incident illustrates everything that is wrong with corporations, globalisation, and capitalism. What is missing from the discussion is any sense of balance.

Many international advocacy organisations are invited to participate in meetings about a wide range of issues on the global stage. 'Of the several thousand NGOs that currently have a formal status within the UN system, only a few hundred are from developing countries, and of the developed country NGOs, an overwhelming majority are from the United States' (Lal 2005: 514).

Few people stop to ask who they represent or their right to speak for anyone other than themselves, or by what mandate they can interfere in or speak about issues that primarily affect developing countries. Few if any journalists mentioned the fact that most of the organisations besieging WTO or World Bank meetings a few years back were from rich industrialised countries, or that the organisations called on to represent 'civil society' in global discussions overwhelmingly represent urban elites predominantly from rich countries. By contrast, Indian trade unions representing millions of people are not being asked to appear on global platforms. There is an enormous discrepancy in resources between NGOs in rich countries and those in poorer ones. The former are generally better funded and staffed than even the largest, most sophisticated of developing world NGOs. Most international

NGO funding comes from wealthy foundations or individuals located in the developed world. Moreover, NGOs in industrialised countries often receive subsidies and even donations from their governments to undertake certain activities – placing question marks against their much-vaunted independence and freedom from material interests.

ANTI-CORPORATE CAMPAIGNS

'If you go to any of the websites of the major activists, you will see the route plan of how to bring a brand to its knees ... when people want to criticize something, they will attach that criticism to the biggest company they can find – 'brandjacking'.

Sarah Murray, *Financial Times* (2004)

It is in this context of a general milieu of distrust of business – its 'ethical deficit' – that we need to place the new and growing phenomenon of corporate campaigns. Having turned their back on electoral politics, where they have not been very successful, many activists are now focusing on anti-corporate campaigns: they identify an issue, select the most visible or vulnerable company related to it, and implement a range of strategies to damage its reputation. This allows activists to pick off large companies one by one, focusing all their energy on the chosen target.

As any good political organiser knows, every campaign needs an enemy. After the Cold War, the Left found that enemy in big business and globalisation, and began to wage war on corporations.

In the view of Jarol Manheim, who has studied what he refers to as 'Biz-war' in the United States, the elements of the attack are well established. 'Biz-war is being waged on all fronts – from the forest and the field to the marketplace, from the bargaining table to the dinner table, from the banks to the churches and the local coffee shops. Corporate greed. Corporate indifference. Corporate welfare. Corporate scandal, corporate malfeasance. Corporate corruption. Corporate crime. These are the images of battle' (Manheim 2004: 3).

This battle assumes many forms: demonstrations, shareholder resolutions, corporate governance initiatives, class action law suits, legislative actions and regulatory complaints, media events, pressures on Wall Street, institutional attacks, and highly personal ones. It is a form of reputation warfare against the corporation as a means of changing corporate policy, company by company, and shaping public policy through the aggregation of these individual campaigns, charges, and attacks. It consists of a wide range of corporate campaigns which have 'at their centre a framing of the corporation as a social outlaw' (ibid).

In the United States the phenomenon known as the corporate campaign was developed primarily within the labour movement in the mid-1970s. The central idea was that, by identifying and undermining a target company's most critical stakeholder relationships – with its customers, suppliers, bankers and the like – and by effectively waging war on its reputation, a union could exert a great deal of pressure on management that might result in a better union contract.

In the course of conducting what by now amounts to well over 200 such campaigns in the United States, organised labour recruited a large number of environmental, human rights and other activist groups, some of which began to learn the techniques used in such campaigns and appreciate their potential to influence corporate decision-makers.

Corporate campaigns have numerous facets, including legal, regulatory and legislative tactics; political, financial, and commercial strategies; and media and public relations activities. The language used about the company and the issue generally includes notions such as justice, rights, community values, and socially responsible behaviour. At no time is a targeted company credited with achieving any of these goals on its own initiative.

These tactics are used by a wide spectrum of organisations. One striking example is an organisation called Empowering Democracy, based in Austin, Texas. Its associates include the AFL-CIO, Global Exchange, Interfaith Center on Corporate Responsibility, Rainforest Action Network, CorpWatch, and Friends of the Earth. Established as an educational base for training anti-corporate campaigners, it defines its mission in these terms:

> **Problem:** Corporate power and influence are increasing to the point of subverting democracy. Although the newly spreading corporate pressure campaign movement is proving it can be effective, we have no infrastructure or process to help the movement mature or to train others in effective corporate campaign strategies and tactics. ...
> **Solution:** Establish an annual conference for corporate campaigners. ... share skills and teach others basic strategies and tactics which organizations and activists can use in corporate accountability campaigns and lay a foundation for an infrastructure for the corporate campaign movement while each year increasing presence and influence at a single company's annual meeting' (ibid: 149).

Companies targeted include Dow, Dupont, Citigroup, ChevronTexaco, Exxon Mobil. Topics at the 2002 conference held in New York included power structure analysis, ways to influence corporate CEOs and directors, internet activism, coalition-building, international coordination, shareholders and governance, researching corporate vulnerabilities, working through local governments to pressure companies, boycotts, legal strategies, organising days of action, and using the media.

The aggressive anti-corporate Rainforest Action Network seeks to protect rainforests, old growth forests, and indigenous people who live in them. Its chosen method is the anti-corporate campaign (ibid: 156). Targets have included the Ford Motor Company and Citigroup. Its Campaign for a Sane Economy targeted the international activities of the financial services industry. A sample of its rhetoric is revealing:

> Mega banks fund the operations of the fossil fuel, logging and mining industries with impunity, refusing to acknowledge their complicity in the destruction of pristine ecosystems and vulnerable human communities the world over. Like a shadowy cartel of drug pushers, these banks keep the industrialized world hooked on an unsustainable and ultimately self-destructive economic model. If we care about the planet we must hold the entire corporate finance sector responsible for their investments (ibid: 156).

It is important to appreciate the interlinked nature of many of these organisations. As long ago as 1980, *Forbes* columnist John Train wrote about encountering reports by Counter Information Services, a British organisation specialising in anti-corporate propaganda. One of the most elaborate was a 69-page booklet about Ford Motor Company. It stated that Ford 'waged war' on its workers, and contained pictures of Generalissimo Franco, a gallows, violent strikers, and soldiers in combat gear. It talked of the irreconcilable conflict between profits and human life. Counter Information Services described itself as an affiliate of the Transnational Institute, an affiliate in turn of the Institute for Policy Studies in Washington. Train eventually discovered that IPS had received a grant from the Ford Foundation whose money came, of course from the Ford family (ibid: 131-3).

It would be an error to misread the fundamental nature of this new wave of pressure on companies.

ESSENTIAL QUESTIONS ABOUT CSR

The notion of CSR is underpinned by a range of questionable assumptions. And while advocates talk about it in terms that broach no questioning of its desirability, feasibility or morality, important questions need to be raised concerning the discourse about companies and their 'responsibilities'.

'Responsibility'

To whom should corporations be responsible? And for what exactly? Is it the local community in which a plant, mine or shop is located, or a broader regional, national, or even global community? Inhabitants of even the smallest village have different interests, perceptions, expectations, needs, demands, and this diversity is multiplied many times over in towns, cities, or countries. To which of these interests should companies respond?

Activists might recommend that a company stays in a given locality even if this is no longer functional. What does this mean for other regions, cities or countries competing to attract the company's business? Why should they lose out?

CSR advocates argue that companies should pay workers in developing countries more than the 'going rate'. This may result in companies hiring fewer workers, and mechanising more rapidly. To whom is such a company most responsible – existing workers, or those denied employment?

The many facets of CSR further complicate the task of definition and evaluation. A company might be considered responsible because of its environmental and community development initiatives; others might label it irresponsible for abandoning its long-standing policy of guaranteeing job security. Many of the same firms that have improved their social practices in developing countries have also cut back on health benefits to employees and retirees in the United States or Britain.

Whose definition of 'responsibility' should a company apply? Consumers and citizens often have different ideas about what they expect from 'responsible' companies. A 2005 survey found that, to Chinese consumers, the hallmark of a socially responsible company is safe, high-quality products. For Germans it is secure employment, and for South Africans it's contribution to health care and education (Donaldson 2005).

For activists, a socially responsible company in the food business needs to sell 'organic' products. Many supermarkets now provide consumers with a choice between conventionally farmed produce and 'organic' food. However, many experts believe organic farming is *not* better for the environment.

Norman Borlaug, father of the 'green revolution' and winner of the Nobel Peace Prize, advocates the use of synthetic fertilisers to increase crop yields. He points out that the use of synthetic fertilisers tripled global cereal production between 1950 and 2000, but the amount of land used increased by only 10 per cent. Using traditional techniques such as crop rotation, compost, and manure to supply the soil with nitrogen and other minerals would have required a tripling of the area under cultivation. 'The more intensively you farm, the more room you have left for rainforest,' he adds (quoted in *The Economist* 2006a).

'Socially responsible behaviour' is inevitably politically defined, and therefore controversial.

'RESPONSIBLE' FOOD SHOPPING AND TRADE-OFFS

In 2006 *The Economist* investigated the notion of 'shopping to help the environment', and discovered that it was far more complicated than it appeared at first sight. Some findings are summarised below.

Is organic farming more energy-efficient?

Activists argue that the natural gas used to make artificial fertilisers is a 'completely unsustainable' resource, but organic farming requires more energy per ton of food produced because yields are lower.

Fair trade?

The British organisation Fairtrade seeks to address 'the injustice of low prices' by guaranteeing that producers in developing countries receive a fair price. This involves paying producers an above market 'Fairtrade' price for their produce, provided they meet particular labour and production standards.

Is this a 'responsible' approach to global trade? The low price of commodities such as coffee is due to overproduction, and ought to be a signal to producers to switch to growing other crops. Paying a guaranteed Fairtrade premium – in effect a subsidy – prevents this signal from getting through and encourages more producers to enter an already overtraded market. This drives down the price of non-Fairtrade coffee even further, making non-Fairtrade farmers poorer.

Fairtrade certification is predicated on political assumptions about the best way to organise production. For some commodities, including coffee, certification is available only to cooperatives of small producers who are deemed most likely to give workers a fair deal when deciding how to spend the Fairtrade premium. Coffee plantations or large family farms cannot be certified. Yet limiting certification to co-ops means 'missing out on helping the vast majority of farm workers who work on plantations,' says the Rainforest Alliance which certifies producers of all kinds.

Local food

Food bought from local producers either directly or at farmers' markets is becoming increasingly popular. Local food is not necessarily organic, but buying directly from small farmers short-circuits industrial production and distribution systems. Local food thus appeals to environmentalists, national farm lobbies, anti-corporate activists, as well as consumers who want to know more about where their food comes from.

However, there is a reason why supermarkets were invented, and global trade expanded. According to Britain's environment and farming ministry, it is better for the environment to truck in tomatoes from Spain during the winter than grow them in heated greenhouses in Britain. A shift towards local food and away from a supermarket-based system with its distribution depots, lean supply chains, and full trucks might actually increase the number of food vehicle miles, because produce would move around in a larger number of smaller less efficiently packed vehicles.

Trade-offs

The Economist concluded: 'All food choices involve trade-offs. Even if organic farming does consume a little less energy and produce a little less pollution, that must be offset against lower yields and greater land use. Fairtrade food may help some poor farmers but may also harm others, and even if local food reduces transport emissions it also reduces the potential for economic development. ...

'Food is central to the debates on the environment, development, trade and globalisation, but the potential for food choices to change the world should not be overestimated. The idea of saving the world by shopping is appealing, but tackling climate change, boosting development, and reforming the global trade system will require difficult political choices' (*The Economist* 2006a).

Democracy

Inherent in the concept of CSR is the assumption of a single definition of 'the public interest'. It is taken for granted that the public interest can be defined quite easily, without trade-offs or serious conflicts, thus clearing the way for companies to adopt and implement appropriate programmes. CSR advocates continually simplify issues and characteristically take it for granted that there are known and agreed 'solutions' to national and international challenges.

Why do we have politics and freedom of expression to air different points of view if the public interest on social, environmental, developmental, and other issues is self-evident? Who decides what 'responsible' practices based on 'universally agreed' principles are? If everyone agreed on solutions for the world's problems and challenges, politics would not be needed at all.

On many CSR issues it is far from obvious that campaigners' agendas are popular, let alone sensible. It's never clear whom exactly they represent. Thus consumer activist Ralph Nader ran for president in the US 2000 elections, but received only 3 per cent of the vote. 'Rather than fight their corner in elections,' says Legrain about corporate activists, 'they bypass them. Bludgeon companies with consumer boycotts, threaten to besmirch their precious brands and then exact a price – we will lay off you if you forward some of our agenda' (2002: 205).

The best policies on global warming are far from clear globally, let alone nationally or in the sphere of the company or individual consumer. Hard-headed negotiation can be anticipated within countries and between developed and developing countries if any practical policies are to be devised. Assuming that individual firms, groups of firms, or partnerships between companies and international NGOs can or should resolve these issues is both wrong and misplaced. Settling such questions exceeds both the competence and the proper remit of private enterprise as well as NGOs. This does not mean that individual companies cannot or should not clean up their emissions and save energy, but this is a different matter from developing international and national measures to combat global warming (*The Economist* 2005b).

Civil society and developing countries

One of the most insidious ideas in the package of assumptions underpinning CSR is the notion that activists or NGOs represent 'civil society'. Companies, journalists, and politicians frequently treat the views and demands of activists and other often hostile critics of business as more rationally based, more representative of society's expectations, and more morally sound than they often are.

NGOs need to be made much more accountable and transparent. The tables should be turned. NGOs need to be interrogated about their contribution to the public good and adherence to universally acceptable values.

Take issues of transparency and governance. Who are their members? Are they individuals, companies or organisations? In which countries do those members reside, and whom do they represent? How are decisions made about policy issues? Do they canvass members for their views, and are these discussed at regular board meetings?

How are they funded? Do they receive government subsidies – and if they do, how much, and from which governments? Are they exempt from paying tax? (another form of subsidy). What are those subsidies meant to achieve?

On what information do they base their assertions and accusations? What research have they done; by whom is it done, and using which methods? Has it been peer-reviewed? Is it reliable? Is it generalisable? When was it done, and is the situation still as they describe? Does it consist of one incident, or can it legitimately be taken to represent what is happening throughout a company's operations or throughout a country?

What is even more questionable is when NGOs based in rich countries presume to speak for and represent the interests of 'the poor' in developing countries. Why should the tastes and preferences of first-world consumers be considered morally superior to the life-determining choices facing poor people in developing countries? And why should the preferences of some people living in the richest countries in the world determine how millions of people in very poor countries find a way out of poverty, malnutrition, and despair? Although the 'needs of the poorest' are often invoked in campaigns in industrialised countries, it is hard to see how NGOs without any representative status in poor countries can have more say on these issues than poor people's own elected governments.

Take the increasingly popular idea of adopting global environmental and labour standards. Setting uniform minimum standards everywhere is a bad idea when countries are so different. Moreover, the balance between the costs and benefits of standards is different in rich and poor countries. As countries become richer, people expect higher standards, and can afford them as well. But while they are still poor they should not have higher standards imposed on them that would make them worse off than they are already. If people in rich countries find social standards in poor countries offensively low, they have several options. They can drop protectionist measures and tariff barriers, thus helping developing countries to grow more quickly leading to a rise in their own standards in a more sustainable way. They could argue within their own countries for a removal of farming subsidies (and other tariff barriers) so that food producers in developing countries can compete on a more even playing field. They can choose not to buy the product in question.

James Shikwati from Kenya asks:

> Why do Europe's developed countries impose their ethics on poor countries that are simply trying to pass through a stage they themselves went through? After taking various risks to reach their current environmental and technological status, why do they tell poor countries to use no energy and no agricultural or pest control technologies that might harm the environment? Why do they tell poor countries to adopt a sustainable development doctrine that really means little or no energy or economic development? (Driessen 2003: 30).

The strange notion of global civil society

A popular idea in CSR circles is the notion of 'global civil society'. Ann Florini of the Brookings Institution has described this as follows:

> What we are seeing is the emergence of a whole series of transnational networks ... out of traditional social institutions such as churches ... that are beginning to develop into something that looks like global civil society ... (and the) creation of citizens' movements that are an essential counterpart to capitalism at the global level ...it can serve as a messy but essentially good enough channel for transnational democratic debate (2003).

The assumptions contained in this statement are far-reaching, but would provoke little if any criticism in political discussions in Washington, Brussels, New York, or London.

Few advocates of global governance talk of global elections. Instead, they talk of tripartite global governance institutions comprising some large companies, some governments, and 'global civil society'. This last component is never defined but tends to comprise representatives of some large NGOs which, it is assumed, can talk on behalf of the world's poor.

The idea that 'the people' are represented by public interest NGOs is hard enough to swallow in a relatively small country such as South Africa, but even more difficult to conceive of across many nations. Moreover, large companies compete intensely with one another and represent a minority of the companies or enterprises in any country, most of which are much smaller. What has emerged in most instances is a relatively small coterie of organisations, large companies, consultants, and advisers who presume to make deals and form partnerships on behalf of this so-called 'emerging global civil society'.

Who elected those who claim to speak for or represent 'global civil society', to make decisions that will affect the lives and prospects of millions of people in developing countries?

For many CSR activists, the absence of instruments of global governance means that other mechanisms need to be put in place, thus justifying their projected role for participant multinational companies and selected NGOs. But the voices heard represent a very small slice of the cacophony of ideas and views across developing countries.

Democratic governments are accountable for their actions, and voters are given regular opportunities to 'throw the rascals' out of power if needs be. To whom are CSR advocates, international NGOs, 'global networks' and others accountable? Companies are accountable to their boards, and operate within a strict, extensive framework of laws, regulations, and other measures. Within what framework of laws, standards, rules and representivity do the international NGOs operate?

Why do so many people in Washington and elsewhere think that Oxfam represents anything other than the views of the mainly first world professionals in its employ? Or that their ideas better represent 'the voices of the poor' than the democratically elected government of Brazil or India?

Democratic elections function as a mechanism that puts NGOs with loud voices in their place as elections determine how acceptable the policies they advocate are to the electorate at large. One can see how this works in a nation state and the healthy relationship between organised citizens exercising their rights of free association on particular issues by forming an NGO and representative politics. But how do we conceive of international NGOs in this light?

Western campaigners focus on what matters to them, not the priorities of the developing world. International NGOs, however large, do not represent the views of national electorates. They and their allies in developing countries represent interests and organisations operating within the civil societies of those countries but they certainly cannot claim to represent 'global civil society' in its rich totality at all.

How generalisable is CSR?

When one digs deeper into the reality of CSR rather than its rhetoric, it is surprising to discover its highly selective, partial nature. Most campaign groups set out to change the processes, values, and activities of companies, and argue that this will radically change the global prognosis on the issue at hand. What they seem to lose sight of is that most of the world's workers are employed by small and medium-sized firms.

Amnesty International once warned companies that '... the

increasing scrutiny of corporate behaviour by the media, consumer groups, community organisations, local and international NGOs, and the immediacy of global communications, leaves companies with little or no hiding place' (Vogel 2005: 158). The common assumption is that this critical scrutiny applies uniformly to all companies and all their activities, and that local events or conditions can be easily and accurately relayed to a global audience. In practice, NGOs tend to focus on issues that can be easily packaged for western audiences. This means that many global companies, many more national companies, and many situations or issues remain out of the public eye because they do not involve high-profile western brands. Activists target some major brands and ignore others. For example, Adidas has not been subject to the kind of scrutiny that Nike has had to endure.

One of the key mechanisms for encouraging CSR is that of voluntary codes. These include the well-known SA 800 voluntary code with certification developed in 1996. By 2004 a total of 4 430 facilities in 40 different countries and 43 industrial sectors had been certified, but this only covered some 270 000 workers – a drop in the ocean (ibid: 83). Voluntary codes primarily govern the manufacturing of products for retailers and branded goods companies that sell to consumers in the United States and Europe. They do not usually affect the production of generic merchandise intermediate goods, or products manufactured by companies whose primary markets are domestic or are exported to other regions, 'all of which remain below the radar screen of western activists' (ibid:76).

They also rarely extend beyond primary contractors, many of whom subcontract to other firms or households. Moreover, they still cover a relatively small number of manufactured products. Most importantly, relatively few codes cover agricultural workers, who constitute the majority of the labour force in most developing countries. Voluntary codes and monitoring primarily influence enclaves in the global economy. They largely focus on workers for first-tier suppliers (ie, big-name brands) and in large factories, which constitute only a small portion of developing country footwear, apparel, toy, and sporting goods exports. They rarely affect the informal or home-based sectors, in which most developing country workers are employed (ibid: 76 ff).

The standards for and scope of corporate environmental reporting are equally uneven. First, 'environmental sustainability' or sustainable development is impossible to define. As Jagdish Bhagwati has remarked, 'Even God does not know what sustainable development means' (2004a: 156). The contortions involved in encouraging companies that extract minerals and other primary resources into devising rhetoric about the sustainability of their activities must either induce Alice in Wonderland humour or involve a definition of sustainability that so stretches the meaning of the term that it becomes something else entirely.

Here again, Vogel (2005) has thoroughly examined the evidence and found that the diversity of corporate environmental impacts means that any discussion of this issue must be highly selective. The available literature primarily deals with business practices in developed countries marked by extensive government regulation. While often labelled as CSR, business decisions in this field frequently represent normal business practices rather than new initiatives in corporate responsibility. Many corporations have voluntarily accepted greater responsibility for the environmental impact of what they produce, purchase, and sell.

The Canadian oil company Talisman had a major oil concession in the Sudan, and was targeted by activists for doing business in that country. This pressure started to affect its stock price. Its CSR report for 2000 lists considerable efforts by the company to illustrate the 'responsibility' of its activities in that country, and how much local communities could benefit from its presence. Nevertheless, it eventually decided that it did not wish to deal with sustained hostile attention, and withdrew from Sudan (Talisman Energy Inc 2000). Not surprisingly, the largest foreign investors in the Sudan are now Chinese firms.

This raises two difficult issues for many CSR activists. What happens if all western oil companies decided to follow the logical outcome of activist pressure and withdraw from all difficult and risky, often horrible places? What will the reality of the growing Chinese business presence – whose style of business, corporate values, and attitudes to human rights, the environment, and other sensitivities make almost any western business look positively soft – mean for corporate responsibility advocates?

What about socially responsible investing, shopping, and employment?

The goal of 'socially responsible investing' (SRI) is to make lucrative investment choices that have a positive impact on the world. The events of the past few decades – from Vietnam to Chernobyl to South Africa – brought the idea of using investment choices to influence corporate behaviour into the mainstream.

It is important to note the criteria for most of the socially responsible investment funds. Enron, for example, was favoured as a socially responsible energy stock until just before it crashed. Vogel (2005) finds that companies involved in arms, tobacco and alcohol are all excluded but that despite these funds claiming to be on the cutting edge of changing public expectations of business, no fund had relaxed its exclusion of military contractors since September 2001. This once again raises the generalisability question – what happens if all investors followed suit?

There is little evidence that the growing numbers of 'ethical' investors are prepared to accept lower returns. Writing in *The Atlantic* (October 2007), Henry Blodgett points out that the single best performing stock in the S and P index for the 46 years through to 2003 has been the tobacco giant Philip Morris, and he questions how many investors would have chosen to exclude dividends from this investment. The market has proved to be remarkably efficient in determining what marks a corporation as 'good'. A recent Wharton study calculated that funds which layer on ideological screens often perform worse than the general market by about 31 basis points a year – a huge discrepancy (Entine 2006).

SRI comes in many forms, but one of the most common is avoiding investments in 'bad' companies. Exactly how to define these 'bad' companies is only one of the challenges facing this kind of investing. Let's go back to Sudan, today's favourite SRI target for exclusion. Will disinvesting in any company doing business with Sudan as many activists are calling for and many investors have already done, help stop the genocide in Darfur? Or will abrupt withdrawal of foreign capital only strengthen the Sudanese government, as investors like Warren Buffett say it would?

To what extent do consumers favour the products of socially responsible firms? Time and again, the evidence points in the same direction. People act differently from how they say they will or how they want to be perceived. A European survey in 2004 found that while 75 per cent of consumers indicated that they were ready to modify their purchasing decisions to align them with environmental or social considerations, only 3 per cent had actually done so (Vogel 2005: 48). J W Connolly, former president of Heinz USA, captured this reality well when he remarked: 'Consumers wanted a dolphin-friendly safe product, but they were not willing to pay more for it. If there was a dolphin-safe can of tuna next to a regular can, people chose the cheaper product. Even if the difference was one penny' (ibid: 135).

What about another frequent claim by CSR adherents, that 'responsible' companies are more attractive places for employees to work, and make it easier to hire the best available talent? In 2004 British American Tobacco (BAT) was asked if it had to pay more to attract and keep staff in a much reviled industry. The firm's chairman said no: 'One thing that surprises me is that we offer a job publicly, and we are inundated' (ibid: 58). If the much vilified tobacco industry has this experience, and in an economic climate of growth and 'talent wars' for qualified people, it is hard to believe the CSR propaganda on this any more.

CONCLUDING REMARKS

There is no persuasive alternative to a market-based approach to economic growth. Despite this, in countries in which capitalist endeavour has produced the highest standards of living the world has ever known, business is on the defensive as a legitimate and moral form of activity.

Large companies are most sharply attacked over their activities in developing countries. They are facing pressure about issues in industrialised countries as well, but the stark contrast between large modern corporations and the poverty of many places outside of North America, Japan and Europe give activists far more scope to portray businesses and their activities in a bad light.

The strange dance around CSR can only be explained by the way in which an anti-business world view has been allowed to grow and flourish in universities, media, and popular culture and the growth of cross-national advocacy and campaigning organisations that have set their sights on business and companies as a means of enforcing the changes they want in the world. Faced with this onslaught many companies regard CSR as the best of a set of bad options, and acquiesce in the package of presumptions which assume that companies need fundamental change in order to play a virtuous role.

When we turn our attention to the core ideas that underpin CSR itself, we find that it is built upon fundamentally questionable notions about responsibility, democracy and civil society. And that its proponents have put forward a number of false claims about its presumed benefits, not only for the world but for companies themselves.

Chapter Four

SIMPLE SLOGANS
CAN BE WRONG

'*Most big companies are falling over themselves to appease
pressure groups and present themselves as friends of
people and the planet. ... Corporate social responsibility
is the product of an undemocratic collaboration between
multinational corporations and campaigning organizations,
the former buying peace and acceptability by succumbing to
the demands of the latter.*'

Harold Geneen, *Financial Times* (2001)

ALTHOUGH SOME CSR activists are opposed to market economics, the movement is not simply the creation of anti-capitalist agitators; its impact has been too widespread. In part, it reflects a genuine change in the environment in which business operates. Today, people in many societies know more about events elsewhere in the world, and therefore demand greater openness on the part of companies (and other institutions), and have a legitimate interest in their broader social impact. At the same time, people in developed countries place less trust in almost all institutions.

I have spent so much time on CSR, the assumptions that underlie it, and the campaigns that characterise it because this shows us how many ideas are wrapped up in this simple slogan. It also reveals the need for thinking much more creatively about business, development, poverty, and the politics of ideas.

CSR and the ideas surrounding it are built upon many other notions about business itself, civil society and the future of developing countries.

WEIGHING UP THE CASE FOR CSR

The conception of reality underpinning the CSR world view is faulty in a number of respects.

- It is a pessimistic, often highly 'alarmist' perspective that does not recognise human progress and innovation over the past century.

- It does not take account of the enormous progress made over the past 50 years in combating global poverty, and the fact that the absolute numbers of people living in poverty have declined even as world population has grown.

- It is built upon an ahistorical vision of the relationship between economic growth and environmental issues. The evidence shows that when economies grow, and citizens gain stronger 'voice', environmental standards improve enormously. Societies begin to allocate resources to improving the environment, and many have been remarkably successful in alleviating difficult environmental challenges.

- It exaggerates the power of companies to change global poverty and 'the environment', and fails to recognise the role of other actors and forces in contributing or responding to poverty and inequality.

- It minimises the role of the state in respect of economic and development issues, and in relation to corporate conduct in developed as well as developing countries.

- It fails to appreciate the scale and nature of development challenges in poorer countries, and thus generally fails to advocate sustained and mass scale approaches to address these challenges.

- There is a lack of appreciation of the realities of global trade, and the precise roles of large and small businesses.

- It underplays the role of the state in successful national development, and does not understand or appreciate the role of large companies in this process, nor the important contribution of market dynamics in general.

A former chief economist of the OECD, David Henderson, has noted:

> Many large corporations that have come out for CSR, whether
> directly or through organisations which they have created and
> continue to finance, have lent support to ideas and beliefs that are
> dubious or false. On behalf of business they have been ready to
> endorse uncritically, ill-defined and questionable objectives; confess
> imaginary sins; admit to nonexistent privileges and illusory gains
> from globalisation that require justification in the eyes of 'society';
> identify the demands of NGOs with 'society's expectations'
> and treat them as beyond question; accept overdramatised and
> misleading interpretations of recent world economic trends and
> their implications for business; and, in some cases, question
> outright the economic system of which private business forms an
> integral part' (2001: 58).

WHY WORRY?

I used to think that CSR consisted merely of businesses adopting
some 'soft' rhetoric and allocating relatively small amounts of money
to the least entrepreneurial people in management to use for 'good
works'. These activities were often not strategic, did not have much
systemic impact, and were frequently intermingled with marketing
and PR efforts, but were also not very harmful except when the funds
were used to support groups that opposed markets and the values that
underpin the market economy. And some of the projects funded by
CSR were positive ones, with beneficial impacts on their recipients
and sometimes broader society.

While this might have been the case in the 1980s, it no longer obtains today. As we have demonstrated, in many countries CSR is not just a growing area of opportunity for consultants, monitoring agencies, and so on; it increasingly involves national legislation, an expanding multilateral consensus, a mindset in the media and academia, and a creeping view within companies themselves and the business schools that serve them, constituting a set of pressures in and around large companies that is very hard to resist.

Throughout society, business is called upon to demonstrate its good corporate citizenship, and almost all large companies want to show that they are. What is going on? Why are business executives going along with this, and does it matter?

We know that the add-on social and environmental practices of the vast majority of companies have not had any positive effect on their bottom line. The public image of companies – whether the products they sell or their business practices – has not affected their ability to hire the staff they want, or retain motivated and competent employees. Remarkably few companies have been punished or rewarded by financial markets for their social performance. All the evidence indicates that of the many factors affecting corporate earnings, CSR is among the last. In short, CSR is neither necessary nor sufficient for business success. And yet very many firms seem to act as if CSR really matters.

A number of reasons can be adduced for this subservience to the 'responsibility' mindset. Fear is a major factor. A survey in 2002 of 1 000 CEOs from 33 countries found that CSR was driven primarily 'by the negative consequences of ignoring the impact of criticism on company reputation' (Vogel 2005: 52). Corporate managers are products of their social environments, and are therefore sometimes uncertain about the legitimacy of business or how to defend it, thus making them susceptible to CSR arguments. Few executives or managers proudly and confidently explain and defend the role of corporations.

It is even more unusual to find business leaders willing to take on the misconceptions informing much of the business responsibility debate.

Companies targeted by activists feel the need to demonstrate their commitment to human rights, the environment, and the latest fad for attacking global poverty on terms they believe will satisfy activists and the doubters within their own ranks. Companies fear they could be next on the hit list, and want to deflect this. Some have been persuaded by PR and advertising agencies that positioning themselves as more responsible than others will pay dividends in the marketplace, or they see CSR activities as a way of differentiating themselves from their competitors, as a form of marketing.

At one level, observers might be tempted to conclude that this doesn't really matter. Although there has been an explosion of demands for business to demonstrate its social responsibility, this has hardly impacted on its core mission. Much of the talk is rhetoric, social and environmental accounting procedures are not tightly monitored, most companies can get away with spending modest amounts of money, and without having to make major adjustments. Many claimed 'responsibility' successes are things companies would have done anyway as new technologies or societal standards changed.

Financially, a lot of corporate social investment is either marketing of the company's brand under another guise, or can be used in that way. And if it cannot, the amounts involved are not large enough to have a significant impact on profitability. Very few companies have taken the injunctions of activists really seriously. And those that have, have quickly demonstrated the economic costs of trying to implement core 'responsibility' injunctions.

THE COMPANY THAT TRIED

Levi Strauss, the famous blue jeans manufacturer, kept taking 'responsible' decisions and then backtracking as it rediscovered the realities of doing business. Initially the company wouldn't move from 'economically inefficient' San Francisco to the American Sunbelt for 'responsibility' reasons, but was compelled to do it for economic reasons a few years later. It again played the same catch-up strategy about moving from those states to lower-cost countries in Asia.

The company said it wouldn't continue manufacturing in China because of human rights issues, but the proposed phased withdrawal never took place as the importance of the Chinese economy became increasingly apparent. Five years later the company reversed its decision, although it initially said it would not sell clothes made in China in the United States. Eventually, under pressure from the market, the company's leaders revised its 'mission and aspirations statement'. They deleted the line that promised to 'conduct our business ethically and demonstrate leadership in satisfying our responsibilities to our communities and to society', and replaced it with a commitment to 'achieve and sustain commercial success as a global marketer of branded apparel' (Schoenberger 2000).

CSR budgets typically comprise tiny portions of company budgets. Some observers have therefore concluded that the whole debate about CSR is overblown; that it's actually a question of rhetoric and gesture, with very little action.

In my view this judgement is a mistake. The victory of the activists goes deeper and further than just words and attitudes. A number of real dangers are looming.

Increased regulation

Any examination of the social reports of the largest, most visible global companies shows how complex many social and environmental issues are, and the detailed attention they need to give to those issues in order to avoid adverse public attention. Activists are demanding higher standards of accountability, and concrete evidence of performance. These will need to be made available to external stakeholders in formats that permit more accurate benchmarking.

Within companies, CSR often increases costs, and impairs commercial performance. Managers have to take account of a wide range of goals and concerns and involve themselves in new, time-consuming processes of consultation with outside stakeholders. New systems of accounting, auditing and monitoring are required, and if firms insist on their partners, suppliers and contractors observing the same standards, this will involve costs for them as well. Running a business in a global market is difficult enough; expecting managers to do this and take seriously a range of CSR injunctions as well, means that something has to give.

For the economy as whole, CSR points the way to anticompetitive tendencies and over-regulation. Insofar as 'socially responsible' businesses find that their new role involves higher costs and lower profits, they have a strong interest in ensuring that their unreformed rivals are compelled to toe the same line, whether through public pressure or government regulation. The large publicly visible firms have an interest in ensuring that smaller rivals do not escape the net, while firms in rich countries have a similar, growing incentive to see to it that competitors in developing countries are made subject to the same pressures.

The demand for formulating and enforcing international standards, rules, and codes emanates from a number of different sources, including the European Commission; UN organisations, World Bank, International Finance Corporation (IFC); some governments; international NGOs; and multinational corporations themselves. In 2001, Nike's CEO, Philip H Knight, commented as follows:

> I know what makes for good performance when I see it on the running track. I know it when I read quarterly results. I have to admit, though, I am not sure how we measure good performance in corporate responsibility. I'm not convinced anybody does. Why not? Because there are no standards, no agreed-on definitions. ... If we have a scorecard that includes all of our main competitors or a set of multinational corporations and a uniform yardstick, I'll at least have a way to frame an answer (quoted in Litvin 2003: 248).

Chris Helzer, Nike's head of external relations in South East Asia, has stated explicitly:

> We are in favour of enforcing minimum labour and environmental standards at the WTO. If we have to pay the costs, we don't see why our competitors shouldn't have to too (quoted in Legrain 2002: 208).

Corporations are already the most accountable institutions in the world. No other organisations are subjected to the same degree of scrutiny, or required to be as transparent. No politician has to seek 're-election' every day, every week, every month, as companies and their products do in the marketplace. Many governments may have moved to deregulate markets, but have simultaneously been regulating companies to a growing degree. The United States government, traditionally one of the least interventionist, has also increased its grip on companies through laws governing health, safety, environment, affirmative action, employee and consumer rights. According to Management and Budget, by the end of the 20th century the cost to

American firms of complying with social regulations was $289 billion a year, a figure others reckoned was only one third of the real amount (Micklethwait & Wooldridge 2005).

Company oversight by the state, which began as a mixture of accident prevention (such as workplace safety rules) and administrative convenience (such as pensions) has sprawled. In the United States laws for companies on everything from disabled people to greenhouse gas amount to a domestic version of the EU's Social Chapter, which formally codifies workers' rights.

Increasingly, then, corporate contributions to social well-being are no longer voluntary but expected, and in some cases demanded. The drive for codes of conduct is spreading, sector by sector. Starting with textiles, we now have similar kinds of campaigns and attempts to introduce standards in fields ranging from forestry through computers to investment. In July 2000 the British Pensions Act was amended to require trustees of occupational pension plans to disclose their policy on social reporting as part of their Statement of Investment Principles. Belgium, France, Germany, and Sweden have adopted similar regulations. The Australian Financial Services Reform Act stipulates that all products with an investment component including pension and mutual funds, must include disclosure of 'the extent to which labour standards or environmental, social or ethical considerations are taken into account in the selection, retention and realisation of the investment' (Dhanarajan 2005). And, in what could be the most expensive incursion of all, we are witnessing the introduction of specific rules and demands for the banking sector. (An ironic development. While banks are signing codes designed to enforce what other companies must do 'ethically', their own behaviour in their core business activity has helped to create a global economic meltdown!)

What is ominous is that many activists are increasingly dissatisfied with the corporate response. They feel they are being conned.

Companies sign voluntary codes of conduct, but don't implement them; they mouth the words of CSR, but don't apply them to 'every business decision', and do not take seriously the injunction to 'make CSR live throughout the company'. As a result, more and more CSR advocates – in academia, NGOs, even in business – are calling for increased state measures to make companies conform with their views.

It is striking that Professor David Vogel's measured and fair book *The Market for Virtue* (2005), which points out many of the false claims made on behalf of CSR, itself ends with a call for far stronger action. He argues that the definition of 'responsible corporations' needs to be expanded; that responsibility should involve much more than going 'beyond compliance', and that this should include efforts to raise compliance standards. CSR needs to be 'redefined to include the responsibilities of business to strengthen civil society and the capacity of governments to require that all firms act more responsibly. Responsible firms also need to support public policies that establish minimum standards for their less virtuous competitors.' In his view, by working with and pressurising governments to enhance their capacity to develop and enforce corporate, environmental, labour and human rights standards, large multinationals can reduce their own monitoring costs, and strengthen the credibility of their codes (ibid: 170-1).

Other dangers

In arguing that companies have a social case to answer, CSR advocates are contributing to the moral delegitimation of business activity. A defensive position on the social role of business, especially large multinationals, hardly helps to consolidate the acceptance of market economics and the positive role of business as instruments of economic progress and innovation. As Clive Crook has stated,

> Private enterprise requires a supporting infrastructure of laws and permissions and more generally the consent of electorates to pursue its business goals, whatever they may be. ... but the informed consent of electorates and an appropriately designed economic infrastructure in turn require an understanding of how capitalism best works to serve the public good. The thinking behind CSR gives an account of this which is muddled and in some important ways downright false (*The Economist* 2005a).

An inflated conception of the power of business and its role in society is being allowed to stand unchallenged. The result is that companies are perpetually on the defensive. The prevailing view of business also distorts perceptions of globalisation, and inevitably puts too much onus on business to right the wrongs of an imperfect world.

The overemphasis on corporations distracts attention from the responsibilities of other institutions in combating poverty, injustice, and inequality. Much more attention should be focused on the role of the state, and the harm done by bad government.

The CSR approach also deflects attention from the core challenges of development, the scale and nature of poverty in many countries, and the kinds of responses that will actually have a sustained impact. The contribution of business through projects is very limited. The role of large companies in a virtuous cycle of sound state policies and enhanced opportunities for domestic and foreign investment would make a far greater contribution to the welfare of citizens of developing countries than CSR projects.

Business has an interest and important role in promoting improved national infrastructure and the further liberalisation of national economies and global trade. Almost every economy offers opportunities for further liberalisation; reforms with respect to starting a business, hiring and firing workers, enforcing contracts, obtaining credit, etc could hugely expand business opportunity, attract far more investment (domestic and foreign), and add greatly to social welfare.

The business contribution to economic progress arises from the 'combination of opportunities and pressures' that a competitive market economy generates. Ensuring that markets are really competitive and that new and small companies can enter them easily are key components of maximising the benefits of market economies.

Last, but very importantly, the CSR debate diverts business attention away from another core issue, namely how business is perceived by the wider society (not just activist NGOs); how it wants to be seen; and how it should best communicate its role. And why it is that such a misconceived set of ideas about companies and their impact on society has been able to develop and spread.

Many of these issues require a much greater understanding of how competitive market economies work. The CSR agenda doesn't help business in focusing attention on the issues that would promote its interests or in persuading the rest of society that the larger public interest is served by expanding corporate activity, not by curbing or continually attacking it.

Richard Lambert, head of the Confederation of British Industry puts this well:

> Business is not a separate vested interest operating on the margins of society. Its interests are not different from those of the general public. ... a healthy business sector lies absolutely at the heart of a healthy society. And society won't work as well as it should if it regards this prime source of its wealth, jobs and taxes with distrust or suspicion (Lambert 2006).

The current 'dance' between CSR activists and large corporations can perhaps be best understood as a complex blend of elements: anti-business sentiment; business acquiescence; a general desire for

more transparent institutions; the appetite of the western media for
exposés; their 'gotcha' mentality when it comes to companies and
their operations in general but particularly in far-off locations; and
the dominance of western 'voices' in global debates.

IS APPEASEMENT WORKING?

The question then becomes whether business appeasement of
its critics is working, for whom, and for how long. Acquiescing
in voluntary codes and self-monitoring has not halted demands for
legislated standards with mandatory monitoring and penalties for
non-compliance. The costs of compliance are not known, but are
certainly growing. A glance at the glossy CSR reports published by
large corporations indicates increasing resources devoted to this topic
– in rather strange documents which generally consist of a series of
anecdotes about uncoordinated projects that demonstrate a company's
social concerns.

The moral opprobrium directed at business does not seem to abate
when business agrees with its critics that it has to do more to ensure
a positive contribution to society. And even when business spends
increasing amounts of after-tax money, when is it enough for the
critics?

Companies think that, by pandering to radicals, they can co-opt
them or reach an accommodation with them; but in many cases
activists see corporate accommodation as weakness and an invitation
to push harder. Evidence shows that the more a company changes
its policies in response to activist pressures, the more likely it is to be

targeted again. There will always be a gap between what a business is doing and what some group – however small – finds offensive, or wants it to do. Ironically then, contrary to the advice of many CSR advisers, the more publicly a firm accounts for its CSR activities, the more vulnerable it will be to being attacked.

Real business concerns

Multinational corporations are powerful mechanisms for progress, prosperity, and innovation, but this does not make current market design a panacea for the world's ills, nor are business people a unique species who never make mistakes or engage in abhorrent deeds.

Some companies do in fact behave in ways that provide cause for concern, but the ever lengthening tentacles of the CSR debate divert attention away from these issues, and finding ways of dealing with them. Examples include the excessive salary benefits of many corporate executives; or how governments of industrialised countries deal with corporate corruption when it takes place in other countries. Whether first-world governments are doing enough to penalise such companies, instead of implicitly endorsing the notion that it is acceptable to bribe people in poorer countries, is worthy of much greater attention and exposure. Of course, developing country governments need to combat corruption more energetically as well.

Probably the most important issue arises from the need to further liberalise domestic economies as well as global trade. Many advocates of good corporate citizenship speak a lot less about removing barriers to competitiveness in their own industries, the need for fairer rules of trade between developed and developing countries, or the need for developing countries to open up their markets to each other.

Sometimes companies and individuals within them simply get things wrong. Every company faces different challenges, depending on its activities and location, and the CSR approach does not really help businesses to deal with them. Should a company invest elsewhere in the world, where the business environment is not as well structured and regulated as in its home country? What are the responsibilities of companies to people it needs to lay off because a factory is no longer profitable? How should they behave in countries with weak, corrupt, or brutal governments? There are no simple answers.

Companies should treat their employees well, observe moral principles in their day-to-day business dealings, avoid unnecessarily damaging the environment, and think about their relationship with governments and communities in which they operate. They should reject the insidious assumption implicit in CSR that business always has a case to answer, and that there is a package of actions that can make a company morally irreproachable.

WHAT ARE THE ALTERNATIVES TO CSR?

Many opponents of CSR refer to a seminal short article written by Milton Friedman in 1970 and published in the *New York Times* in which he argued that 'the social responsibility of business is to increase profits' (Friedman 1970), that in a free enterprise system a corporate executive is an employee of the owners of the business, and thus directly responsible to them. In the vast majority of cases, those employers want to make as much money as possible while conforming to the basic rules of the society in question, 'both those embodied in law and those embodied in ethical custom'. In his view, to suggest that an executive has a 'social responsibility' is either pure rhetoric or requires that he must act in some way that is not in the interests of his employers.

> For example, that he is to refrain from increasing the price of the product in order to contribute to the social objective of preventing inflation even though a price increase would be in the best interests of the corporation. Or that he is to make expenditures on reducing pollution beyond the amount that is in the best interests of the corporation or that is required by law in order to contribute to the social objective of improving the environment (ibid).

In Friedman's view, in each of these cases the corporate executive would be spending other people's money for a general social purpose, and this causes two problems. The executive is effectively imposing a tax, and deciding how it should be spent, thus bypassing elaborate constitutional, parliamentary, and judicial provisions (in democratic states) to control these functions, and ensure that taxes are imposed in line with the preferences and wishes of the general public.

Second, he asks whether the executive is capable of implementing his 'social responsibilities'. While he is an expert in running his company, 'nothing about his selection makes him an expert on inflation' (ibid). And how much cost is he justified in imposing on his stockholders, customers, and employees for this social purpose?

Some might argue that social problems are too urgent for the slow course of political processes, and that CSR is a quicker, more effective way of addressing them. In his view this amounts to an assertion that those who favour CSR have failed to persuade most of their fellow citizens to agree, and are therefore seeking to attain by undemocratic procedures what they cannot attain by democratic ones.

Friedman is undoubtedly broadly correct when he asserts that the primary role of business is to run a profitable enterprise, that the discussion by business and its critics is characterised by a lack of rigour, that the call for social responsibility is mainly directed at corporations rather than individual proprietors, who comprise the vast majority of enterprises, and that it is impossible to decide precisely what a business's responsibilities are, once one acknowledges the diversity of choices and preferences on any social issue.

However, his approach – as evidenced in this article – to the topic is too narrow. He fails to provide useful insights into the realities of doing business in a multinational, multicultural world. He is too quick to jump to accusations of socialism rather than appreciating the depth of the relationship between effective, enabling states and working markets, and does not provide a useful perspective on the complexity of modern societies and the role of large companies within them. He and his followers slip too easily into claiming both that markets always work and that only markets work.

His supporters tend to a rather fundamentalist approach. They recite the dogma that 'the business of business is business' (a phrase he did not use) and see the world and the role of business in terms that are too simplistic to have much of an impact on the current debate. In some respects, it is not difficult to see why 'the other side' is winning.

There are at least six vital issues which this approach either does not deal with or glosses over too quickly.

They tend to ignore the situation of developing countries. Friedman's article argues that 'there is one and only one social responsibility of business – to use its resources and engage in activities designed to increase its profits; so long as it stays within the rules of the game, namely engaging in open and free competition without deception or fraud'. However, in many poorer countries, there are no 'clear rules of the game'. Companies can do secret deals and establish monopolies; they can exploit the absence of any rules at all; they can slant things so that the opportunities available to small and new businesses are harder than they would ordinarily be; or they can take advantage of very weak rules to do many things that they would not get away with in more developed societies.

They assume a uniformity of ethics and culture. Friedman argues that an executive's responsibility is to make as much money as possible while conforming to the basic rules of society, 'both those embodied in law and ... ethical custom'. This is one of the key dilemmas in the 'responsibility' debate. When we start talking about extra-legal issues, whose ethical customs should prevail? Should it be the ethics of a company as determined by its current managers? Should it be those of the community or country in which the business is operating? This instruction is not as simple as it might appear if one is running a company active in different countries, staffed by people from different nationalities who might and probably do differ on the nuances of ethics and custom.

The efficacy and existence of the state is taken for granted. Probably because they do not deal with the situation in developing countries, business fundamentalists assume the existence of an effective state. In many societies across the world, weak states are often a greater threat to citizens' lives than strong ones – anarchy is sometimes worse than authoritarianism. At the very least the state must provide security for its citizens and their activities, including enterprises. In many developing or transitional economies, crime escalates and crime prevention imposes huge costs on large and smaller businesses alike. This kind of situation is also found in parts of cities – American ghettoes, or French *banlieus* – where middle-class assumptions about law and order do not apply. In his article Friedman does not examine the role of companies in promoting or lobbying for effective state performance with respect to crime, national security, border control, or customs enforcement, or what businesses should do to protect themselves and the neighbourhoods in which they operate if the state cannot maintain effective law and order. There are a range of other areas in which a state that works is essential for economic activity.

They generally deal too hastily and briefly with the interaction of companies and communities at the local level. In both developing and developed countries, companies are part of the social fabric of a local place. Exactly how to play the most constructive role and use company resources most effectively requires more in-depth attention than his short article provides. Business does indeed need a 'licence to operate' from the local polity; how to do that is worthy of more intense focus.

The complexity of the debate about what is in a company's short-term and longer-term interest is simplified. Friedman rightly argues that in many cases a company will call something a part of its social responsibility when it is in fact something the company is doing to promote its survival and success. These kinds of actions can span a wide field. His examples derive from conditions and experiences in the United States, a rich industrialised country, and he therefore mentions company contributions to community amenities, or improving local government. These are small amounts in rich countries. 'Fixing local government' in most or all developing countries would be an enormous challenge, going far further than Friedman's notion.

Friedman's approach to democracy appears naive. He argues that in a free society it is hard for 'evil' people to do 'evil', especially since one man's good is another man's evil. In a majoritarian democracy, especially in a country with ethnic, linguistic, or other minorities, it is quite possible for government to adopt policies that have evil consequences for large numbers of people.

The reality of our global world and the role and impact of companies within society is more complex than the Friedman article or his somewhat fundamentalist followers allow. The widespread demand for greater openness on the part of companies and the legitimate interest in the broader social impact of their operations and activities requires an expansion and adaptation of the basic Friedman formulation.

Is 'do no harm' the right advice?

Some of the most thoughtful critics of CSR – including Martin Wolf of the *Financial Times* and Clive Crook, previously with *The Economist* – as well as some of the more sensible CSR advocates start off by providing companies with sound advice.

A good guiding principle, they say, should be how corporate executives would feel if what they are doing – whether in a developing or developed country – would be splashed all over the newspapers. If they would be embarrassed about this information being made public, and how this would affect the company's reputation, then they shouldn't do it.

However, they then go on to say that companies should operate on the principle, taken from the Hippocratic Oath for doctors, of 'above all, do no harm'. Neither of them says exactly what they mean, but I am concerned about this phrase and the advice inherent in it.

The essence of capitalism is the continual invention of new ways of doing things. Joseph Schumpeter outlined the essential features of capitalist evolution which he characterised as a process of creative destruction – 'the fundamental impulse that sets and keeps the capitalist engine in motion comes from the new consumer goods, the new methods of production or transportation, the new markets, the new forms of industrial organisation that capitalist enterprise creates' (see Henderson 2004: 83).

The factory wiped out the blacksmith's shop, the car superseded the horse and buggy, the corporation overthrew proprietorship. 'Creative destruction is the essential fact about capitalism. Stabilised capitalism is a contradiction in terms' (Schumpeter 1942, quoted in McCraw 2007: 3). The destructive part of this process is that existing factories are closed, workers lose their jobs, entrepreneurs go out of business, and some small shopkeepers cannot make a living when supermarkets or Wal-Mart come to town.

Some of the critics of capitalism and globalisation want to stop the current process. But what would have happened if we had stopped the process when electricity replaced lamplighters? As Norberg has put it, 'Without creative destruction we would all be stuck with a lower standard of living ... the idea that we should halt change now is as misguided as the idea that we should have obstructed agricultural advances two centuries ago to protect the 80 per cent of the population employed on the land at the time' (2004: 141).

He has also remarked that 'Capitalism is easy to defend, but hard to love' (2003b). This is partly because economic growth is driven by a process that rejects the old and inefficient and moves towards the new. Societies and the entrepreneurs within them learn from this process of rapid succession and competition between different ways of doing things, and how markets reward those who adopt the most successful methods. Open, competitive societies function as laboratories where the unsuccessful learn from the more successful, and the successful are motivated to achieve even more. They provide an environment in which individuals and companies are free to make the necessary changes and adjustments. As Michael O'Dowd has noted, 'it is ideas that survive and perish depending on their fitness; individuals adapt and learn' (O'Dowd 1996: 95).

Take the current debate about outsourcing from the United States to Asia. In a recent study for the Institute for International Economics, Catherine L Mann offered this optimistic perspective:

Frequently cited projections indicate that millions of jobs will be lost to offshore workers. What these projections ignore is that the globalization of software and its services in conjunction with the diffusion of it to new sectors and businesses will yield even stronger job demand in the US for its proficient workers. ... The global integration of IT software and services will lead to a decline in the prices of software and services, thus promoting further diffusion of its use in more companies and more sectors. This will result in a new wave of productivity growth, generating faster economic growth and more employment. In the US the Bureau of Labour Statistics predicts the net creation of 22 million new jobs over the next decade, mostly in business services, health care, social services, transportation and communications. In particular, demand for computer support specialists and software engineers is expected to double between 2000 and 2010 (quoted in ICC 2004).

Manufacturing in industrialised countries is not losing its competitive edge. It is shifting to higher-value products such as airplanes, fibre-optic equipment, or luxury goods. In the process companies create better paid jobs with better working conditions. In parallel, manufacturing companies are devoting more resources to tasks upstream (conception) and downstream (marketing) of the production process, thus creating millions of new jobs for the educated workforce of industrialised countries.

In a dynamic economy, jobs are continuously lost and created. Trade expansion and increased business activity over the last 20 years have substantially accelerated the pace of job creation across the world. Between 1982 and 1999 an average of 34 million jobs were created every year in manufacturing and services worldwide (ibid).

It is easier to see the destructive part of capitalism rather than its creative side, but it is far more creative than destructive. Newspapers report on people who lose their jobs when a factory closes down. It is less sensational and therefore harder to report on the multiplicity of new jobs created when innovations provide entrepreneurs with fodder for new businesses.

Companies are the main vehicles, the principal initiating agents, for the continuing process of change that improves productivity and creates greater social welfare. To advise these businesses to 'do no harm' makes no sense.

Of course, corporations should not wilfully or unnecessarily do harm, and should mitigate any harm they do inflict through better practices. But the very essence of the process at work requires disruptive change, and this inevitably involves harm to some people, areas, communities, and environments. Many of those people will find new jobs or take advantage of new opportunities. Some towns will die and some of their inhabitants will struggle to make the adjustments required to find new or equivalent jobs. We should not stop the engine of progress and increased productivity for this reason.

Governments need policies and strategies to deal with these realities. Companies need to do what is appropriate and right in particular circumstances – whether enjoined by law, self-interest and reputation, economics or management values. Greater attention is required to this dimension of market development; in other words, the relationship between destruction and creation. And those in favour of markets need to get much better at communicating how the engine of capitalism works – 'creates' – to benefit the vast majority of people and places, most of the time.

Competitive advantage is the engine that produces success in business. It is this success that generates the profits and growth which enable governments and companies to transform a barren landscape into a thriving city, to change the future of a hitherto poor country, to modernise individuals and societies. In business, survival really matters. Everything else is distraction.

CONCLUDING REMARKS

One of the core aims of this book is to develop the perspective, overarching framework, ideas and language business needs to better communicate its real contribution and to provide guidelines to clearer thinking about business and society. In its response to the activists and their concerns, business is often addressing issues it would not otherwise have chosen as priorities. When it comes to CSR – just whose agenda is this?

In adopting many of the ideas, words, policies and mindset of CSR, business leaders and their companies are choosing a defensive, apologetic approach to competitive capitalism and its place in modern societies.

There are other choices for business.

We need to move beyond the sterile, entrenched positions in the Friedman-versus-CSR debate. Both sides fail to provide practical guidelines to CEOs or governments on how to define and shape relationships among markets, states, and citizens. As Bobby Godsell, former chief executive of AngloGold Ashanti, has noted:

> A large part of the debate about business and society has been caught in a conceptual trap. The business of business is business, argues the business fundamentalist camp. Here business purpose is the creation of shareholder wealth. Yet the impact of business and the challenges to business are far broader than those either felt by or imposed by shareholders, argue the stakeholders camp. This dichotomy confuses the essential identity of business with its social consequences and its absolutely necessary relationships with both society and polity (2007).

A new and different lens is required to illuminate the contribution of multinationals to developing countries – which exemplifies the broader role of business in all societies – and to think effectively about the rights and responsibilities of corporations in the 21st century.

Business leaders and their advisers need to move beyond appeasement and defence. They need to build a more positive, more compelling set of ideas within which to locate business as a part of the civil world, outside the state but intimately engaged with rules and regulations established by governments, and operating in an environment shaped by national politics, policies and culture.

It is vital to explore the development problematic; to place business, markets, civil society, and state actors within a developmental framework; and to ensure that the discussion is market-affirming rather than market-undermining, developmentally sensible, and economically rational.

The rest of this book turns to the development of such a new approach to defining and communicating a more realistic, comprehensive and positive vision of business and its role in society. This discussion has to be situated within a different set of ideas about development, the way forward for developing countries, and full-blooded support for companies and profit-making as a vital contributor to the public good.

As Crook notes:

> The conditions that must be satisfied if capitalism is to serve the public good are not trivial. A comprehending and supportive climate of opinion must be added to the list. That is why the battle of ideas matters so much (*The Economist* 2005a).

PART
T W O

Business is good for society
and essential for sustained
development

Chapter Five

TRANSFORMING LIVES
The Direct Impact of
Modern Corporations

*'Nandani Nilekani, chairman and founder of pioneering
Indian multinational Infosys, says his company's greatest
achievement is not its $2 billion turnover, but the fact that it
has taught Indians to redefine the possible.'*

The Economist, 'Business and Society: The Search
for Talent' (2006b)

COMPANIES OPERATING in markets are now responsible for most of what can be described as world prosperity. This is especially true in the wealthiest countries, but is also increasingly the case in those parts of the world where wealth remains rare and recent. This must surely underpin the case for promoting and expanding business activities. However, there are few sustained arguments that make the case for business in this way. This chapter will outline the direct ways in which businesses change people's lives for the better.

A REVOLUTIONARY INVENTION

An organisational invention devised just before the industrial revolution was as important for subsequent worldwide economic growth as any engineering discovery.

The principle of limited liability has been the bedrock of the phenomenal growth and success of the modern corporation. This principle established the right in law to establish an economic enterprise where if something is owed to the enterprise, it is not owed to the individuals nor do the individuals owe what the company owes. Thus the principle of limited liability as applied in modern companies is the instrument through which the savings of individuals are converted into the capital that powers the corporation and its numerous investments, and which, in turn, can secure the general well-being of entire societies, communities, and individuals.

In their book *The Company: A Short History of a Revolutionary Idea* (2005), Micklethwait and Wooldridge argue that 'the limited liability corporation is the greatest single discovery of modern times'. It is the mechanism through which companies increase the pool of capital available for productive investment; it allows investors to spread their risk by purchasing small and easily marketable shares in several enterprises; provides a way of imposing effective management structures on large organisations; and it has the capacity to fail with relatively low social costs.

It is through this mechanism that today's corporations can finance and manage their large-scale operations. Companies are uniquely effective in making human effort productive. Specialised resources in the form of labour, raw and finished materials, capital and knowledge come together in a remarkable process that transforms these components into goods and services of greater value. In so doing they make a revolutionary contribution to the world in which we all live.

SEARCHING FOR THE GOOD THAT COMPANIES DO

Internet searches based on keywords such as 'positive impact of business' or 'business does good' mostly produce links to NGO websites and those of other critics who believe businesses must be regulated to become 'ethical'. There are few public advocates for business who emphasise the way in which their companies improve people's lives in the course of pursuing profits.

Free market advocates, who are naturally opposed to regulation, tend to focus on the *potential* impact of unregulated innovation rather than pointing to the ways in which private enterprise has already generated innovations such as the telephone, automobiles, airplanes, radio, television, computers, refrigeration, central heating, air-conditioning, and life-saving drugs.

New products are not the only ways in which businesses transform lives. Millions of people's lives are improved whenever 'a businessman discovers how to get a product to his customer more quickly, when he finds a way to cut costs somewhere so he can reduce his prices, when he develops a new system that allows people to obtain what they want more easily' (Browne 2001).

An exception appears in the World Business Council for Sustainable Development's (WBCSD) publication *From Challenge to Opportunity: The Role of Business in Tomorrow's Society* (2006). Under the heading 'Business Does Good By Doing Business', the report spells out the positive impact of business in the following unambiguous terms:

> Most companies benefit society simply by doing business. We meet customers' needs for goods and services. We create jobs. We pay wages and salaries. We provide for employees and families

through pensions and health plans. We innovate to create products that contribute to human progress. We pay taxes that fund public services and infrastructure. We create work for millions of suppliers, many of them small- and medium-sized companies.

But, in the rest of the WBCSD report, this insight evaporates. Rather than arguing for the expansion of business to enhance the good it does, it contains numerous calls to impose corporate responsibility programmes and restrict business activities in the name of 'ethics'.

The impact of business on American prosperity

Merely by doing business, companies improve the lives of Americans. The direct effects of business can be defined as the intended outcomes of efforts to enhance their competitiveness. These include jobs; cheaper, better goods and services; better training methods, improved productivity; opportunities for other businesses; profits generated for shareholders, many of whom are small investors and members of retirement funds; and taxes paid to government. It is easy to take these contributions for granted.

General Electric is one of the oldest and biggest American corporations. It has 320 000 employees, with 700 000 dependants; more than 5 million shareholders, including many retirees; and is responsible for the pensions of more than 600 000 people. It powers commercial aircraft carrying 660 million people every year; some 230 million people have medical scans on GE imaging machines annually; and nearly one third of the world's electricity is generated by its energy products. It is one of the most innovative companies in the world; it has created thousands of products – starting with the light bulb – that have changed people's lives, and runs huge research facilities in four different countries (Heineman 2005).

John Heineman Jr, senior vice-president for law and public affairs at GE, has stated:

> The myriad benefits conferred on stakeholders across the globe by [GE's] sustained economic performance is in sharp contrast to the devastation of poor or short-term results from the Enrons and WorldComs ... and makes clear why this should be the first dimension of good corporate citizenship (ibid).

Another multinational that has contributed hugely to American prosperity is British Petroleum. Operating in 100 countries, and employing 100 000 people, it produces about 3 per cent of the oil and gas consumed globally every day. It is the largest producer and supplier of oil and gas in the United States. It employs some 43 000 Americans; supplies 15 000 gas stations across the country, which supply Americans with 46 million gallons of gas every day; and has $40 billion of fixed assets. Its presence brings jobs, wealth, and tax revenue, with the wages paid out for its oil business alone amounting to more than $3 billion a year (Browne 2004). In 2004 the then chairman of BP, Sir John Browne, stated:

> BP has a direct impact on the lives of millions of people. We are major investors, and our decisions can shape local economies. We produce, transport, and sell fuels; and at every stage in the chain the way in which we work [shapes those economies]. We generate profits on behalf of our shareholders who are mostly pensioners and those saving for the future (ibid).

Microsoft has commissioned a study that speaks of the Microsoft 'ecosystem', comprising companies selling products that use, service, or distribute company software. The 'ecosystem' contains at least half a million companies, including those selling PCs and servers; software vendors; retail outlets and resellers; and service and training firms. Most of these are small, local firms. In 2007, 42 per cent of the 35,4 million people in the global IT sector were employed in the Microsoft ecosystem, generating some $514 billion in taxes (IDC 2007: 1).

In 2007 a subset of the Microsoft ecosystem excluding 'channel firms', whose revenues could not be tracked, generated $425 billion in revenue. This helped to fund about $100 billion invested in research and development, marketing, sales, and support in 2008. Most of this money will be spent in the regions where the revenues were generated.

For every dollar that Microsoft made in 2007, the ecosystem will make $7,79. This enormous impact on job creation, revenue generation, and business opportunity is likely to continue. The IT market will drive the creation of more than 100 000 new businesses between 2007 and 2011. Many of these companies will be small and locally owned (ibid).

Wal-Mart is the world's largest retailer. It has lowered the prices of a wide range of goods and services, which has had numerous direct and indirect effects on economic growth and social welfare. It has enhanced the shopping experience of poor people, and made them feel that their needs have been taken into account. The journalist Sebastian Mallaby has written:

> Wal-Mart's critics allege the retailer is bad for poor Americans. This claim is backward. ... Wal-Mart's discounting on food alone boosts the welfare of American shoppers by at least $50 billion a year. The savings are possibly five times that much if you count all of Wal-Mart's products. ... Wal-Mart's 'every day low prices' make the biggest difference to the poor, since they spend a higher proportion of income on food and other basics. As a force of poverty relief, Wal-Mart's $200 billion-plus assistance to consumers may rival many federal programmes (2005).

Wal-Mart started in rural America, and became successful by opening cut-price stores in rural towns rather than large cities. It pioneered a number of practices that enabled it to sell goods at lower prices than its competitors. These included bargaining with suppliers, cutting out wholesalers, and doing very little advertising. The company began operating its own non-unionised trucking fleets, using computers to order goods and keep track of stock and sales (minimising inventories and increasing customer satisfaction), and cutting transport costs to the bone (Lichtenstein 2006).

A new Wal-Mart store typically reduces city-wide prices by two to three per cent in the short term, and about ten per cent in the long term (Basker 2005). The company has been credited with helping to restrain inflation during the time that oil prices soared.

With domestic sales of about \$229 billion in 2004, Wal-Mart accounted for about 8,66 per cent of America's retail sales (not including automobiles and auto parts). Its obsession with low prices forces its competitors to lower theirs as well, even when the prices of the material needed to make those products – gas, plastics, steel, and construction materials – are rising. Wal-Mart absorbs rising inflation by adhering to three disciplines. It buys aggressively from China – to the tune of \$18 billion in 2004. It continually pressurises its 61 000 American suppliers (with which it spent \$150 billion in 2004) into producing at lower costs and accepting smaller profits. It accepts low margins for itself – Wal-Mart's operating income is about 6 per cent of sales (Gross 2005).

Probably the most emotional issue that mobilises Wal-Mart's critics is the way in which it devastates small retail businesses, and changes 'Main Street' in small American towns. However, Sobel and Dean (2008) have found that Wal-Mart has no statistically significant long-term impact on the size and profitability of the small business sector in the United States. They argue that 'Main Street' is transformed rather than destroyed. While small businesses that used to sell building supplies, toiletries, groceries, clothing and electronics are particularly hard hit, new stores and services emerge.

Prior to the opening of Wal-Mart stores, downtown retail space is generally taken up by stores providing the merchandise now sold by the giant corporation. When these valuable sites are freed by Wal-Mart's entry, they become economically viable locations for many other types of small businesses. This provides opportunities for new entrepreneurs in other sectors (ibid).

An analysis of 25 new Wal-Mart supercentres in 2002 showed that, apart from the unquestioned gains in consumer welfare, their opening had more positive than negative economic consequences for the communities involved. Employment grew more rapidly in Wal-Mart communities, and wages in the retail sector were more likely to have risen than fallen. In their study of the Wal-Mart 'revolution', Vedder and Cox argue:

> Wal-Mart is a plus for American society. The huge gains in consumer welfare, measured by Hausman and Leibtag in billions of dollars annually are unquestionably greater than other, relatively small net economic costs (which the evidence suggests are probably close to zero and more likely negative) that Wal-Mart imposes on society. In our judgement, it is hard to conclude that Wal-Mart has not been good for America (2006: 16).

The presence of modern corporations in America creates the jobs, wealth, products, and services on which prosperity depends.

What happens when these corporations go out of business, or move elsewhere? Numerous examples show that besides the specific loss of jobs, goods, pensions, and other benefits, the loss of a corporation tends to trigger the collapse of entire local communities, thus demonstrating the remarkable impact of companies on local development.

A case in point is the closure of a copper smelter at Anaconda, Montana, in 1980. A local company had operated it for more than 75 years, but in 1978 it was bought by the Atlantic Richfield Company (ARCO). Two years later, ARCO announced it was closing the plant. The consequences for this community of 12 000 people were far-reaching (see Bluestone & Harrison 1982: 69-71).

The closure of the ARCO smelter 'echoed through the city'. It erased 1 500 jobs, eliminating 80 per cent of the total local payroll. Before long, one in six members of the workforce was unemployed, and food-stamp rolls grew by 190 to 434 families. By December 1980 some 36 other businesses (excluding the railroad) had laid off 20 per cent of their employees. A quarter of businesses anticipated further lay-offs, and one third cancelled expansion plans. Most reported that their business had already declined by 10-50 per cent, despite the severance payments made by ARCO and the various forms of unemployment insurance and public aid supplied to those directly and indirectly affected. Workers sold their $55 000 houses for $35 000 in order to take jobs elsewhere. Businesses that normally would have provided a comfortable retirement for their owners went bankrupt, leaving them with nothing more than social security for their old age (ibid).

Modern corporations as efficient bureaucracies

One of the main functions of modern corporations has been to harness bureaucracy to the task of enhancing material welfare. Alfred Chandler has shown, in his numerous studies, how companies that built up their bureaucratic or organisational capabilities were able to use more sophisticated machinery; exploit efficiency-enhancing complementarities between various production processes; and institutionalise processes of organisational learning, thus enabling them to produce better goods and lower prices.

The German chemical company Bayer AG is an instructive early example. By the turn of the 19th century it had the most extensive, most carefully planned managerial hierarchies the world had yet seen. This flowed from the creation of a massive new industrial plant on the banks of the Rhine. The plant was designed to assure a steady flow of materials from point of arrival through processes of production to storage and shipment of final products. It comprised seven departments: five processing departments, a sixth consisting of workshops and offices required to service the processing plants, and a central administration. Each department had its own laboratories and engineering staff, so as 'to make possible a common working of various people, and encourage each individual by mutual stimulation' (Chandler 1992). The offices of the production engineers were also close to the chemical laboratories so 'that works chemists can at any time get into direct communication with the works engineers'. The plant covered 760 acres, and employed almost 8 000 workers. By that time Bayer's global sales force of experienced chemists were working with more than 20 000 customers.

The formation of this efficient new bureaucracy resulted in a dramatic reduction in the cost of dyes, and the destruction of many smaller dye companies, most of them in Britain. Much the same thing happened in other sectors in which Bayer was active, including pharmaceuticals, film, agricultural chemicals, and electrochemicals. Bayer continued to expand throughout the world using its research and development capacity to generate new products such as Aspirin. It was a dominant global player for most of the 20th century.

Not all business bureaucracies are efficient, and there are many examples of companies becoming unwieldy. Unlike government bureaucracies, these companies quickly find themselves facing a difficult choice – either improve their performance, or go out of business. Modern corporations have created efficient dynamic bureaucracies because they operate in competitive markets (ibid).

Most economic processes consist of thousands of interactions and activities, some organised by corporations and others emanating from market processes involving many smaller companies, even individual actors.

However, as the Bayer example shows, corporations are often able to coordinate processes more effectively internally than through external markets. Consider the case of Wal-Mart. The benefits this company generates are largely the product of a very large, sophisticated system of coordination that regulates interactions among many actors, from Chinese suppliers to massive retail stores in Canada, Mexico, the United States, and elsewhere (Lichtenstein 2006).

Much of Wal-Mart's success hinges on its size and control over a huge, highly intricate global supply chain. It sells about 15 per cent of the general merchandise and food in the United States. In some categories, such as household staples and basic apparel, its market share is closer to 30 per cent. Even the biggest suppliers become dependent on Wal-Mart's demands, and this is even stronger among the smaller firms that make up the majority of Wal-Mart's 20 000 global suppliers (ibid).

Wal-Mart wants its suppliers to offer low prices and to be technically and operationally compatible with its own processes. It often requires suppliers to open their books and submit to a rigorous cost analysis. Once a cost structure for a product is established, Wal-Mart requires acceptance of its own business strategy: small profits, rapid turnovers, and high sales volumes. Wal-Mart controls this process via the largest private data processing centre in the world, second only to the Pentagon. It collects and organises information from 140 000 systems, and records 20 million customer transactions every day. Several hundred thousand data mining questions are sent to it every week. This database is available to Wal-Mart's thousands of vendors. They can use it to reduce their own inventory management costs, enhance operational efficiency, and test the potential of a new product in a way that is more precise and less costly than standard product marketing tools (ibid).

Responding creatively to real needs

Companies build organisations that can generate cheaper and better products, more and improved career opportunities, and new forms of wealth. The market system in which such companies are embedded provides incentives to create such bureaucracies, and pursue increases in organisational efficiency. Companies also respond creatively to societies' changing needs, even where such needs have never been articulated. The market provides the space and the rewards to ensure that companies achieve this crucial function. Markets are decentralised systems, allowing people from different regions and stations to formulate new ideas and test them in the marketplace (Hayek 1945). If these ideas connect to a social need, the company succeeds; if they don't, or cease to do so, the company fails.

There are three ways in which companies find new ways of meeting social needs. The first is when a company is formed by an entrepreneur specifically to meet a perceived need. The second is when companies reinvent themselves in response to changing circumstances. Lastly, large companies can innovate through systematic R&D that builds on their existing knowledge of production processes as well as customers' needs.

Nurturing entrepreneurs

Netscape was started by Jim Barksdale. He first helped Federal Express to develop its package tracking system, and then moved to McCaw Cellular, a mobile phone company that he helped merge with AT&T. Next, he took over a new company called Mosaic Communications, formed by Jim Clark and Marc Andreessen, which developed the first really effective and user-friendly web browser. Mosaic, under Barksdale, then changed its name to Netscape (Friedman 2006: 63). Tom Friedman has called the simplified web browser technology pioneered by Netscape 'one of the most important inventions in history' (ibid: 61). Netscape brought this technology to its customers and began to make the Internet truly usable for the first time. It then collaborated with its competitors to expand the size and functionality of the Internet. Netscape, Microsoft and Sun Systems all realised that the public, which suddenly could not get enough of email and browsing, wanted Internet companies to work together to create one interoperable network. They wanted companies to compete with each other over different applications, that is, over what consumers could do once they were on the Internet, not over how they got on the Internet in the first place. As a result, by the late 1990s the Internet computing platform was seamlessly integrated; anyone was able to connect with anyone else, anywhere, and on any machine (ibid: 68).

Corporate reinvention

Companies can reinvent themselves, drawing on existing knowledge in order to meet a new need. A well-known example is United Parcel Services (UPS). UPS started out as a delivery service, and pursues this activity on a massive scale. It operates a fleet of 270 cargo jets, the eleventh largest in the world, and ships more than 13,5 million packages a day. Through its extensive interaction with customers, UPS came to see that it could also advise them on how to improve their logistics and supply procedures, including customising products for specific customers. Now, as Friedman puts it, 'UPS people are not just synchronising your packages – they are synchronising your whole company, and its interaction with both customers and suppliers' (Friedman 2006: 168).

UPS CEO Mike Eskew has explained the new service as follows: 'This is no longer a vendor – customer relationship. We answer your phones, we talk to your customers, we house your inventory, and we tell you what sells and doesn't sell' (quoted in ibid: 175-6). Consequently, businesses have been able to reduce costs and increase productivity, both of which help to expand prosperity.

Research and innovation

The third way in which companies respond to new needs is through a process of continual innovation, normally epitomised by in-house R&D programmes dedicated to producing a constant stream of new products and more efficient processes. Large companies have an advantage in this area as they can afford to finance extensive R&D, and integrate this with their knowledge of customers' needs and production processes. However, in order for large companies to assume this kind of risk, they need to operate within the right kind of incentive structure. This is why American pharmaceutical companies have generated a continuous stream of new cures and life-enhancing medications.

In 2006 America's pharmaceutical and biotechnology research companies invested a record $55,2 billion in the development of new medicines and vaccines. America's biopharmaceutical companies spend far more on biomedical research than National Institutes of Health and pharmaceutical research companies in all other countries. In 2007 Billy Tauzin, CEO of the Pharmaceutical Research and Manufacturers of America, pointed out that 'well over half of the world's new medicines are developed by our country's innovative companies … This year's increased investment continues more than 25 years of strong growth in R&D spending as our scientists and bench researchers continue the hunt for better treatments for cancer, HIV/AIDS, Alzheimer's disease, Parkinson's disease, and many other medical conditions' (PhRMA 2007).

Eli Lilly & Co CEO Sidney Taurel has explained the leading role of American pharmaceutical companies as follows:

> When all is said and done, there is only one market in the world that supports pharmaceutical innovation – the United States. We still speak of it as the 'last free market,' and indeed, though hardly 'free' of government intervention, it is the one market where global innovators find the incentive they need to keep pushing the boundaries (Taurel 2005: 327).

Private companies have led the fight against HIV/AIDS. The pharmaceutical industry has developed 91 per cent of HIV medication. Mortality declined dramatically after the introduction of antiretrovirals, while monthly costs for AIDS patients decreased by 16 per cent after Highly Active Antiretroviral Therapy (HAART) was introduced in 1996-7. While pharmaceutical companies are continually criticised over the high cost of their products, it is clear that without them there would be fewer or no therapies for those diseases at all, and those therapies that did exist would be much more expensive (Beaumont, personal communication).

IMPROVING LIVES IN THE DEVELOPING WORLD

In the parts of the world where western-style prosperity remains elusive, big corporations are nevertheless at the forefront of creating the development that these countries need. One way in which they do this is through investment, devoting resources to finding and unlocking the economic potential that often lies dormant in these countries. Large extractive companies (minerals and energy) have played a particularly important role in this regard.

The South African mining house AngloGold Ashanti is one of the world's largest gold producers, with production of 5,64 million ounces of gold in 2006. It operates open pit and underground mines and surface reclamation plants in Argentina, Australia, Brazil, Ghana, Guinea, Mali, Namibia, South Africa, Tanzania, and the United States, and employs about 61 000 people (AngloGold Ashanti 2006a).

One of its major contributions is finding and investing in new sources of gold across the globe. It constantly develops large capital projects, and runs extensive exploration programmes in 15 countries. The company also creates opportunities through its strategy of seeking out partnerships with junior exploration and mining companies in regions outside mainstream mining areas. During 2006 the company diversified in this way into Laos, China, the Philippines, and Alaska.

AngloGold Ashanti's strategic objectives are to drive down costs, lower mining and geopolitical risk by diversification, and invest directly in, or partner, downstream retail operations. As part of its value-adding growth strategy, the company is continually on the lookout for additional opportunities. Together with Mintek, South Africa's national metallurgical research organisation, it has launched a project to research and develop new industrial applications for gold. AngloGold Ashanti also holds a 25 per cent stake in OroAfrica, the largest manufacturer of gold jewellery in South Africa, and has collaborated with it on a number of projects, including the development of an African gold jewellery brand. OroAfrica has established a Jewellery Design Centre, aimed at improving product standards through technology, design, and innovation (ibid).

AngloGold's other major contribution has been to develop the market for gold. Through its own international gold marketing initiatives, and in collaboration with the World Gold Council, it has improved its own customer base as well as those of other gold producers. Its marketing programme aims to increase the desirability of its product, sustain and grow demand, and support the deregulation of the market in key economies. From 2004 to 2006 AngloGold Ashanti spent some $44 million on gold marketing initiatives, most of it via the World Gold Council (AngloGold Ashanti 2006a, b).

Besides extracting gases and minerals that would otherwise lie dormant, large corporations have triggered progress and prosperity in many developing countries. Two examples are Coca-Cola's activities in China, and Unilever's in Indonesia.

Coca-Cola in China

The impact of Coca-Cola on the Chinese economy in 2000 has been jointly studied by researchers of Peking University, Tsinghua University, and the University of Carolina. Their findings can be summarised as follows:

- The Coca-Cola system directly employed 14 046 people. This included permanent, temporary, skilled and unskilled workers. More than 62 per cent were skilled workers, most of whom were permanently employed.

- Some 350 000 people were employed in the bottling system, and the sale of Coca-Cola products in China supported at least 50 000 jobs in wholesale and retail sectors.
- About 414 000 direct and indirect jobs were sustained by Coca-Cola's production and distribution in China.
- In 1998 the Coca-Cola bottling system injected 8,16 billion RMB into the Chinese economy. This investment generated additional Chinese output of about 21,7 billion RMB.
- In 1998 Coca-Cola bottlers paid 387 million RMB in taxes to the Chinese government. The additional economic activity stimulated by Coca-Cola's activities generated an additional 1,2 billion RMB in tax (Peking University et al 2000).

Coca-Cola's presence has had numerous equally important qualitative effects on the Chinese economy. Many Coca-Cola bottling plants started off as inefficient and technologically backward state-owned enterprises. As a result of their association with Coca-Cola, they have been transformed into the market-oriented businesses that Coca-Cola requires. Managers of bottling plants have been made financially accountable, and have instituted better inventory and quality control, and cost management systems. They have learnt to track consumer preferences, and pay attention to their product's distribution. Workers have learnt that they will be rewarded for hard work. Prior to their association with Coca-Cola, managers tended to focus simply on increasing output, regardless of market conditions. Now they have been pushed into recognising that the quality and acceptability of their products is a vital aspect of success in a more market-based system.

Coca-Cola has played a role in stimulating small business. Many vendors selling Coca-Cola products were previously unemployed. On average, 28 per cent of the owners of retail shops and restaurants in Harbin, Guangdong province, Shanghai, and Xian were jobless before starting their ventures. Many subsequently depended on selling Coca-Cola products for their livelihood. In addition, among the 400 retailers canvassed at random, most agreed or strongly agreed that 'Coca-Cola products attract customers to the store' (ibid).

Coca-Cola has also contributed to more substantial business development. For example, in 1986 the Zhong Fu Industrial Group began supplying bottles to Coca-Cola. It then began to follow Coca-Cola, setting up bottle making plants near every new Coca-Cola plant. By 1999 Zhong Fu had 36 plants across the country, and began to export bottles to Japan and South East Asia (ibid).

Lastly, Coca-Cola has helped to strengthen and expand Chinese markets by providing training to tens of thousands of Chinese in its 'world-renowned' marketing methods, and by investing its capital and experience in developing localised soft-drink brands.

Unilever in Indonesia

Unilever produces more than 400 food, household and personal care brands (from Lipton's Soup to Dove soap); has operations in about 100 countries and sells in 50 more. Agriculture provides more than two thirds of the raw material for Unilever's branded products. It buys 28 per cent of the world's spinach; 13 per cent of the world's peas; 7 per cent of the world's tomatoes; and 13 per cent of the world's black tea (Unilever 2007). As Unilever's CEO, Niall Fitzgerald, has put it:

> The very business of doing business has a huge impact on society. Three quarters of our sales revenue goes straight out again to pay for goods and services for suppliers. And of the wealth we create each year by adding value to those goods and services, around 70 per cent of it is channelled back into society through employee

wages, shareholder dividends, government taxes and community investment. We generate employment. For every job we create in Unilever we indirectly create several more in our supply chains and distribution channels. ... More than 100 years ago the founder's vision for the company was an expression of his values: '... to make cleanliness commonplace; to lessen work for women; to foster health and contribute to personal attractiveness, that life may be more enjoyable and rewarding to the people who use our products (Fitzgerald 2003).

This assessment is borne out by an Oxfam study of Unilever's impact on Indonesia (Clay 2005). Despite Oxfam's generally anti-business bias, it discovered the following:

- Unilever Indonesia's core workforce comprises about 5 000 people, of whom 60 per cent are direct employees, and 40 per cent are contract workers. Indirectly, the full-time equivalent of about 300 000 people earn a living from Unilever's value chain.
- More than half of this employment occurs in the distribution and retail chain. This includes an estimated 1,8 million small stores and street vendors.
- The closer and more formally workers in the value chain are linked to Unilever, the more they benefit. Two thirds of the value generated along the chain is distributed to participants other than Unilever's direct producers, suppliers, distributors, and retailers.
- Taxes paid by Unilever to the Indonesian government account for 26 per cent of the value generated in the chain.

The Oxfam research included a case study of the production of Kecap Bango, a sweet soy sauce brand that Unilever had acquired. Because sales were growing rapidly, Unilever needed to find a steady and consistent supply of high-quality black soybeans. In partnership with researchers at a local university, it started to work with a small group of producers, offering them a secure market, credit, and technical assistance (ibid).

Some 95 per cent of Indonesians use at least one Unilever product. Many are basic goods such as hand soap, laundry products, and tea. Many of the company's products have become affordable for people living in poverty, in part because they are sold in smaller packages.

Researchers conducted interviews in a number of communities living within one kilometre of Unilever Indonesia's facilities. Of those interviewed, half claimed to have benefited directly from Unilever's presence. These benefits included direct employment, increased sales in local shops, larger numbers of passengers for motorbike taxis, and opportunities to maintain or repair the bicycles or motorbikes of Unilever employees (ibid).

Daewoo in Bangladesh

Another example of how the activities of large multinationals can stimulate business activity in Asia comes from Bangladesh. Easterly tells the story of how the training and example provided by the Korean company Daewoo sparked the growth of an entire export-oriented industry in one of the world's poorest countries. In 1979 Daewoo was looking for a new base to circumvent garment import quotas. These quotas did not cover Bangladesh, so Daewoo entered into a collaborative agreement with a Bangladeshi company, Desh Garments. Daewoo helped Desh Garments set up a new factory, and took 130 Desh workers to Korea for training. Desh's garment production expanded quickly, from 43 000 shirts in 1980 to 2,3 million in 1987. Subsequently, 115 of the Desh workers who had received training from Daewoo set up their own garment export firms. Diversifying into gloves, coats, trousers, they created a new Bangladeshi industry that, by the late 1990s, had generated $2 billion in sales (Easterly 2001: 137-8).

Transformation in Eastern Europe

Another part of the world transformed by multinationals is the former communist-controlled countries of eastern Europe. They did so by means of training, modernisation, jobs, welfare, environmental responsibility, and providing products in ways that contrasted starkly with the way things worked (or did not work) under communism. Charles Lewis shows that the entry of multinationals opened opportunities for educated, ambitious young people to obtain relevant training; apply their knowledge to new, dynamic opportunities; become part of the modern economic world; build careers; and achieve material rewards. Multinationals revolutionised the world of many young east Europeans in ways they could not have dreamt about under communism (2005).

In the early 1990s, the majority of female students at the prestigious Moscow State University chose 'hard currency prostitute' as their most favoured profession; this was the best job they could imagine obtaining (ibid: 36). Multinationals changed all that by providing leadership positions to people with some skills and knowledge; flying people with aptitude to training institutes in America, Britain, and Germany; putting them on a career path where they earned top salaries if they performed; and pushing them to become part of the international business world. Lewis argues that multinationals did more than any other agency to create a new meritocracy in which hard work, ethical behaviour, and a desire to learn were amply rewarded.

Multinationals provided new jobs that were better paid and offered better working conditions than the state had provided or continued to provide. Unions, where they actually represented workers' interests, were often the strongest supporters of the entry of multinational corporations. When VW took over Czechoslovakia's Skoda works, union leaders were taken to VW headquarters in Germany to ensure their support for the deal. The conditions they found there were 'like paradise' compared with their wages and working conditions, and the leaders who saw what could be possible became the most ardent supporters of foreign investment in their country (ibid: 48).

Eastern European consumers have also benefited greatly from the entry of western shopping chains and consumer companies. As Lewis puts it, consumers 'welcomed the new hypermarkets with open bags'. Shoppers particularly liked the wider product ranges; helpful staff; bright, clean, well-organised stores, and longer trading hours (ibid: 136).

As a result of the greater efficiency and increased competition introduced by these stores, the food component of many countries' inflation baskets has fallen by two or three percentage points since the early 1990s. Lewis concludes that 'sentimental western observers who would like a return to the quaint, slow-paced shopping experience of the past should listen to a Slovak mother recall the humiliation of waiting three hours on a Christmas night in the hope of buying three oranges for a family treat' (ibid: 141).

SABMiller in South Africa

Large companies have also played a crucial role in improving lives in southern Africa. The South African subsidiary of the large multinational brewer SABMiller has created countless benefits within the South African economy. SAB employs 8 611 workers in South Africa; its first round suppliers have created an additional 46 000 jobs, and these suppliers in turn have created further business and employment opportunities. On the basis of these multiplier effects, in 2005 SAB's activities in the country created 362 000 full-time jobs, some 3 per cent of the country's total employment. Besides this, its output was estimated at R44 billion for 2005, some 3,3 per cent of South Africa's GDP for that year. The taxes that SAB paid in that year amounted to R8,5 billion, with an additional R12,2 billion collected from businesses linked to SAB's operations. This total of R20,7 billion constituted 4,8 per cent of the country's total government tax revenue in 2005 (SABMiller 2007).

SAB produces a wide range of products at competitive prices. The company has an excellent record of continuous innovation in terms of brands and packaging, thus generating benefits for consumers that are difficult to quantify.

SAB's creation of new business opportunities in South Africa has often been part of a deliberate plan. In 2007 the company spent R1,96 billion on commercial equity for more than 4 000 black suppliers. Its managing director, Tony van Kralingen, asserted:

> SAB's focus on outsourcing key services and creating wealth for new players is not new. In 1987 we introduced our owner-driver project, which saw former employees of SAB form their own companies to distribute SAB's product brands to the trade. To date, SAB's investment of well over R3 billion has resulted in about 235 individual companies with 352 vehicles distributing some 60 per cent of SAB's volumes (ibid).

This project has since been expanded to include Distribution Operators, involving owner-drivers who have more than one vehicle.

Since 1995 SAB has invested more than R38,5 million to help

launch more than 3 200 businesses. More than 85 per cent of the businesses started since 2003 are still in business (some are now multimillion-rand enterprises), and almost one third supply goods or services to SAB (ibid).

De Beers in Botswana

Possibly the most dramatic example of a large multinational transforming the economic fortunes of a southern African country is that of the South African diamond mining conglomerate De Beers in Botswana. As the president of Botswana, Festus Mogae, put it in June 2006: 'For our people, every diamond purchase represents food on the table; better living conditions; better health care; safe drinking water; more roads to connect our remote communities; and much more' (DiamondFacts Organisation). The facts bear this out. Diamonds account for 76 per cent of Botswana's export revenue, 45 per cent of government revenue and 33 per cent of gross domestic product. Since the discovery of diamonds in Botswana in 1966, GDP has grown by 7 per cent a year on average. Debswana, a Botswana diamond company co-owned with De Beers, is the largest corporate contributor to socioeconomic development in Botswana. Without the legitimate diamond trade, Botswana would lose about $13 billion of revenue a year. The loss would impact on everything, from social programmes to government investments in infrastructure.

In 1966, when diamonds were first discovered, there were only three secondary schools in the entire country. Forty years later, thanks to revenues from diamonds, there were 300. Moreover, every child up to the age of 13 receives free schooling. Thomas Tlou, a Botswana citizen, says: 'At independence in 1966, Botswana was one of the poorest countries in the world. Thanks to diamonds, Botswana is now regarded as a middle-income country and provides its people with a good standard of living' (quoted in ibid).

A recent study argues that De Beers has probably generated the most spectacular direct benefits for the government of a developing country in history. It was instrumental in creating Botwana's national diamond producer, Debswana, in 1969. As the value of Botswana's diamond deposits became apparent, the government made use of a renegotiation clause in its contract with De Beers to improve the arrangement. An estimated 70 to 80 per cent of profits accrue to the government (Noland & Spencer 2006).

When indirect effects are taken into account, the diamond industry generates a quarter of the country's jobs. Ancillary activities include security, catering, and maintenance. Without diamond mining, Botswana's economy would be at a completely different stage of development. Debswana's demand for electricity has boosted the growth of the Botswana Power Corporation, which has benefited non-mining sectors of the economy.

Debswana has established an active training and localisation programme, and funds Botswana students both at home and abroad. Most Debswana employees are citizens of Botswana. Similarly, the Botswana Diamond Valuing Company and the Diamond Trading Company Botswana are almost entirely staffed by Batswana (ibid).

COMPANIES PROVIDING TRAINING IN SOUTH AFRICA

The skills shortage in South Africa is a serious impediment to further growth and development. Some local commentators have suggested that part of the problem is a lack of commitment among private sector companies to training and further educating their employees.

A survey conducted to test this claim found the opposite to be true. Eighty-two companies employing 874 078 people responded to the survey. They indicated that 178 820 of their employees had participated in both accredited and non-accredited skills acquisition programmes. A further 55 876 had received support (other than direct training) for courses in this category and a further 12 403 employees had received either direct training or support towards programmes and qualifications falling into the higher education and training levels of skills development. In total, 247 099 of the 874 078 employees in the respondent companies had received skills training or support during the previous year. The participating companies had either funded or supplied skills training for an additional 46 703 people classified as 'non-employees'.

The 70 companies which provided data reported that they had spent R3,7 billion on training and education. A further R453 million was indicated by companies who provided this data from their CSR budgets. Although these companies are only a fraction of the private sector (they employ 10 per cent of the formally employed), their expenditure nearly matched the R5 billion spent on training by the government's training institutions (Godsell & Fourie 2007).

THE DIRECT IMPACT OF BUSINESS:
FINAL THOUGHTS

Successful companies are remarkable institutions, representing achievement and human progress. Their direct impact on society can be seen in the goods they produce and the scale on which they operate. Public companies provide the means by which millions of small investors can part-own and share in their success, and by so doing save money for their retirement. So the corporation has enabled the democratisation of investment. As Michael Novak's US example illustrates: 'The ownership of publicly owned companies extends through more than half the American adult population ... the largest holders of stocks and bonds are the pension plans of workers in the public and private sectors. 'Shareholders are no small, narrow band of the American population, but a large majority' (Novak 1997a: 41).

Large companies have also democratised consumption. It is increasingly rare for important commodities to be available only to the very rich – those which are tend to be extreme examples of what everyone else can have in a more basic model. The way in which we all live, and increasingly not only in the richest countries of the world but developing countries as well, has been shaped by the ability of companies to take ideas and turn them into viable products that can be delivered to markets on a big enough scale to make them affordable.

Micklethwait and Wooldridge have noted that 'Henry Ford's $5 wage was a force for good; but his cheap cars helped change the lives of the poor in ways that socialists could only dream about' (2005: 190). The same can be said about pharmaceutical companies providing modern medicines to 'everyman', airplane companies powering a global revolution in cheap flights; computer companies changing the way in which we store, retrieve, and think about information.

And then, in the latest example of the direct impact of business on society, especially its poorest members, we have mobile phones. Whereas Nokia, Motorola, and other manufacturers are interested in the number of phones they can sell across the globe, and how often their customers come back to buy a new phone, the impact of this technology – invented, produced, marketed, distributed, and sold by companies – on the poor is only now starting to unfold. Mobile phones have become tools of modernisation throughout Africa and other poor regions. In communities where the state or a state monopoly has been unable to deliver land line telephony, innovative affordable cellphone contracts and equipment are reaching the remotest villages. And, through this acquisition of a mobile phone that works and a company with good service to maintain it, poor people can run a business from the side of a rural road or urban sidewalk; can call for help when in trouble; can connect to a bank and the benefits of banking services; and keep in touch with whomever they want (Vodafone 2005).

Recalling the key findings of a recent IFC publication entitled *Paths out of Poverty* on the role of private enterprise in developing countries (IFC 2000) is a good way to end this chapter. The IFC report is built upon two studies examining empirical data from more than 40 countries for some material, and over 80 countries for other trends. Some of the key conclusions are directly relevant to our concerns. These include:

- Growth is good for the poor, and long-term economic growth is an essential condition for poverty reduction.
- Private enterprise has proved to be the strongest contributor to sustainable economic expansion.
- Private firms play a unique, irreplaceable role in the processes of economic and social mobility that lift people out of poverty, and this role assumes more significance because another route out of poverty

– income redistribution – has proved so problematic.

- Private enterprise is by far the largest source of employment and investment, a significant source of tax revenue, and a major contributor to research and development.

- Private enterprise is also an important source of less tangible but vital factors such as openness to ideas, innovation, opportunity, and empowerment.

- The private sector is the best job creator across many different countries, and more and better jobs offer the best – often the only – opportunity for upward mobility for poor people and their children.

- Private investment has a major role to play in economic growth. Recent studies have shown that it is more closely associated with growth than public investment is.

- When dynamic private enterprises are allowed to flourish, they tap into people's initiative, ingenuity, and self-reliance. When people can participate in an economy by creating or joining an enterprise, they gain a voice.

- Private enterprise spans a wide array of activities and forms – all can contribute to poverty reduction.

- *Large firms contribute decisively to development.* In competitive conditions they are able to take knowledge from more advanced economies and adapt it to their own. Subsidiaries of international firms play a particularly active role in the transmission of knowledge. Large firms that receive foreign direct investment (FDI) ranging from labour-intensive enterprises to capital-intensive high technology firms also play a major role in reducing poverty. FDI flows to developing countries are two and a half times larger than foreign aid in the form of loans and grants.

- There would be no sustainable, reliable base for funding programmes that benefit poor people such as health, education, social safety nets, and agricultural research without a foundation of private economic activities.

- Private enterprises extend direct benefits to employees, customers, and suppliers and indirect benefits to society, among them support to social services, and the mobilisation of capital.

- Financial institutions and capital markets play a special role in development and poverty reduction by mobilising savings, including the savings of poor people, and allocating resources. In this sector too the most sustainable and sustained expansion is by private institutions.

- In order to maximise the poverty-fighting capacity of private enterprise, competition is essential. In the long run, monopolies, oligopolies, protection against competing imports, and government subsidies all undermine the poverty-reducing capacity of private firms. One key to improvement is a more competitive environment.

- The fundamental contribution that the state can make to enterprise development is to secure contract enforcement between private parties and between private parties and the state – most basically clearly defined property rights. There is a strong empirical correlation between the degree to which the rule of law is enforced and long-term development. Enforcement of the rule of law benefits poor people as much as it benefits the entire population.

The social benefits of private enterprise – including long-term economic growth, employment, and empowerment – can be increased when appropriate government policies are adopted and enforced. The mammoth World Bank investigation into the lives and aspirations of poor people across the globe, captured in *Voices of the Poor,* confirms these findings (Narayan 1999; Narayan et al 1999). The attribute of overcoming poverty most frequently mentioned by poor people quoted in *Voices of the Poor* is 'economic livelihood', defined as employment, income generation, and participation in the cash economy.

Those who make development policy would best serve the interests of the poor by recognising the power of private enterprise to promote economic growth and reduce poverty, and doing everything possible to help them attain these goals.

Chapter Six

TRANSMISSION BELTS OF MODERNITY
the indirect impact

'It wasn't just jobs the Chinese were after, it was modernization itself. When foreign companies sought to open factories in China, the government insisted that they use and teach Chinese workers how to use their latest techniques, flooding a technologically antiquated country with know-how and spurring a speedy transfer latter-day industrial revolution.'

Robyn Meredith, *The Elephant and the Dragon: The Rise of India and China and What It Means for All of Us* (2007)

MOST DISCUSSIONS of business ignore a crucial dimension of the relationship between business and society that I will refer to as 'invisible corporate citizenship'. This involves the unintended consequences of doing business.

In rich, highly advanced societies, these processes are taken for granted to such an extent that their relationship to economic activity is rarely perceived. This relationship can be more clearly described and identified in a developing society or newly democratic market economy, where modern corporate activity is more recent.

When I attended the World Economic Forum meetings in Davos, Switzerland, in January 2008, the unintended consequences of business activity were strongly evident. Among some of the 'largest egos in the world', Indian and Chinese leaders were confidently talking about their companies and their countries in a way that would not have been the case even five years ago. This is a direct result of economic success and the expansion of domestic companies into the global arena. No one intended this to happen; it is one of the results of economic growth and corporate success in these countries – or 'invisible corporate citizenship'.

There are at least seven areas in which business existence and activity have positive unintended outcomes.

BUSINESS AND NATIONAL ECONOMIC DEVELOPMENT

When foreign companies invest for the long term in a developing country, they can fuel a virtuous circle of economic activity. Workers benefit from jobs, skills, knowledge transfer and training; local suppliers benefit from commercial loan and banking facilities, contract based investment possibilities, and access to leading international practice. Local consumers can access more and better products at affordable prices.

Transforming the prospects of millions

Companies make a subtle contribution to society that is generally overlooked. Firms are optimistic by nature, the very opposite of the fatalism that characterises more traditional societies, or those that have laboured for decades under socialist rule or other kinds of ineffective, corrupt, and debilitating governments that clamp down on initiative and achievement.

Companies – managers, entrepreneurs, institutions – turn ideas into realities, provide real-life choices, take good notions and make them work as viable, safe, affordable products that can be distributed to consumers throughout the world. In his study of the automotive, computer, electronic, and textile industries in South East Asia and Latin America, Theodore Moran has shown how foreign investment through companies can

> transform the overall development profile of an entire host country, thereby redefining the economic prospects of hundreds of thousands and even millions of workers who are not directly employed in foreign plants (2002: 8).

Similarly, Paul Romer has shown how foreign textile investors have helped to transform the economy of Mauritius with a 'package' of benefits, including new production techniques, international contracts, and experience in navigating the complex terrain of textile quotas in international markets. Within 15 years, this new dynamic revolutionised the Mauritian economy from slow-growing agricultural activities and high unemployment to 'high-growth garment export activities, a tight labour market, and rising wages' (1992). The potential to alter a host country's development trajectory is even more pronounced when foreign companies invest in more sophisticated industries, such as electrical equipment, electronics, auto parts, industrial machinery, chemicals, medical equipment, and pharmaceuticals (Moran 2002).

In Asia the development of what economists call backward linkages with the local economy began tentatively in the computer and electronics sectors, but soon expanded. For example, by 1981 one American semiconductor investor in Singapore bought components from 200 local suppliers. Six of the largest were affiliates of other Japanese, American, or European corporations, but four more were Singaporean companies. The investor provided local firms with technical plans, detailed specifications for parts, and helped them to introduce effective quality control procedures, including 'troubleshooting' by American engineers.

A second consumer electronics manufacturer, a European multinational, made four of its largest contract manufacturing arrangements with other foreign affiliates, and four with Singaporean firms. It helped the Singaporean suppliers to automate their production facilities, even buying the necessary machinery, renting it to suppliers, and taking payment in the form of future deliveries. It also helped them retrain their workers in order to achieve the necessary economies of scale. Both European and American investors 'walked' their Singaporean suppliers through the process of penetrating international markets. The latter initially supplied sister plants of the foreign parent firms, but then began selling to independent foreign buyers. Three indigenous firms that began by supplying the local affiliates of foreign firms reached the ranks of the top ten contract electronics manufacturers in the world (ibid: 124-5).

The consequences of these development trajectories are profound. Think of the implications of this comment by an executive of the American computer firm Texas Instruments: 'We came for the cheap labour and tax advantages, but we are staying because of the expertise we have built up [in Malaysia]. As far as assemblage and testing are concerned, we have more expertise here than we have in the United States – we sometimes have to send Malaysian engineers to the States to solve their problems' (ibid: 123).

Developing domestic business sectors

At first sight it may seem as if the only contribution of foreign investors in developing countries is to employ unskilled or semi-skilled labour, thus augmenting local savings. In fact, according to Moran, they offer

Integrated packages that include hard to replicate technologies, business techniques, management skills, HR policies and marketing capabilities. As they introduce these assets into the local economy, foreign investors may position the host country at the frontier of best practices in international industries. ... Foreign investors may find that it is in their own best interest to develop local supplier networks and to supervise and help improve the performance of those networks. The foreign firms may thus generate backward linkages, spillovers and positive externalities for host country workers, managers and firms that exceed what is reflected in the parent firms' profits. Foreign direct investment and the globalization of industry consequently not only allow a host economy to do what it already does more efficiently, but make it possible for the host country to transform the set of activities that can be performed within the country's borders (ibid: 108).

Investment by foreign firms in developing countries has hugely positive results. Its value goes far further than the much-needed provision of employment in those firms' own plants and suppliers, and helps to change the range of productive activities taking place in their new host country. If this potential is handled well by the host government, increased foreign direct investment can transform the future of an entire country, and the life chances of all its citizens.

The relationship between the parent multinational company and its subsidiaries does not lead merely to a once-off contribution of even the most advanced 'off the shelf' technology and business practices; it results in a continuous upgrading of technology and business practices in a dynamic process that soon embraces local supplier companies as well.

Among the most important indicators of the business environment in a country are the international businesses already operating there. The role of successful companies goes even further than that. South African companies, many of which have expanded successfully into other African countries, and some of which have become successful global players, see themselves as 'ambassadors' for the country and the whole continent.

Similarly, the emergence of big Indian multinationals has changed the way in which other countries and companies view not just those Indian companies but India itself, as a place to do business, and a growing locus of tourism, fashion, and culture. Corporate success is changing the way in which Indians, Africans, and Brazilians view themselves, and how investors, citizens and governments in rich countries view these increasingly successful parts of the developing world and their inhabitants.

COMPANIES AS AGENTS FOR CHANGE AND MODERNISATION

In 1980 Deng Xiaoping, influential leader of the Chinese Communist Party, declared: 'Foreign capital ... will bring some decadent capitalist influences into China. We are aware of this possibility. It is nothing to be afraid of' (quoted in Santoro 2000: 44).

Companies have an impact on society that goes way beyond economics. In many respects they are revolutionary hidden agents of change.

Transmission belts of human rights and modernity

One part of the 'corporate transmission belt' conveys the latest manufacturing and marketing techniques – we have already examined the powerful impact of these elements on emerging economies. However, modern companies also bring with them what one might call the associated 'software' of effective corporate cultures and human relations practices based on 21st-century notions of individual rights and responsibilities.

When a multinational enters a new society, it needs to select and then train its workforce to ensure their productivity, which requires that employees are satisfied with their working conditions and their future prospects. In the course of formal and on-the-job training, companies influence the values and behaviour of their employees. As Debra Spar, a professor at the Harvard Business School, puts it:

> American firms' normal business procedures incorporate a sort of grass roots meritocracy and openness not found in many host country companies. US and western multinational corporations reward employees based on performance, not out of patronage or other nonprofessional considerations. Multinationals emphasize training and workplace benefits, further reinforcing the idea that every individual has intrinsic potential and human dignity (quoted in Novak 1996b: 160).

Michael Santoro, associate professor at the Rutgers Business School, recently spent time in China talking to company executives and workers. I will use material from his subsequent book to illustrate the collateral benefits of normal business operations of western multinationals operating in that country.

Empowering individuals

According to the American electronics multinational Motorola, its operations in China are guided by the same beliefs that underpin its activities elsewhere: respect for individuals, and uncompromising integrity in everything they do. As a company manager stated: 'These beliefs help create an environment of empowerment for all in a culture of participation. … Motorola's commitment to teamwork and continuous learning is key to developing the company's operations in China and its partnership with the Chinese people' (Santoro 2000: 4).

Every Motorola worker receives a booklet describing the company's 'I Recommend' programme which encourages workers to suggest improvements in the workplace. Chinese language posters persuade workers to speak out if there are dangerous conditions in any part of their plant, or some process that can be improved. Motorola wants its managers 'to take the initiative, exert leadership, assume responsibility, manage rapid change, and work in teams' (ibid: 6). All of this is typical of western companies, but what is the norm in a western democracy is built upon very different values and assumptions about individual action and behaviour than a Chinese worker would typically learn by working in a state-owned enterprise and living in Chinese society.

American companies send many of their Chinese employees abroad, thus exposing them to western society and global market forces. According to Business Roundtable, every year 300 to 400 Chinese workers tour Caterpillar's main assembly facility in the United States, and selected managers spend six months in the United States where they attend courses and programmes. General Motors conducts programmes to familiarise Chinese government officials with American business practices and United States government approaches to industrial standards and regulations. Seminars are held in China to discuss vehicle sales, distribution, consumer protection, and the contribution of the automobile to society (Business Roundtable 2000: 30).

New values

What are the values and ideas that Motorola and other western employers are communicating to their new employees in China through learning on the job? Western employers are encouraging radical new ideas in their Chinese employees:

- *Speak up if something is wrong or not efficient.* In traditional Confucian culture, good subordinates obey and respect the boss. In a repressive, one-party communist state, the boss gives orders, makes decisions, looks after subordinates, and expects mute obedience from employees. The modern business ethic contradicts both ideas, and leads to greater individual freedom.
- *Individuals matter.* Santoro quotes an employee as saying: 'Working for a foreign company is a major change for Chinese ... you are respected as an individual and a human being' (Santoro 2000: 43).
- *Merit counts.* Foreign business are helping to create a class of white-collar staff and technical workers who have reached their positions through talent and hard work – a rather different approach to that of a communist party which uses access to and retention of jobs as a means of social and political control. Santoro quotes a young Chinese who previously worked for a state-owned enterprise: 'As long as you perform [in a western company], you will be promoted. SOEs are large and old. You are behind a lot of people for promotion' (ibid: 11). Santoro writes: 'For the first time in modern Chinese history, a young man or woman can achieve financial and career success without joining the Communist Party. This sense of the worth of the

individual is a cornerstone of a culture that respects individual civil and political rights' (ibid: 43).

- *Work in teams, share information.* Authoritarian states maintain social control by controlling access to information. Many western companies operating in China provide employees with email, Internet, photocopiers and mobile phones and demonstrate the positive effects of easy communication and information flow. These facilities are essential for their effective operation and competitiveness, but are also encouraging a more open Chinese society.

- *Take responsibility, problems can be solved, individuals matter.* Employees are encouraged not to wait for company leaders to act, and channels are provided for feedback and dialogue – very different from the political culture outside the factory gate.

- *Assume leadership by speaking out and thinking differently – reason and facts matter.* Santoro quotes a female worker: 'In Chinese firms the boss can do and say what he likes; he doesn't care if his advances are unwanted, because he is the boss. In an American firm I feel well protected against that. I know my rights' (ibid: 59).

New ideas in closed societies

Less than one per cent of China's labour force is employed by foreign companies. But, writes Santoro, 'who is to say what the impact will be when a couple of guys are talking over beer after work and comparing their experiences of working in a state-owned company with those of a foreign company?' (ibid: 68). And who can predict the exact impact of foreign companies on the many other firms, individuals, and families who are affected by their presence and ways of doing business in the city in which they are operating? Or the impact on officials with whom the company comes into contact in the national government or the ruling party?

There can be no doubt that the presence of foreign companies and investors in China is helping the spread of new and radical ideas in a closed society. This is not the intention of these companies, but it is a consequence of their approach to running their businesses.

The broader impact of work practices

The values, ideas, and practices inherent in modern western business practice can profoundly influence workers, their families, other networks, and ultimately their entire society. These include:

- Modern recruitment methods – based on individual achievement and not group ascription such as tribal affiliation, gender, or connection to local 'big men'.
- Training – centred on individuals and their performance, and provides space for people to determine their own destiny.
- New forms of organisation – the replacement of traditional work gangs with modern self-directed work teams carries with it a new set of social assumptions, with spillover effects for the individuals concerned (Godsell 2007).
- Emergence of an information society – development of knowledge workers as individual centres of power within a company helps to democratise the workplace (ibid).
- New forms of management – if management must explain, campaign, and gain assent for activities and roles, this has implications for other forms of authority in society from national and local government to the family and the school (ibid).
- Market and business development result in new forms of organisation including business organisations, trade unions, consumer organisations, all of which can exercise their power on a wider social stage.

- In authoritarian states, workplaces can become 'liberated zones' – the training, testing, and assembly grounds for forms of social power and social organisation outside the state.

Workplace practices become a way of propelling people along the road towards modern citizenship. These inadvertent consequences of corporate activity become powerful transmission belts of modernisation and change in all societies, but particularly those that are not democratic, egalitarian, or marked by freedom of speech and organisation.

Large companies can have an impact in other unexpected areas. In the new market economies of eastern Europe, people place considerable trust in western global brands. People in these societies admire business; they see large corporations as providing jobs, creating wealth, opportunities for workers to grow and progress; and a sense of direction, purpose and meaning (Hilton & Gibbons 2005: xi).

Following South Africa's transition to democracy, a successful black business woman, head of the Institute of People Management, awarded a lifetime achievement award to a white supermarket executive. She said the supermarkets managed by his company were the first facilities in the country where she experienced what it was like to be treated with respect, where her custom was valued as highly as those of white shoppers. This led her to question why, if she could be treated with dignity in a store, the government could not treat her in the same way.

BUSINESS AND THE RULE OF LAW

In developed market economies, the confidence of shareholders is boosted by a range of intermediary institutions. Stock exchanges require companies seeking a listing to submit extensive, stringent financial reports. Specialised firms vouch in various ways for the information reported by corporations. Financial statements are audited. Investment banking firms underwrite share issues. Law firms approve company prospectuses. The business media are also part of the oversight system, with journalists seeking to expose fraud and incompetence. These market-based devices are reinforced by various public ones. Governments make laws defining and protecting shareholders' rights, making accounting and auditing firms liable for any faulty disclosures they endorse; and defining what managers may and may not do to benefit themselves. False disclosure and insider trading are penalised, and individuals may sue companies or managers for losses due to illegal actions. In the most sophisticated markets, financial regulators also play a significant role in ensuring effective and honest markets (McMillan 2002: 176).

The process of listing a firm on a public stock exchange in a less developed economy is an instructive example of the invisible role of business. It requires a network of institutions, rules, monitoring processes, values, and procedures. Gordon Redding, former head of the University of Hong Kong Business School, has described this process in respect of a listing on the Chinese stock exchange (1998):

> A large multinational corporation needs certainty in order to invest
> in China. Providing this certainty requires rules and standards.
> The company therefore pushes for effective property laws and
> laws governing contracts. Rules and standards require the means

to create, monitor and maintain them. Evolving, monitoring and maintaining such rules and standards require institutions and associations. Institutions and associations require independent professionals. This in turn requires an independent judiciary and reliable information. And this requires reasonably open, free media and public debate (quoted in CDE 1996a).

Thus normal business activity requires and creates a complex web of institutions, organisations, self-regulating mechanisms, processes of transparency and openness, and professionals and their organisations that comprise important components of modern society. In so doing they help – unintentionally – to strengthen civil society.

These economic kinds of organisations are not discussed in civil society literature, but they certainly count among the institutions and associations that function outside direct state organisation, funding and control, and therefore constitute an important part of the non-state sector.

BUSINESS AND INSTITUTION-BUILDING

Foreign direct investment and legal reform

John Hewko has worked in Moscow, Kiev, and Prague as a partner in the global law firm Baker and McKenzie. In this capacity he has served as legal adviser to the Ukrainian parliament, and member of the drafting committees of the original Ukrainian foreign investment laws. Based on this experience, he argues that foreign investors are not 'passive spectators' in the legislative and institutional reform process.

Instead, foreign investment has been a 'dynamic force in the forefront of the push for change, and an agent for such reform' (2002: 5).

Early investors in post-communist countries were generally large multinationals and individual entrepreneurs. While multinationals do regard legal considerations as important, they generally take a back seat to market potential. These companies are investing in the long term and have the resources needed to deal with bureaucratic red tape, inefficiency, and other difficulties (ibid: 9).

Foreign companies pay lawyers and accountants large sums of money to identify specific risks and problems relating to their investments. As a result, 'foreign investors and their advisers ... are best suited to identify the exact changes needed in the legislative framework in order to facilitate FDI, and address foreign investor concerns' (ibid: 5).

Foreign investors often end up facilitating legislative and institutional changes in ways that are more efficient, relevant, and cost-effective than the efforts of the international development community. Hewko notes that foreign investors are not altruistic, and their interests may not always coincide with those of society as a whole or with those of domestic investors. He is therefore not suggesting that the legislative and institutional reform process should be left exclusively to foreign investors; domestic institutions, especially representative governments and other local and even international organisations have important roles to play. Companies and investors from different countries will introduce different values and ideas, and have varying degrees of tolerance for imperfections in the host state's legal system.

Generally, new Ukrainian laws were based on USSR legislation adopted during the two years preceding the break-up of the Soviet Union, and it was 'painfully obvious' that Ukrainian parliamentarians and committee members drafting the legislation did not understand how foreign investors, corporations, and a market system operated. Hewko argues that the foreign business community and its legal and accounting advisers represent the most efficient mechanism for identifying inadequacies and problems in existing commercial legislation and regulations (ibid: 13). No other actor is better placed to understand and explain the exact changes needed in a given country than the companies investing in it.

Building institutions and professions

According to Hewko, the literature on institution-building ignores the role that foreign investment can and does play in this process. This role is particularly significant in two key respects: the development of a culture of respect for the law, and development of the legal and accounting professions (ibid: 20).

Serious foreign investors (largely multinational firms) play a vital role in training and educating individuals, and in developing a cadre of citizens who understand and accept those practices and concepts. They transfer to employees not only valuable business know-how and technical expertise but also expose them to a certain work ethic, business practices, ethical standards, and codes of conduct. Over time, these actions create a critical mass of citizens who have been inculcated with a reform mentality, and who will support and demand reforms in the country's laws and enforcement institutions.

Foreign investors are also extremely effective in providing training and transferring know-how. 'The fact that McDonalds has trained thousands of young people throughout eastern Europe has meant far more and had a far greater impact on the process of creating the appropriate cultural framework for institutional reform than most of the efforts of the international development community' (ibid: 21).

Foreign investment and the legal and accounting professions

Almost all post-communist countries now have a significant number of well-trained, sophisticated accountants and auditors. According to Hewko, this is due almost exclusively to two factors: foreign investors, and the then Big Five accounting firms.

Each of the Big Five had substantial operations in all the countries in eastern Europe. They employed thousands of accountants, consultants, auditors, and support staff, almost all of them local people. Foreign investors need to comply with tax, accounting, and auditing requirements of the host country and with those of their home country as well. Since local accountants were generally incapable of providing those services to the standards required by foreign investors, the task fell on the Big Five. In the process they trained English-speaking, market-savvy accountants and auditors, and revolutionised accounting practices in those countries. They also played a significant role in training the management of their client companies, exposing managers and staff to modern western concepts, practices, and procedures.

The same phenomenon has occurred on a smaller scale with respect to the legal profession. Demand fuelled an invasion of western law firms. Like the accounting profession, these firms (at least in the early years) had an 'almost exclusive monopoly on major inbound investments, privatizations and cross-border financing work, and had a significant impact on developing and training sophisticated local attorneys with a deep understanding of how law is to be practiced, the role of law in society, and the need for legal reform' (ibid: 21-2).

In Hewko's view, much of the literature on legal and institutional reform – and on development more generally – ignores the extraordinary contribution of foreign investors and foreign accounting and legal firms to the development of the legal and accounting professions in the host countries. Compared with this, the influence of training programmes funded by the international development community has been insignificant (ibid: 23).

He concludes: 'If the goal is to increase the quality of the legal and accounting profession in a given country, there is no faster or more efficient mechanism than to encourage in that country a critical level of foreign investment and foreign law and accounting firms' (ibid).

BUSINESS OPPORTUNITIES AND PRACTICES EMPOWERING WOMEN

Market economies break down barriers to the more efficient use of resources. Many critics of markets and globalisation complain that international companies 'interfere' with 'traditional ways of life'. One of the traditions challenged by business practices is the long-standing subjugation of women in many developing societies.

A silent revolution

Helen Rahman of Shoishab, an Oxfam-funded organisation working in Bangladesh, maintains that the emergence of the country's textile industry during the past 20 years has significantly improved the status of women. According to her, the garment industry has stimulated a 'silent revolution of social change'. It used to be unacceptable for women to work outside their neighbourhoods, and those who left the countryside to go to the city were assumed to be prostitutes. Now it is acceptable for women to rent a house together. Moreover, their income gives them new-found social status and bargaining power (quoted in Norberg 2003b: 46)

Although no major comparative studies exist of the consequences of foreign investment for women, this area of business impact has perhaps been the most fully explored, partly because activists have claimed that these consequences have largely been negative. By contrast, the experience and responses of women workers in developing countries differ greatly from western reactions to isolated cases of physical abuse, unsafe working conditions, or withheld wages.

New and better choices

An ethnographer of the working conditions of women in Java, Indonesia, notes that while factory work is exploitative, young women clearly prefer it to their other meagre choices. 'Although factory work, organisation and discipline are strict and often brutal, female workers perceive factory employment as a progressive change in their lives, not as a gaping unhealed wound' (Litvin 2003: 236).

The most striking evidence that factory work can transform women's lives comes from a study by a British academic of employees in export-oriented garment factories in Bangladesh. Until recently, strict Muslim traditions of *purdah* made it socially unacceptable for many women to work outside their homes. Foreign investors and their local subcontractors lobbied at the highest national levels to change this. Today, some 95 per cent of the 1,4 million garment sector employees in Bangladesh are women (Moran 2002: 15). Moran quotes a garment worker as stating:

If garments had not come to Bangladesh, many women would have had to eat [by] sacrificing their honour or eating off their brothers. Without these factories, they would have had no honour. Now their value has risen (ibid: 238).

Self-respect and freedom

Jagdish Bhagwati, professor of economics at Columbia University, believes that legitimate, income-generating work has transformed the adolescent experience of Bangladeshi girls, and provided them with a degree of autonomy, self-respect, and freedom from the back-breaking physical work traditionally reserved for women (2004a: 85).

Other studies in Indonesia, Mexico, and Malaysia have reported similar positive effects. Besides improving the overall welfare of workers, employment in foreign-owned plants has provided many female workers with what Nobel Prize winner Amartya Sen has called 'enhanced agency' (quoted in Moran 2002: 15).

Social impact

The social benefit of employing women in low-skilled jobs in export factories extends beyond increased individual status and autonomy. When women work, a larger proportion of their household income is directed towards health, nutrition, and education, which reduces the intergenerational transmission of poverty. Working in factories also appears to militate against early marriage, and may raise awareness of family planning (ibid).

New networks, new opportunities

Factory development creates new opportunities for the advancement of women. In the Philippines, data from the 1980s showed a clear division of labour by gender, with men predominating in supervisory roles, and women in lower-skilled positions. By 1998, across all sectors of specially created Export Processing Zones where foreign investors were clustered, these proportions have changed radically (ibid: 31).

In 1999-2000 Linda Lim, professor at the University of Michigan Business School, visited Nike factories in Vietnam and Indonesia, and interviewed management personnel in Singapore, as part of the university's response to student protests triggered by media reports about conditions in those factories. Besides confirming the positive findings of others, she notes that in her previous studies in Malaysia a significant portion of women factory workers used the networks they had developed at work to provide goods and services to one another; one of the attractions of factory jobs was the access it provided to much wider networks that could be used for these commercial purposes (ibid: 3).

Other opportunities for women

Vinod Khosla founded the high-tech company Sun Micro Systems in the United States, and later became a partner in a global venture capital firm. In the latter capacity he came to know a commercial micro lending firm in India, with 128 different branches in three different states, serving 200 000 clients in about 3 000 villages. Almost all the clients are women. He reports that the lending programme has not only changed their financial status but also their mental orientation.

'Entrepreneurship is about self-confidence ... I have no doubt that this will have all kinds of other consequences' (Khosla 2004).

Hindustan Lever recruits women in Indian villages as freelance direct sales operators. According to Niall Fitzgerald, Unilever's CEO at the time, the company decided to train these women, facilitate their access to micro credit, and deliver its products to their doorstep to sell to their neighbours (Fitzgerald 2003). The project faced several seemingly substantial obstacles; women in these communities are not normally breadwinners, and many were reluctant to borrow money. Moreover, most were uneasy about selling goods to their friends and neighbours at a profit. Nonetheless, the initiative went ahead and, according to Unilever, has had a significant impact on women's lives (ibid).

By treating people as individuals, and opening up jobs to women, modern companies are providing women in many developing regions with opportunities they have never had before. The consequences of this are profound, not only for this generation of women but also their children.

BUSINESS EMPOWERS THE POOR AS CONSUMERS

Business activities strengthen markets and, because suppliers in those markets need and depend on customers, they also create consumer power.

An interesting example can be found in 1980s apartheid South Africa. At a time when state repression was making it increasingly

difficult for internal opposition movements to sustain any form of
protest, some local organisations came up with the idea of organising
consumer boycotts of white-owned stores.

The organisers usually compiled long lists of demands, some
relating to local business, some relating to local conditions and some
concerned with fundamental changes in national policies. In most
cases these committees were not directly concerned to attack or change
local business practices, but the boycotts often had the effect of getting
white people in cities and small towns to talk to black opposition
movements, listen to the concerns of ordinary black people, and
develop joint strategies.

It was remarkable how rapidly most white shop owners were
prepared to ditch racist practices and racist views when their black
customers abandoned them. Rather than polarising towns, the
consumer boycotts often led to whites and blacks working together
towards ending local apartheid and improving living conditions. The
economic ties between white business owners and black customers
were more powerful than the laws and prejudices that separated them.

In the mid-1980s, at least 22 towns were hit by these consumer
boycotts. Most were in the Eastern Cape, and the most successful
instances occurred in small towns whose white and black populations
were segregated, but nevertheless lived in close proximity. In these
towns many small businesses depended very heavily on black
customers.

One prominent boycott occurred in the small town of Port Alfred.
The Port Alfred Civic Organisation called for the boycott in May
1984, and laid out a series of demands which had to be met before
they would call it off. By mid-August, with their businesses facing
bankruptcy, shopkeepers relented. They first met with black leaders
to negotiate a way out of the boycott. They pledged to end segregation
in their shops, committed themselves to creating local jobs, appealing

to the authorities on behalf of the black community on issues such as rent arrears, and making informal approaches to the police, after which police behaviour in the township reportedly improved. They also declared their support for a single, non-racial municipality. By the third week of August, the protest was suspended and boycott leaders joined business leaders on a committee to create a public works programme.

When poor black consumers in a racially divided, undemocratic society used their market power, they pushed businesses into listening to and forging closer links with their customers. The result was a series of new relationships between black and white leaders in hitherto totally divided communities; new respect for black communities; recognition of their consumer power by white businesses and politicians; and meaningful local development.

In a deeply discriminatory society, black consumers were able to use their consumer power to change perceptions of blacks by whites as well as prospects for progress in local communities; ultimately they helped to change the direction of an entire society.

BUSINESS — AN INDEPENDENT SPACE FROM THE STATE

Peter Drucker has argued that the creation of private companies was a major social innovation – they were the first autonomous institutions in hundreds of years, and the first to 'create power centres that were within society, yet independent of the central government or the national state' (Micklethwait & Wooldridge 2005: 54).

In the heated debates about business and its social role, it is often forgotten that companies are voluntary institutions independent of the state – mediating structures between individuals and the state. Michael Novak argues that after the family, businesses may well be the most important civil society institutions.

New forms of individuality

In earlier societies, people were entirely defined by their status as peasants, artisans, or merchants. Being a member of a guild, for example, encompassed a complete set of economic, legal, political, even religious codes. Modern market society is based upon looser, more temporary associations founded to pursue specific economic, cultural, or political interests. The concept of limited liability inherent in modern corporations is a model for other forms of association in capitalist societies where individuals cooperate with a part of their lives for common but limited purposes – 'participation without absorption' in Muller's words (2003).

Without this, civil society could scarcely have emerged. The economic freedom to start enterprises and participate freely in labour markets produce further possibilities for expanding human freedom and extending the field of human experience. Muller concludes that 'many of the moral advantages and conceptions of selfhood that those in capitalist societies take for granted are due in no small part to capitalism itself' (ibid).

Business, pluralism, and civil society

Novak has argued that business is the first political institution of civil society. The founders of the United States sought to establish a 'commercial republic' because they thought it would be more safely based on commerce than on aristocracy, religion, or the military.

> Following Montesquieu, they held that commerce inherently cries out for law and teaches respect for law; benefits by peace and is destroyed by war; teaches prudence and attention to small losses and small gains; softens manners; diverts attention from issues of glory and spiritual divisiveness to seek modest progress on humble but useful matters and distributes the practical interests of people even in the same families among different industries and different firms (1997a: 39).

His final remark points to an important added dimension of the broader social role of business. Although we might talk of 'business' as though it were a single entity, this shorthand term is misleading. The highly diversified nature of commerce and industry results in the interests of citizens involved in these different enterprises and sectors taking different forms. As a result, 'the sheer dynamism of economic invention (facilitated by markets) makes far less probable the coalescing of a simple majority which could act as a tyrant to minorities' (Novak 1996b: 93). And this is a vital ingredient in building more plural societies.

Companies and the private wealth they create play a critical role in securing independent thinking and political freedom. In many countries it is hard to imagine a vibrant, flourishing civil society representing the interests, ideas and energies of thousands of individuals and communities without corporate funding.

Listed companies give individuals, families and communities a chance to acquire private wealth as shareholders. In so doing, they expand the space for independence and private action.

Business and communities of interest

Companies and the communities they form are an integral part of the social order, vital to both civic and public life. Although critics often portray business people as driven individuals motivated solely by self-interest, business requires the building of networks, associations, and 'communities' of common interest.

Business owners or managers must build a community of work, and a great deal depends on the level of creativity, teamwork, and morale a firm's leaders can inspire. Firms also depend on larger communities of suppliers and customers, bankers and government officials, transport systems, and the rule of law. In many ways, business is, in Novak's words,

> a community activity, and capitalism is not solely about the individual. It is about a creative form of community. The institution that is capitalism's main contribution to the human race is not individualism; it is the private business corporation independent of the state. The main thing to notice about this invention is that it generates a new and important form of human community – one of whose main purposes is to create new wealth beyond the wealth that existed before it came into being (1996b: 126-7).

In short, a decentralised economic system makes possible the establishment of groups independent of political power, which in turn provides the potential for political pluralism.

Business as an independent player

South African businessman Bobby Godsell has described the workplace in an authoritarian state as a 'zone of liberation', where workers and trade unions can learn new forms of negotiation and decision-making (Godsell 2007). This works in a larger context as well. Companies function as alternative centres of power, influence, and resources to those of the state.

Business, by dint of its existence outside the ambit of the state, can contribute to greater pluralism, freedom of expression, and diversity, thus strengthening pressures for democratisation or democratic consolidation. The Chinese state is trying to retain control over all the dynamics taking place as more economic freedom is allowed, but even there one can observe how the hold of the state over the lives of individuals is relaxed as a modern business culture spreads.

Apartheid South Africa provides another perspective on this issue. As the country developed the South African economy required growing numbers of skilled and semi-skilled workers, and businesses increasingly found that these people could no longer be drawn from the white community alone. Business also needs a stable workforce. As a result, South African businesses increasingly began to employ blacks in skilled and semi-skilled positions, and advocate the creation of stable – and therefore permanent – black urban communities.

The first places where black and white South Africans worked and ate together were in large companies, where people were treated as individuals rather than units of labour. Companies – local and foreign – led the way in training black people, promoting them, integrating the workplace, and recognising black trade unions. By demonstrating that black South Africans could perform as well as others when given training and opportunities, companies – not by design but in effect –

showed white South Africans that a non-racial future was possible, that a racially integrated society could function without conflict.

CONCLUDING REMARKS

'In eastern Europe, the ability to buy a Big Mac, shop at Tesco and buy real Levis rather than fake ones was not just a welcome extension of consumer choice, but the most tangible possible symbol of individual and political freedom – a daily reminder of the freedom to choose.'

Steven Hilton and Giles Gibbons, *Good Business: Your World Needs You* (2005)

The current conversation about business and its role in society ignores the hidden dimension of what I have called 'invisible corporate citizenship'. This chapter has only touched the surface – one could find many more examples around the world of how ordinary business activities are changing people's lives without this ever once being discussed in a corporate boardroom or documented in an annual report – and certainly not acknowledged by any business critic.

This chapter has illustrated the profound contribution that ordinary business activities can make in countries struggling to improve their circumstances. It also points to the diverse ways in which corporate activities have helped to shape richer societies and their prospects for the future.

Through the unintended consequences of its everyday activities, business can:

Provide the potential to transform the trajectory of national economies, with impact on people's lives beyond the individual firm

Correctly managed by a reasonably competent state, foreign direct investment can transform the development pattern of an entire host country, thus helping to redefine the economic prospects of millions. The presence of large foreign companies can provide a bridge from the most advanced societies to poorer countries that enable the latter to jumpstart industrialisation and establish platforms for sustained economic development. Successful companies can act as ambassadors for countries and entire continents, changing international perceptions and encouraging others to invest.

Fuel the forces and dynamics of modernisation

Large companies can be 'transmission belts to modernity'. They introduce and maintain standards in various areas, exposing a widening circle of people and organisations to new and better ways of doing things. Modern ideas on how to manage people and workplaces (careers, training, personal growth, consultation, communication) and values about individuals, education, rights and equal treatment irrespective of social status will not stop at the factory gate.

Expand and strengthen civil society

Companies are independent pillars of civil society, important constructs and promoters of pluralism and voluntary institutions. In some circumstances, they can even act as 'zones of liberation', demonstrating new paradigms of organisation and behaviour.

Firms need an enabling environment made up of laws, regulations, rules and vital institutions of education, training and accreditation to ensure standards are maintained. In the process – inadvertently – they promote the rule of law, greater media freedom, a more transparent law-making process, foster the development of a cadre of managers and other professionals and their involvement in institutions that contribute to an effective business environment. They help to establish an increasingly independent middle class, which plays a vital role in development and growth.

Expand human rights, and unleash pressures for democratisation

Business has a continuing interest in sourcing workers, irrespective of gender, ethnicity, or religion. In the process, it helps to break down social barriers in host societies. In unintended ways, modern work processes encourage individual and collective human rights, as well as the development of managerial and negotiating skills that can be applied in the wider political arena. Markets empower entrepreneurs, and the governments that benefit from them. They empower consumers who can use their new-found power to influence companies and societies at large. The way in which companies interact with customers can lead to them expecting similar levels of service, courtesy and efficiency from government or other institutions.

In order to function effectively, modern businesses require independent networks, associations, and communities of interest. The business sector contains many different players, thus creating a diversity of interests which contributes to greater pluralism generally.

Ordinary business activities can therefore be said to have five major unintended or incidental consequences: changing a country's development path; boosting forces of modernisation; strengthening civil society; expanding human rights and rule by law; unleashing pressures for democratisation. In this sense, business is a constant agent of social change.

This idea is rather different from the notion of business as a conservative force working to preserve the status quo, or an essentially malign power which needs to pay a social penalty to offset the negative consequences of its pursuit of profit.

Economic rationality inadvertently leads to individuals with modern attitudes and institutions of civil society. They in turn inadvertently facilitate human rights, pluralism and democracy. 'In this sense, the market – in its capital raising, skills allocation, workplace training, institution building and goods trading sense – is a stalking horse for democracy' (Bernstein & Berger 1998: 6).

Chapter Seven

IF GLOBAL POVERTY
IS THE ISSUE,
CSR IS NOT THE ANSWER

*'We got more done for the poor by pursuing the competition
agenda for a few years than we got done by pursuing a
poverty agenda for decades.'*

Vijay Kelkar, adviser to the Indian Minister of Finance (2005)

IN THE GUILT-LADEN, emotionally charged world of 'responsible' corporations and their role in global poverty, the Millennium Development Goals (MDGs) are a vital component of the package of new responsibilities being deposited at the corporate door. Many activists, journalists, and corporate managers regard the MDGs as the primary framework for 'the business response to global poverty'. Leading company executives routinely endorse the MDGs, and talk about how they are helping to achieve them.

In this chapter I will examine the thinking behind these goals, and argue that this essentially welfarist, aid-based approach to development is not an agenda that business (or developing country governments) should sign up for. I then turn to one of the latest examples of the drive for global standards, the Equator Principles. Once again, activist-inspired rules for development now being adopted by leading global financial institutions are contrary to the interests of developing countries. Lastly, I examine some of the dubious assumptions about business and 'global poverty' emerging from a leading academic institution and its work on CSR.

These examples of the shaky foundations on which the current discourse on business, global poverty and development are built, illustrate our broad argument. We need a new framework within which to conduct the conversation about business and society, and the role of companies in developing countries.

WHOSE VISION OF DEVELOPMENT?

The logic behind the MDGs is that by setting up measurable targets in the struggle against disease, illiteracy and poverty, the chances of actually achieving results will be improved. The goals were agreed with much fanfare by world leaders at a United Nations conference in 2000. The MDGs have become the equivalent of the 'ten commandments' for those involved in the aid business.

THE UN MILLENNIUM DEVELOPMENT GOALS

1. Eradicate extreme poverty and hunger
   - Reduce by half the proportion of people living on less than one US dollar a day.
   - Reduce by half the proportion of people who suffer from hunger.
   - Increase the amount of food for those who suffer from hunger.
2. Achieve universal primary education
   - Ensure that all boys and girls complete a full course of Primary Schooling.
   - Increased enrolment must be accompanied by efforts to ensure that all children remain in school and receive a

---

high-quality education.

3. Promote gender equality and empower women
    - Eliminate gender disparity in primary and secondary education preferably by 2005, and at all levels by 2015.
4. Reduce child mortality
    - Reduce the mortality rate among children under five by two thirds.
5. Improve maternal health
    - Reduce by three quarters the maternal mortality ratio.
6. Combat HIV/AIDS, malaria, and other diseases
    - Halt and begin to reverse the spread of HIV/AIDS.
    - Halt and begin to reverse the incidence of malaria and other major diseases.
7. Ensure environmental sustainability
    - Integrate the principles of sustainable development into country policies and programmes; reverse loss of environmental resources.
    - Reduce by half the proportion of people without sustainable access to safe drinking water.
    - Achieve significant improvement in the lives of at least 100 million slum dwellers, by 2020.
8. Develop a global partnership for development
    - Develop further an open trading and financial system that is rule-based, predictable and non-discriminatory. Includes a commitment to good governance, development and poverty reduction – nationally and internationally.
    - Address the least developed countries' special needs. This includes tariff- and quota-free access for their exports; enhanced debt relief for heavily indebted poor countries; cancellation of official bilateral debt; and more generous official development assistance for countries committed to poverty reduction.
    - Address the special needs of landlocked and small island developing states.

> □   Deal comprehensively with developing countries' debt
>   problems through national and international measures to
>   make debt sustainable in the long term.
>
> □   In cooperation with the developing countries, develop
>   decent and productive work for youth.
>
> □   In cooperation with pharmaceutical companies, provide
>   access to affordable essential drugs in developing
>   countries.
>
> □   In cooperation with the private sector, make available the
>   benefits of new technologies – especially information and
>   communications technologies.

At face value, one might ask who could possibly be opposed to these worthy goals. Yet a closer look reveals that they are based on numerous faulty assumptions, strengthening the conclusion that we need to build a different perspective on the role of business in development.

Unrealistic approach

The MDGs were adopted by the United Nations General Assembly in 2000. In 2002 the UN Secretary-General launched the Millennium Project, aimed at developing a concrete plan of action to achieve the MDGs. The project was managed by an independent advisory body headed by Professor Jeffrey Sachs, director of the Earth Institute at Columbia University. In 2004 the project released an interim report entitled *Millennium Development Goals Needs Assessment*. In 2005 the advisory body presented its final recommendations to the Secretary-General in a report entitled *Investing in Development: A Practical Plan to Achieve the Millennium Development Goals*.

The MDGs represent what used to be called 'rational comprehensive planning' for national governments, but function on a global as well as national scale. One of the fundamental problems inherent in this approach emerges from the needs assessment. It states that:

> In each of these countries, the Project and local research partners built upon international best practices to identify ... the input targets that would be needed for the country to achieve the MDGs by 2015. ... The second stage of the planning process will be for each country to develop a long term (10-12 year) framework for action for achieving the MDGs, building upon the results of the MDG needs assessment. ... This MDG framework should include a policy and public sector management framework to scale up public spending and services, as well as a broadly defined financing strategy to underpin the plan. The third stage of the planning process will be for each country to construct its medium term (3-5 year) poverty reduction strategy (PRS) and, where appropriate, its Poverty Reduction Strategy Paper (PRSP) based on the long term MDG plan ... and should be attached to a Medium Term Expenditure Framework (MTEF). ... Fourth, both the 10-year framework and three-year PRS should include a public sector management strategy. ... Bringing together a wide variety of inputs from expert resources, the Millennium Project secretariat has been coordinating a multi-step process to develop a methodology for country-level MDG needs assessments (UN Millennium Project 2004: 2-3).

This approach reflects a remarkable level of faith in planning and bureaucracy, and ignores the endemic inability of outsiders to understand the dynamics of, let alone assist with, domestic reform.

One of the many assumptions behind the MDGs is that they are all interrelated – it is not possible to halve poverty in Africa without beating AIDS, improving women's participation in education, or reducing maternal mortality. Thus, in a report on the MDGs released in 2006, the UN loftily declared that 'each investment cluster depends on the others. ... Reaching the Millennium Development Goals thus depends on ambitious action across many sectors' (UN 2006: 2).

Naive faith in collective action

The MDGs are built upon a confidence in 'collective action' by the United Nations and other global institutions that is surprisingly naive. Thus, in a book on the MDGs and related issues entitled *The End of Poverty: Economic Possibilities for our Time* (2005a), Sachs declares that:

> Collective action, through effective government provision of health, education, infrastructure, as well as foreign assistance when needed, underpins economic success (2005a: 2-3).
>
> ... Each low-income country should have the benefit of a united and effective UN country team, which coordinates in one place the work of ... UN specialized agencies, the IMF, and World Bank. In each country, the UN country team should be led by a single UN resident coordinator who reports to the United Nations Development Program, who in turn reports to the UN secretary general (ibid: 285).

How will all this be achieved? The entire final report reflects utopian thinking, urging, among other things, that 'MDG-based poverty reduction strategies should anchor the scaling up of public investments, capacity building, domestic resource mobilization, and official development assistance' (UN Millennium Project 2005a: xx).

'We know how to undertake development'

For the Millennium Project team, development is a technical problem, one that, given the necessary financing, can easily be solved. Thus the overview confidently declares:

> Every country's MDG-based poverty reduction strategy needs to outline the … steps required to reach the Goals. Fortunately, these steps are known. … We know how to triple African maize yields. We know how to provide rural clinics and hospitals with uninterrupted electricity (2005b: 25).

Central to the strategy is the notion that poor countries are caught in a 'poverty trap', and unless their income grows above a certain level they have no chance of raising themselves out of poverty. This is used to justify a call on industrialised countries to step up aid to poor nations. This not only reintroduces a strategy that has mainly failed in Africa, but also places the onus of improving the lot of poor countries on the 'international community', and the willingness of 'rich' countries to give them more money.

The Millennium Villages project

In 2004 Sachs and others started a project called Millennium Villages. While it is meant to work towards achieving the MDGs, Sachs seems to have reversed his position reflected in the final Millennium Project report. He now wants to tackle development on a village-by-village basis, with initiatives coming from villagers (assisted by experts), and seems to recognise that bureaucracies are unreliable. The basic idea appears to be that various development specialists and agencies will collaborate by focusing on selected villages, simultaneously improving agriculture, food production, service quality, education, health, and community-led development (Sachs 2005a).

In the end, though, Sachs continues to view poverty as something that can be overcome by throwing money, technology, and smart people at the problem, regardless of the institutional context.

Business should not sign on to this approach

Formulating some laudable goals does not mean that they will actually be achieved, or that every country should aim to achieve all of them simultaneously. Development is a process, not a series of ticks on an ideal list of benchmarks. Nor does it imply that these are necessarily the right goals. Where in the MDGs does it say anything about fighting crime, building roads, or a reliable electricity supply; achieving high rates of labour-intensive growth; or the necessity of an entrepreneurial middle class or political stability?

One of the most difficult challenges facing developing country governments concerns the identification of priorities. An abiding characteristic of such governments is a lack of capacity. They need to focus on a few realistic targets, ensure that they achieve them, and then move on to the next with greater confidence, more experience, and enhanced managerial skills.

Developing countries need to achieve the highest possible rates of economic growth. This is the only way to move very large numbers of people out of poverty.

Let's turn the MDG strategy on its head. What have we learnt from China, India, Hong Kong, Singapore, Vietnam, Taiwan, and South Korea? Get the basic entrepreneurial, governance and investment climate right so that economic growth takes off, enabling millions of individuals to change their own lives and start to build the independence that in time can lead to more effective pressures on governments for better schooling or services; and start to provide the revenues countries need if they are to afford a sustainable approach to delivering schooling, health, infrastructure, and other services which help to lift people out of poverty.

The MDGs embody a laundry list approach to development: list everything you want to achieve, give them all equal weight, and somehow it will all get done. Instead, what is required is a selective, properly sequenced, politically feasible approach which communicates clearly that if we set out to achieve these few realistic goals, we can go on to achieve others, and our benefits will begin to accumulate.

Key country priorities

What are the key priorities if domestic and foreign investment are to take place, and growth rates start to climb?

The first is infrastructure – road, rail, power, telecommunications. These must be supplied in the key centres of opportunity, and then in more remote rural areas. Imagine if Africa had a continent wide rail system like the United States, opening up countries and regions to investment, settlement, trade, and industry. Poverty could be reduced very rapidly. Without focusing directly on the checklist of poverty indicators, other processes – economic, infrastructural, governance – can lead to better, faster results.

The second is education. Education systems in developing countries cannot cope with the massive expansion of learners, and quality – such as it is – invariably suffers. What is important is to get incrementally growing numbers of learners into functioning schools where learning actually takes place. Quality of schooling is essential for access to deliver results. And why do the MDGs only focus on primary education? Growth will require diverse priorities: primary schooling, higher levels of education, tertiary education in universities and technical colleges.

Why the MDG commitment to free education? One of the most enduring lessons emanating from extensive World Bank research is the importance of the 'user pays' principle as a stepping stone towards sustained development. People value what they pay for; whether drinking water or schooling, poor people can muster the resources to buy what they consume, albeit, if necessary at a subsidised rate. Why perpetuate the myth of 'free' education, which is either paid for in other ways (school uniforms, textbooks, dilapidated under resourced schools), or leads to dependency and a culture of entitlement?

The third priority is to create a business-friendly environment, not just for foreign investors but for domestic businesses too. This means doing away with regulations that make it hard to open up new enterprises or close down failing ones; ensuring security of people and property; establishing a legal system that protects private property and risk-taking in general.

Fourth, as any manager in a large organisation knows, achieving more than a handful of goals in a one to three-year time frame is a lot to ask. What makes anyone think that developing countries – characterised by their lack of capacity – could undertake hundreds of actions required to achieve the Sachs vision of development? If developing countries were given free rein to define their development priorities, would they start with the MDGs? I doubt it.

The MDGs assume that most developing countries are the same, when in fact we know that effective reform and development needs to be accurately situated in a particular society's circumstances and politics. Country differences – in capacity, history, culture (an issue not considered at all in the MDGs) – will affect priorities and strategies for development in fundamental ways.

Fifth, in his enthusiasm to illustrate a 'technical' solution to poverty, Sachs bizarrely underemphasises economics, and almost totally ignores politics. Poverty exists because of a host of interlinked factors, ranging from a lack of education to the absence of property rights, corruption, unaccountable officials and politicians, state failure to provide infrastructure and services and so on. All these factors and others tend to block opportunities for poor people and prevent them from lifting themselves and their communities out of poverty.

The MDG approach assumes that money and technical know-how is what really counts; the much trickier issues of context and culture are not factored in sufficiently. *The Economist* puts this well: 'Brazil is four times richer than Sri Lanka, but its children are more than twice as likely to die before their fifth birthday. Improving sanitation is about breaking habits as much as building latrines. Although aid money can send a doctor to the boondocks, it cannot make him show up for work' (*The Economist* 2007).

Role of business underplayed

In the MDG approach the role of private enterprise in development is totally underplayed. Even though the past two decades have witnessed an enormous shift in resources away from the public to the private sector, and private investment flows to developing countries are now more than twice the level of public flows, little attention has been focused on the most dynamic engine of growth and poverty alleviation: the private sector. The private sector is only mentioned twice in the MDGs – in targets 17 and 18 respectively, donor governments are directed to work in partnership with pharmaceutical companies in providing essential medicines, and with the private sector in making available the benefits of new technologies (UN Millennium Project 2005a: xix).

It seems as if states are meant to achieve the MDGs. *Investing in Development* asserts that 'civil society and business' (always in that order) should be included as 'partners', but this role is not defined, and there is little sense of the fundamental importance of the state creating a context in which markets and businesses will spearhead development (ibid). The role of private enterprise is seen as relatively unimportant, lagging far behind foreign aid, international bureaucratic intervention, foreign experts, and so on. The role of market forces and entrepreneurs in providing education, training, health care, welfare, and infrastructure is either not on the agenda or so heavily coded as to be hidden from view. Thus Sachs states that the '… effective *government* provision of health, education, infrastructure as well as foreign assistance when needed, underpins economic success' (2005a: 3, emphasis added).

What about private provision of health or education? What about the private sector's ability to leverage new money into these arenas? The provision of infrastructure is seen as something that government both decides upon and provides. This underestimates the advantages that the private sector often has in at least assisting with infrastructure provision, and in influencing decisions about how and where infrastructure is provided.

Most developing countries do not have enough experienced, qualified people to run effective states, and even fewer to manage the complicated process of coordinating international consultants and development agencies with local plans and people.

Experienced development practitioners know that sustainability is one of the most difficult things to achieve. The issue is not only how many clinics, schools, or water installations one can finance and build, and how quickly. The much tougher issue is who 'owns' and maintains these facilities once the donor, 'Millennium A team', national government, or large company has left town.

And what about urbanisation?

The correlation between increased rates of urbanisation and economic growth is as close to a natural law as any in human development (CDE 2002: 55). And yet the MDGs emphasise rural over urban development, and advocate 'balanced development' across a given country without considering where economic growth will take place, and why.

The MDGs do not see urban growth as both a challenge to be managed and an opportunity for development. If cities and large towns are managed reasonably well, the prospects for both urban residents of long standing and new migrants improve dramatically. Migrants are generally acting rationally when they 'move to town', where each person has a greater chance of economic, educational and other opportunities than in neglected rural areas.

Urban people frequently have a louder political 'voice' than rural communities In most countries successful rural development will require greater numbers of people to urbanise in order to free up rural land for new agricultural strategies. Societies that fail to deal with the reality and consequences of urbanisation tend to fail with respect to both urban management issues as well as effective rural development. The MDGs seems to fall into this camp.

The MDGs should not be a business project

Companies should not unthinkingly sign on to the MDGs and the approach to development inherent in the programme, nor should developing country governments. 'Making poverty history' requires a political and economic strategy driven by the actions and decisions made by countries themselves, finding a path out of poverty by their own efforts, which is the only way any country has ever done it. Business should put forward its own agenda for development and growth.

ARE THE EQUATOR PRINCIPLES GOOD FOR THE DEVELOPING WORLD?

Getting private investors to bet on poorer countries is a difficult proposition largely because of perceptions of unacceptably high risk. Helping such countries to source funds from sceptical private investors should surely rate as a top priority for those seeking to promote development. However, under pressure from interest groups and international NGOs, development agencies and other organisations are constantly placing barriers in the way of companies contemplating direct investment in poor countries.

Onerous new global standards

The push for global standards (designed in first world capitals) has moved from a focus on large individual global companies to include financial markets. The Equator Principles are a case in point. These comprise a voluntary set of guidelines for managing environmental and social issues in project lending.

They arose out of a meeting convened by the International Finance Corporation (IFC), the private sector financing arm of the World Bank Group, in November 2003. According to the IFC, it will subject all the projects it finances to 'environmental and social standards to minimise their impact on the environment and on affected communities' (IFC 2009a). It claims the Equator standards are 'stronger, better, and more comprehensive than those of any other international finance institution working with the private sector. They clearly define the roles and responsibilities of the IFC and its client companies' (Giraud & Shanahan 2006).

The Equator Principles are very detailed, covering every phase of project implementation. They apply to all countries, sectors and project financing with capital costs of more than US$10 million, and aim to ensure that only projects which comply with the nine principles will be funded (IFC 2006).

Adopting these principles will impose significant new costs on firms and make demands on them that will be impossible or very difficult to meet. This is underlined by the fact that companies wishing to access project funds in terms of this process are now required to undergo training so that they can better understand what the Equator Principles ask of them.

Banks fall into line

Banks have acquiesced in these principles, primarily as a way to minimise risks. By April 2006 they had been adopted by 40 banks, which arranged more than 75 per cent of the world's project loans (Gore & Blood 2006). As Chris Beale, head of Citigroup's global project finance business, said in June 2003,

> Banks believe that [signing on to the Equator Principles] will lead to more secure investments on the part of our customers and safer loans on the part of the banks, because if you finance something that's dirty or something that harms people, there's a likelihood that the host government or local people will interfere with it or even take it away from you (quoted in Phillips & Pacelle 2003).

According to Jonathan Lash, president of the World Resources Institute, companies are committing to these types of agreements to 'protect their brands, and their global right to operate' (quoted in Ignatius 2005).

Developing countries and the poor lose out

Such risk aversion and voluntary self-regulation may cost the banks some business, but the real losers are those living in the world's poorest regions. For example, the Competitive Enterprise Institute claims that

> banking giant Citigroup has implemented the Equator Principles, much to the detriment of the developing world. According to a 2005 Citigroup report, the bank denied financing to 54 of the 74 projects reviewed according to the Equator Principles – projects worth as

much as $75 billion in financing and that are economically sound (Milloy 2007).

In some areas it does not even matter whether companies wanting to undertake projects are ready to comply with all these principles. The IFC has decreed that it will not provide financing under any circumstances to projects in 'undesirable' fields, which include:

- production or trade in weapons and munitions;
- production or trade in alcoholic beverages (excluding beer and wine);
- production or trade in tobacco;
- gambling, casinos, and equivalent enterprises;
- trade in wildlife or wildlife products regulated under CITES;
- production or trade in radioactive materials; and
- purchase of logging equipment for use in primary tropical moist forest (IFC 2009b).

In addition, the IFC instructs all financial intermediaries to apply the following exclusions:

- production or activities involving harmful or exploitative forms of forced labour or harmful child labour;
- production or trade in products containing polychlorinated biphenyls (PCBs); and
- production or trade in ozone-depleting substances subject to international phase-out (ibid).

Producing some of these substances may cause more harm than good, but the list surely pushes out many activities (such as the production of tobacco, alcohol or weapons) that could boost the economies of poor countries that cannot afford to be too selective about which economic opportunities they access. Moreover, these products are produced by many rich countries.

By excluding activities such as alcohol, tobacco and casinos, the IFC is imposing a selective morality on poorer countries and restricting the options available to countries that already find themselves in a disadvantaged position within the global economy. If funding for logging had been prohibited during the early phases of Canada's development, would that country have been able to modernise and grow? How would Scotland and Portugal have fared if they were barred from producing whisky and port? And how would the government of Monaco have felt if it was told casinos were not allowed? Or South Africa's democratic government, which has used casinos as a means of black economic empowerment?

In February 2004 the World Bank rejected a recommendation that it should stop funding oil and coal projects in developing countries. However, the Bank only decided this after being pushed in the opposite direction. In response to pressure to restrict funding for projects that impact on the environment, the Bank had set up an 'extractive industries review'. After considering the issue for two years, a response was leaked from the authors of the World Bank's Extractive Industries Review which recommended 'that the World Bank cancel all funding for oil and coal projects in order to lower global carbon dioxide emissions' (Beattie 2004).

Luckily, sanity prevailed and the Bank's managers concluded that 'adopting this policy would not be consistent with the World Bank Group mission of helping to fight poverty and improve the living standards of people in the developing world' (ibid).

NGOs hold back development

Pressure groups, almost all of which are based in rich western countries, are primarily behind imposing restrictions such as the

Equator Principles. The idea of a set of environmental principles initially emerged from a loose affiliation called BankTrack. Its members include the Rainforest Action Network (United States), the Berne Declaration (Switzerland), the Campaign to Reform the World Bank (Italy), the United Kingdom and United States branches of the Friends of the Earth, the International Rivers Network (United States), the Millieudefensie (Netherlands), Netwerk Vlaanderen (Belgium), Platform (United Kingdom), Urgewald (Germany), and the World Wildlife Fund (United Kingdom) (BankTrack 2008). Not many rural peasants are represented here!

These organisations have consistently criticised banks that have adopted the Equator Principles and have sought to block projects in Iceland, Kazakhstan, Papua New Guinea, Brazil, the Philippines, Thailand, Bolivia, Russia, India, Laos and Peru (Milloy 2007). It is hard to see how these organisations can speak for the hundreds of millions of citizens in these countries.

Compliance with the Equator Principles is beyond the reach of most private enterprises – only very large multinational companies have the resources and personnel to do so. And even for them, compliance is costly and time-consuming. The principles are so complicated and ambitious that they can be neither monitored nor enforced. This means that they will serve to block efficient, ethical companies while opening the way for companies that have no qualms about manufacturing the appearance of compliance or paying bribes. Even when companies are fully compliant, it would be wrong to assume that NGOs would be satisfied and ready to become constructive partners in development.

All three of these realities are illustrated by Exxon's attempts to become compliant with the Equator Principles while constructing an oil pipeline in Chad. The story of Exxon's engagement with the Equator Principles has been told by Sebastian Mallaby, who explains that when Exxon decided to undertake the building of the pipeline in

Chad in collaboration with the World Bank it set out to demonstrate their full compliance with the Equator Principles (Mallaby 2004). To do the job properly, it hired an anthropologist, Ellen Brown, who had been conducting research in Chad for more than 20 years. Besides Brown's extensive work on the project's anticipated social impact, Exxon paid for numerous environmental studies and consultations with 'concerned groups' outside the country. Mallaby catalogues the following unrelenting efforts:

> Exxon sought the advice of primate experts so that the pipeline could avoid gorillas; it consulted Cameroonian anthropologists about the Pygmies in the rain forests. The World Bank had said there must be a 'Category A' environmental assessment ... Exxon promptly commissioned one; the Bank said the assessment's verdict wasn't positive enough, Exxon agreed to reroute the pipeline. The Bank wanted the firm to invite NGO input, Exxon assigned Miles Shaw ... to globe trot around North America and Europe, visiting every outfit that might take an interest in a central African pipeline. However high the Bank set the bar, the oilmen jumped over it – even when the Bank repeatedly moved the bar higher as the project went ahead (ibid: 346-7).

After six years, and 19 volumes of research and commitments, Exxon justifiably felt it had taken every possible step, provided every possible safeguard, fairly compensated all those who would be negatively affected, and had responded to every possible criticism. At that point a group of NGOs with no real stake in or understanding of either the oil project or Chad launched a full frontal attack on Exxon and the World Bank. An NGO calling itself the Environmental Defence Fund as well as an initial instigator behind the Equator Principles, the Rainforest Action Network, launched a public campaign proclaiming that 'development was impossible' in the corrupt Chadian environment. Thanks to the extensive research and compensation undertaken by

Exxon, the company was able to offer effective counters to these NGO attacks.

As Mallaby puts it, Exxon 'had the facts, they had Ellen Brown and all her data, and many of the NGO screamers had never been to Chad'. These rebuttals did not, however, secure the future of the project. Exxon's two partners, Shell and Elf, pulled out 'possibly because of NGO pressure' (ibid: 354). It was only once the World Bank had changed tack and became less concerned about NGO criticism and more determined to push the project through that the Chad pipeline went ahead. Exxon had done everything and more than could be expected of it; it had incurred heavy costs, and it was still not secure from NGO sabotage. Many reasonable companies must surely have concluded from that experience that investment in poor countries is not worth the effort.

NORWEGIAN COMPANY REMAINS 'PURE' RATHER THAN DOING BUSINESS IN DEVELOPING COUNTRIES

Idar Kreutzer, CEO of Storebrand, a Norwegian Financial Services company with 1 327 employees, has decided that his company will not do business with anyone that is not capable of meeting CSR reporting requirements, which effectively means his company refuses to invest in developing countries. He explained his decision as follows:

'Storebrand has been engaged in socially responsible investments (SRI) since 1995, including best-in-class analyses and negative screening (avoiding the worst performers). When assessing its investments in companies, Storebrand applies a "minimum decency" standard, ensuring that its investments are free of human rights violations, corruption, production of landmines, cluster munitions, nuclear weapons, tobacco, and the 10 per cent worst performers of eight high risk industries. When it comes to SRI, Storebrand Life Insurance is among the leaders in its industry.

'Storebrand recently decided not to enter into an investment product with the potential to assist developing countries. This would have involved investing in "emerging market debt", chiefly bonds issued by governments of emerging and developing economies. In line with its usual practice, Storebrand investigated the records of the countries involved to assess whether the investment would be a socially responsible one. After considerable research, we found that none of the investment suppliers could provide SRI screening, and thus it was not possible to guarantee that the emerging markets fund invested only in countries that could meet the same minimum decency threshold.

'Storebrand's dilemma is that our underlying desire to do business in a way that supports the population in developing countries is frustrated by concerns over the possibility of human rights abuses or corruption. The Storebrand board was not prepared to jeopardise the company's integrity or reputation by offering a product that did not meet SRI criteria. But the board also realised that few other investors have taken SRI activities to the same level as Storebrand.

'Storebrand decided not to invest in emerging market debts until we can find investment suppliers with sufficient SRI criteria. At the same time, Storebrand seeks to challenge all our investment suppliers to develop SRI criteria (which will then also keep them out of developing countries)' (WBCSD 2006: 27).

Can any project meet all these criteria?

Exxon's experience in Chad shows that many campaigning NGOs are actually opposed to any development, no matter how sensitively it is undertaken. Ilyse Hogue, 'a global finance campaigner' for Rainforest Action Network, wants parts of the world declared 'no-go zones' – areas deemed by first world based NGOs to be so critical for long-term sustainability that *any* gains from investment will not outweigh the long-term benefits of leaving them intact (Baue 2004).

Such expressions against investment and development lend credence to the views of Steven J Milloy (2007), who claims that he has 'yet to find a significant development project anywhere in the world that (US) environmentalists and their NGO allies support as sustainable', and that the Equator Principles serve 'as a means for NGOs to stop most economic development projects'. He goes on to argue that 'not only do the Equator Principles deny first-world funding to developing nations, they also drive desperately poor nations to seek financing from alternative (and less desirable) sources like China … not known to apply first-world environmental standards to the projects it finances' (Milloy 2007).

SOUTH AFRICA – A REVEALING CASE

Governments in developing countries can also fall into the kind of trap represented by the Equator Principles.

In South Africa the need for environmental legislation was seen as crucial by a few influential people within the newly elected ANC government, supported by idealistic experts from Canada's International Development Research Centre (IDRC). They set out a number of principles on the basis of which the environment would be protected. These principles were developed into a green paper on environmental affairs, which was widely discussed by environmental groups, followed by the National Environment Management Act (NEMA) of 1998. The act was ambitious, modern, driven by environmentalist zeal, but did not take into account that a developing country like South Africa might have other priorities relating to economic growth and reducing poverty, or appreciate that the country did not have the bureaucratic structures needed to undertake such advanced environmental regulation and monitoring (Deneys Reitz Attorneys 2008).

One of NEMA's central requirements is that 'any activity' that could be regarded as 'having a significant impact on the environment' must undergo an Environmental Impact Assessment (EIA). This places heavy demands on farmers, small business owners, or new black enterprises seeking to launch initiatives that may have some kind of environmental consequence. Moreover, it places a massive administrative burden on government bureaucracies struggling to cope with their most basic functions.

Administrative burden paralyses development

The administrative burden created by NEMA has resulted in paralysis and confusion, which has benefited neither the environment nor economic development. In the mining industry, for example, the lack of clarity surrounding environmental legislation (among others) has inhibited new investment. Peter Leon, vice-chairman of the mining law committee of the International Bar Association, stated at the 2007 Mining Indaba that countries such as Australia, Ghana and Tanzania were doing much better than South Africa in attracting investment because of the *clarity* of their regulatory regimes (Brown 2007). The Chamber of Mines (representing South Africa's largest mining companies) has repeatedly argued that the extra red tape involved in complying with the Mineral and Petroleum Resources Development Act, water licences, and environmental legislation all substantially inhibited the development of new mines (ibid).

Numerous commentators have pointed to the inability of the bureaucracy to cope with the requirements placed on them by South Africa's environmental legislation. Analysts from one of South Africa's leading law firms have stated that 'the environmental assessment application process has been riddled with delays and problems' related to 'severe capacity restraints within the Department of Environmental Affairs and Tourism' (Kirby & Sauer 2006). Other departments have buckled under the weight of the requirements imposed on them by environmental regulations, and are increasingly ascribing 'their failure to deliver basic services to the environmental laws they are supposed to implement and enforce' (*Engineering News* 2006). According to a draft report commissioned by the South African Presidency in 2007, 'Environmental Impact Assessment backlogs and delays have contributed to delayed supply-side capacity expansions and investments within the Cement and Clay Brick Industries' (SUDEO 2007). Thulani Gcabashe, then CEO of Eskom, the government-controlled monopoly provider of electricity, stated that EIAs were standing in the way of Eskom's R97 000 million expansion plans (ibid). The urgent need to overcome South Africa's power shortages has persuaded the minister of environmental affairs to push environmental issues on to the back burner.

Overambitious environmental laws hold back growth

In 2006, the South African president, Thabo Mbeki, complained that the country's 'green laws' were causing development delays and slowing down economic activity (*Engineering News* 2006). The Minister of Housing told the construction industry that efforts to meet the country's shortage of more than two and a half million homes would no longer be 'held hostage by butterfly eggs' (quoted in MacLeod 2006).

South Africa demonstrates the danger of overzealous environmental regulation that cannot be properly implemented and enforced, and does not mesh with the country's development priorities.

Companies should not appease activists in rich countries too quickly. The stakes are too high. Developing country governments with influence at the IFC should not allow the Equator Principles to stand. Business should support them in getting rid of these obstacles to development.

WITH FRIENDS LIKE THESE, WHO NEEDS ENEMIES?

In 2004 the Kennedy School of Government of Harvard University established a CSR Initiative. It represents some of the most thoughtful and seemingly business-friendly approaches to CSR, and is influential with the International Business Leaders Forum, the World Economic Forum, the United Nations, and major companies. And yet its work raises important questions.

The head of the initiative, Professor John Ruggie, believes business has created a single global economic space, but the social and political means to govern that space is lacking. In his view, 'rollback', a shift away from globalisation (and market liberalisation) is likely unless the fabric of the global community is strengthened. He also believes 'nobody is better positioned or has greater capacity to play the lead role today than business itself', because it has the scope and capacity for more effective global action than the 'highly fragmented so-called system of global governance' (2004a: 10). He suggests three ways for business to do this:

- *Accountability* to voluntary and other codes of behaviour according to universal standards. In his view 'the investment community' is uniquely positioned to push this. 'Smarter regulations are more likely to result from business itself moving towards greater coverage and convergence – and for governments then to level the playing field between leaders and laggards by codifying best practices.'
- *Building social capacity:* A key challenge for the 'global corporate sector' is inequality. 'The transnational corporate sector has global reach and capacity, and is capable of making and implementing decisions at a pace that neither governments nor international agencies can possibly match. As a result, a variety of other social actors are looking for ways to leverage this platform in order to advance broader social objectives – to help fill governance gaps and compensate for governance failures. And a growing number of firms have become willing accomplices.'
- *Imbalanced rule-making:* Global rule-making has become increasingly imbalanced, privileging capital and global market expansion over social concerns such as labour standards, human rights, environmental quality, or poverty reduction (ibid).

It is hard to understand how a concern with the future of globalisation and increasingly open markets translates into these particular prescriptions. Preserving open markets, encouraging freer global trade, combating global poverty, dealing with the politics of trade in domestic economies are all worthy objectives. However, they will surely require rather different kinds of activities than those Ruggie suggests. It is hard to see how business can play the 'lead role'. What about the role of governments and democratic politics?

Ruggie's colleague Jane Nelson, one of the foremost proponents of CSR, holds similar views. Although always quick to acknowledge all sorts of positive contributions business makes, she too wants companies to 'do more', to get involved in partnerships to deal with 'global poverty', and find ' new ways' for business and business skills to support international development goals (Nelson 2006).

There are problems with this perspective. Ruggie argues that there is increasing social demand for private enterprise to 'create greater public value beyond traditional forms of compliance and philanthropy' (2004:a 4). Here we have an excellent example of an approach to business that ignores the many contributions companies make to the societies in which they operate through their everyday business activities. These are taken for granted, and a long list of additional issues added to the pressures on business to 'contribute'.

It is accepted without question that rules and regulations are desirable and that these should be codified, and extended to all sectors that have hitherto escaped this net. As I have demonstrated in the case of 'sweatshops' and the Equator Principles, 'global' labour, and environmental standards are detrimental to development in poorer countries.

What are all these additional business activities meant to achieve? Should business protect the market system or globalisation by loudly proclaiming its commitment to development and the abolition of poverty? Is this for reasons of corporate survival, good PR, or does success in national and international development demand this?

Companies and entrepreneurs have always looked for new opportunities, and successful enterprises have always met community needs. Why should companies now be required to adopt new rules and objectives?

Nelson approvingly quotes the 2005 World Development Report, which lauds the virtues of business as business:

Private firms are at the heart of the development process. Driven by the quest for profits, firms of all types – from farmers and micro-entrepreneurs to local manufacturing companies and multinational enterprises – invest in new ideas and new facilities that strengthen the foundation of economic growth and prosperity. They provide more than 90 per cent of jobs – creating opportunities for people to apply their talents and improve their situations. They provide the goods and services needed to sustain life and improve living standards. They are also the main source of tax revenues, contributing to public funding for health, education and other services. Firms are thus central actors in the quest for growth and poverty reduction (Nelson 2006: 6).

However, this begs the question: *If things are improving, and business is already playing such an important, positive role, what exactly is wrong with what companies have always been doing?* How do we get from the rise of multinationals and the long list of their achievements to the need to sign on to elaborate new development goals?

There is an unquestioning faith in international collective action and the United Nations system. Why is this self-evident? Surely an academic initiative needs to justify its support for a particular perspective on development, or explain its faith in the United Nations system and its aid-based approach that has failed so often and in so many places.

At no point is it clear how diverse company initiatives will impact on 'global poverty' or the backlash against globalisation in any meaningful way. Companies involved in the CSR 'movement' are a tiny minority – some 2 000 of the world's 60 000 multinational corporations (CSRI 2004). How could they conceivably affect large international markets in the manner suggested?

Missing issues

Many issues are not discussed in the Kennedy School approach. The first is corporate interests: what is in a company's interest to undertake in the development field, and why?

Another silent topic is politics: the politics of a specific company in a particular local, national or global market; the politics of a particular business sector, and how it can deal with its challenges; the politics of a segment of business in a country with ethnic, racial, or linguistic divisions. Or the politics of governments or communities in respect of how they deal with businesses. Or the rather large question of competition – between rich countries and emerging markets, between established multinationals needing to deal with growing competition from developing country companies.

How much is enough? One word we never hear is 'trade-off'. When do all the demands on business for involvement in non-essential activities start to undermine the risk-taking nature of entrepreneurial activity? And hence delay or slow down economic growth in countries that desperately need it?

What about development? Little attention is paid to what this word means, what this process involves, and exactly what companies can do that is sustained, and relevant to the scale of mass poverty. What are all these corporate initiatives actually achieving?

One frequently gets the impression that any and all actions by business in this arena of social impact are desirable. Companies must just show a willingness to appease their critics – energy and commitment counts, not results.

And yet, as I have argued throughout and as participants in Kennedy School conferences point out, CSR and its partnerships are 'drops in the bucket, nibbling at the edges of major public problems. They are not the road out. The road out is a functioning government, a good court system, economic opportunity for growth' (ibid: 7). What is getting in the way of results? 'Widespread corruption, poor education, very little accountability in much of the developing world. ... For companies and business associations operating in such conditions, a critical leadership question is how to build public capacity rather than shoulder the burden of trying to replace it on an ongoing basis' (ibid).

Why so much pressure on companies?

Why are those at the leading edge of the CSR movement directing so much pressure at corporations when they are aware that it is the quality of national governments that really make the difference? There is an enormous gap between the 'extramural' projects of most individual companies – however excellent and well-intentioned – and the overblown rhetoric predicting an impact on 'global inequality and poverty' through their cumulative social impact.

Private CSR projects cannot impact at scale on national poverty, never mind global poverty. Why are companies participating in discussions that set them up to fail, and perpetually place them at the receiving end of claims that they are not doing enough?

CONCLUDING REMARKS

This chapter has tried to illuminate some of the problems surrounding the popular view of business and global poverty. This is a perspective that:

- *minimises* the role of states, governments, and national politics;
- *exaggerates* the power of business to deal with global poverty or inequality;
- *minimises* the role business plays just by doing business;
- *inflates* any potential role it might play 'extramurally';
- *conflates* international NGOs and activist groups with the concerns, interests and needs of governments and citizens of developing countries (and probably the majority of citizens of developed countries too);
- *misses* out the many steps involved in moving from the necessarily limited interventions of companies in specific places at specific times to how this will affect sustained development and empowerment of countries, millions of individuals, and very many communities in the longer term;
- *dismisses* the hard realities in developing countries, and glosses over the difficult challenges of sustained development after the international actors have left town.

Most importantly, it *ignores* the phenomenal economic and developmental achievements of successful developing countries which engaged with the very companies that are now deemed inadequate.

The MDGs, the Equator Principles, the adoption of global labour and environmental standards, the endless injunctions for business to 'do more' and act directly to deal with 'global poverty', do not stand up to scrutiny. They are generally not good for developing countries, pose real dangers to the risk-taking spirit of successful enterprise, and are not the key priorities on the real business agenda.

If we are seriously worried about pressures to close down liberalisation and restrict global trade, then focusing attention on CSR-type activities by companies is a colossal misdirection. If we are genuinely concerned about the plight of billions of people whose lives consist of relentless poverty, 'shouting' at a small minority of large companies to conform to activists' expectations and western preferences is a distraction.

Business leaders need a different perspective on all of this.

Why listen to voices emanating from international institutions whose legitimacy and contribution to development pale in comparison with those of business? What business leaders need are voices and perspectives that will inform significant actions of real value in communities and countries, and provide a base for building alliances with governments and citizens of developing countries; assisting them to mould their own development strategies in line with their needs and circumstances, rather than kow-towing to pressures from small interest groups in very rich places.

Business needs its own agenda, one that will have much more to do with governance, an improved environment in which to do business, and national competitiveness.

Chapter Eight

A DEVELOPING COUNTRY
PERSPECTIVE ON
BUSINESS AND DEVELOPMENT

*'By far the greatest contribution business can make to
development is through the very act of running its businesses
– paying suppliers, paying wages, paying taxes. ... There is
no contradiction between what is good for business and what
is good for development.'*

Graham MacKay, CEO, SABMiller (2005)

THE DISCUSSION about business and development being conducted mainly in richer countries is strangely lopsided. In this discourse multinational corporations matter more than any other kinds of enterprise and receive more attention than any other participant in the development process, including national governments. What business does in its strictly business activities and the myriad positive consequences of this are not subject to much discussion or generally taken into account in the 'ledger' of what business contributes to societies.

Most curiously, the conversation has little to offer on business and the politics of national or global development. As a result, far too little attention is paid to trade-offs and the processes of bargaining and compromise that characterise development in any country.

In this chapter I intend to go back to basics and provide a framework for thinking about business and development issues in a different way. There are indeed important challenges facing companies in all societies, particularly those wishing to operate in or which originate within developing countries.

A different starting point

I want to propose a perspective on business based on the following propositions:

- Economic growth is good for human development. High rates of growth have hugely desirable consequences for societies and the vast majority of their members.
- Enterprise and competition promote efficiency and innovation, and are therefore good for society.
- Large companies are successful forms of enterprise that should be applauded and encouraged.
- Developing countries need the foreign investment, cutting-edge technology, and best practices that only multinationals can provide.
- The best way to 'socialise' big companies is to have more of them operating within competitive markets, in countries with smart (preferably democratic) states.
- Far from being rogue institutions, large companies are generally – not always – model citizens, complying rigorously with the law in whichever country they operate.

This positive attitude to business is linked to a different perspective on development which stresses: the role of individuals and their attitudes, values, beliefs, and need for opportunities; the importance of nation-states and political and policy choices made at all levels of government; dynamic markets and the supporting institutions that help them to function well.

Certain factors hampering development need to be borne in mind: the complexity of the development process, and the reality that most outside interventions have been unsuccessful; communities generally consist of different interests and points of view; and the need for some humility in any social intervention, without letting this paralyse progress and leadership.

This amounts to an approach to development which is profit-driven, pragmatic, incremental, experimental and involves learning by doing. Viewed in this light, it is important to:

- think more about markets and encourage competitive enterprises of all sizes to play a larger role in meeting social needs from health to education;
- acknowledge the special nature of private money and resources in development and how best to leverage this for maximum benefit;
- emphasise the importance of accountability to all those directly affected by the development process.

Like any other sector, business is not immune to the predations of dishonest, callous, or uncaring people. But just as the existence of crooks in politics or NGOs does not make me despair about democracy or civil society, bad people in business do not undermine the value of capitalism.

If one starts the conversation about business and development with negative presumptions and faulty ideas about development, one ends up with more and more rules about how business should behave in developing countries. On the other hand, if one starts with a positive approach to business and an appreciation of the risk-taking and precarious nature of companies, this leads one to think about creating environments in which competitive enterprises can flourish and help build the wealth and social capital that make nations great.

Let's start building this alternative approach to the role of business in development.

MISSING ISSUES IN THE CURRENT CONVERSATION

Markets and states

Successful societies need markets *and* states. Two propositions identify the strengths of markets as well as their limits. McMillan puts this well:

> First, their vigour comes from their decentralized nature – they empower people to find creative solutions to problems. This is opposite to the state, which is intrinsically centralized. So resilient are markets that sometimes they operate without the support of the state ... [Nonetheless] the state is indispensable, providing goods and services that markets would undersupply, and acting in the background as market rule-setter and referee (2002: 149).

States frequently lay the foundations for successful enterprise – the American interstate highway system built in the 1950s facilitated long-distance commerce, the aerospace industry was built on military procurement. Sometimes the activities of companies create negative externalities that require state intervention.

Some of the side-effects of market activity cannot be left to the market. State intervention is essential in the public interest. Some externalities can be corrected by defining and enforcing property rights. In other cases the harmful activity can be taxed, thus providing public authorities with resources to deal with its effects. In extreme cases, the only solution is to ban the activity concerned (ibid).

Markets cannot provide everything. The state must protect its citizens by providing national defence and policing; it must also manage the money supply and the value of the national currency.

The ideal scope of the state is a highly contentious issue. Some governments are too big and too ambitious, trying to provide goods and services better left to the private sector. Other governments are weak, and neglect the basic functions of protecting and securing people and property, and providing the goods and services which only the state can provide. The collapse of socialist central planning is sometimes held up as proof that governments should stay right out of the economy. The fact that governments fail, though, does not prove that the ideal state is a minimal state (ibid).

To frame the choice as 'planned economies versus free markets' is simplistic and wrong. Certain essential public goods offering widespread benefits must be provided by the state, or at least funded by it.

However, public provision does not necessarily entail public production or ongoing maintenance. Social goods are sometimes most efficiently produced by the private sector, but their public nature calls for the government to help pay for them. The state should provide the foundation for market action by supplying the monetary, legal, and regulatory infrastructure.

In a democratic society there is no single way to structure state and market relations, or integrate them with the international economy. Democratic processes will generate diverse solutions in different national, regional, and cultural contexts.

Economic growth is essential for successful development

Poverty need not be a 'trap'. Growth can be achieved and when it is, poverty can be dramatically reduced.

According to the World Bank, China's rapid growth in the 1980s and 1990s resulted in more than 200 million people escaping poverty. Foreign companies poured more than $600 billion into China since 1978 – eclipsing American expenditure on the Marshall Plan for rebuilding Europe after World War Two. Foreigners built hundreds of thousands of factories throughout China, and hired millions of people. The average Chinese worker earned nearly five times more than previously, and millions bought mobile phones, computers, automobiles, and apartments (Meredith 2007: 10).

Over the past half century a growing number of previously poor countries have achieved unprecedented rates of growth, and improvements in standards of living. According to the UNDP's *Human Development Report* for 2004, the proportion of people in extreme poverty fell from 29,6 per cent in 1990 to 23,2 per cent in 1999, and the number of people living on $1 a day slipped from 1,29 billion to 1,17 billion a decade earlier (ibid: 6).

The evidence is compelling. In East Asia and the Pacific, the region with the strongest growth in the 1990s, annual per capita GDP growth of 6,4 per cent resulted in a 15 per cent decline in the rate of poverty (using the $2 per day criterion), and in south Asia 3,3 per cent annual growth led to an 8,4 per cent decline. At the same time, negative growth increased poverty rates by 1,6 per cent in sub-Saharan Africa and 13,5 per cent in Europe and central Asia. 'The message is clear: sustained economic growth reduces poverty' (ibid: 7).

As David Henderson has put it:

> Material progress of people everywhere, rich and poor alike, depends above all on the dynamism of the economies in which they live and work. Rapid progress is now expected wherever the political and economic conditions exist for a market economy to operate effectively (2004: 15).

Economic performance has been uneven, and not all countries have shared equally in rising prosperity. The extraordinary progress made by many previously poor countries owes little or nothing to foreign aid. Economic progress in recent decades has stemmed from profit-oriented activities and initiatives on the part of entrepreneurs and companies working in competitive market economies, framed by stable states and political systems. This business contribution has resulted from the twin stimuli provided by a market economy: wide-ranging economic opportunities, and pervasive competitive pressures.

The importance of entrepreneurs and enterprise

In 2004 the United Nations appointed a special commission of inquiry into the role of the private sector in development. Its report is a milestone in development thinking within the world body, and directly relevant to our concerns. It starts by stating that:

> The saving, investment and innovation that lead to development are undertaken largely by private individuals, corporations and communities ... the private sector can alleviate poverty by contributing to economic growth, job creation and poor people's incomes. ... The primary responsibility for achieving growth and equitable development lies with developing countries ...[and] includes creating the conditions that make it possible to secure financial resources for investment (UNDP 2004: 1-2).

The private sector meets the needs of poor people in places governments do not reach.

> In the slums there are frequently few if any health services, public education or infrastructure. In many cases where services exist

they are provided by unregulated often informal private sources. Anywhere from 15 per cent to 90 per cent of primary education is provided in private schools. Some 63 per cent of health care expenditures in the poorest countries are private, almost twice the 33 per cent in high income countries that belong to the OECD. With the right attention and regulatory requirements, privately provided services can help meet the needs of poor people (ibid: 8).

The report demonstrates how private enterprise can alleviate poverty. In Cambodia, hundreds of small providers offer services ranging from battery recharging to fully metered electricity provision for entire communities. These providers now serve an estimated 115 000 customers – more than a third of electricity customers nationwide. Fierce competition between private locally owned mobile phone companies in Somalia has driven the costs of international phone calls down to less than $1 a minute, about a sixth that in many other African countries. This is a country with no official banking or postal system, and in which many people do not have running water or electricity (ibid: 6).

The private sector can thus alleviate poverty by contributing to economic growth, and providing poor people with better, cheaper goods and services.

Although the reigning 'business and development' discourse focuses almost exclusively on multinational corporations, domestic business sectors are vital. The United Nations report contains a number of interesting recommendations on how to unleash the potential of domestic private sectors. It argues that governments should facilitate private sector development, and avoid actions that would impede this. They should foster competitive markets, and create enabling operating and investment environments in which all private enterprises (big and small) can flourish (ibid).

It recommends stable, predictable political dispensations, with governments formulating sound macroeconomic policies, rules encouraging competition, and other measures conducive to the development of enterprise and the financing of human and physical infrastructure.

The report argues for properly functioning legal and judicial systems; protection of property rights; the effective resolution of contractual disputes. It calls for an environment that facilitates the movement of private capital of all kinds, not just FDI, and that positively influences regional and global risk assessments of the country concerned.

It calls for targeted subsidies and tax incentives when these are needed to correct market imperfections, and welcomes the private provision of essential infrastructure – power, water, communications, and transport – through public-private partnerships, innovative regulatory models, and other means aimed at ensuring that private enterprise is not placed at a competitive disadvantage vis-à-vis the state (ibid: 23).

Governments really matter

The contribution of business to economic progress emanates from the combination of opportunities and pressures generated by competitive market economies. As economies become freer, and the scope of markets extended, opportunities are widened and competitive pressures increase. Hence economic liberalisation is key to enlarging and strengthening the primary role of business.

Virtually every economy presents large, unrealised possibilities for deregulation and liberalisation. The World Bank's Doing Business report provides a useful insight into the ease of doing business in 145 countries. These excellent reports provide us with comparative information and benchmarks on the effects of regulations in five key areas: starting up a business; hiring and firing workers; enforcing contracts; obtaining credit; and closing a business.

These annual reports highlight inefficient and inappropriate regulations in countries around the globe, and the costs they inflict on entrepreneurship, economic growth, and individual freedom. There are staggering differences worldwide. Starting a business requires $5 531 in Angola and about $28 in New Zealand (ibid: 17). It takes two days to start a business in Australia, 168 days in Indonesia, and 215 days in Congo (ICC 2004). It takes 21 procedures to register commercial property in Abuja, but three procedures in Helsinki (World Bank 2005: 3). In Mozambique a customs reform project reduced the amount of time required to clear goods 40-fold, resulting in a 175 per cent increase in revenue for Mozambique's government (Fitzgerald 2003).

Doing business in one country differs from doing business in another. A regulatory framework that encourages private enterprise is vital for economic growth and job creation. Excessive business regulations are counterproductive: protecting well-connected large companies able to circumvent the rules but making life particularly difficult for smaller enterprises, the main engines of economic growth in most developing countries.

Two more examples demonstrate the important role of national governments. Many industrialised countries protect their agricultural sectors by means of export subsidies, price support mechanisms, and other trade-distorting support measures. This adversely affects agricultural sectors in poorer countries as they encourage overproduction and the reduction of prices to levels which farmers in developing countries cannot match.

The second example concerns another aspect of global trade which is seldom discussed. Developing countries tend to protect their own markets against one another. Despite a steady increase throughout the 1990s, South-South trade still represents a tiny share of world trade. The expansion of trade between developing countries would enable poorer countries to reduce their dependence on markets in industrialised countries, and diversify their export base. According to an UNCTAD report (2008), South-South trade more than tripled between 1996 and 2006, reaching a total of more than US$2 trillion. However, despite this rapid increase, South-South exchanges still made up only 17 per cent of global exports in 2005.

These three examples expose two popular fallacies: that states and national politics matter less and less in an era of globalisation; and that poverty in developing countries is primarily caused by the activities of predatory multinational corporations in cahoots with rich country governments.

'Business' is a complex category

The term 'business' is used very loosely. It can be used to refer to two different entities:

- Individual firms, ranging from multinational corporations to one-person enterprises. In many societies different forms of private enterprise coexist in a symbiotic relationship – multinationals, large domestic companies, small and medium enterprises, formal and informal micro enterprises.
- Business organisations, or the voluntary associations of a number of firms in certain sectors or countries. Some associations are formed to capture the state or protect their members against competition; others seek to improve the functioning of markets by lobbying for contracts to be enforced more efficiently, or transaction costs to be reduced.

These bodies generally define and promote a set of longer-term goals
which they try to justify in terms of a broader public interest rather
than mere market share or profitability.

Four other factors need to be considered when using the term
'business'. The first is ethnicity. In many ethnically divided societies,
most corporations and retail businesses are owned and managed by
members of an ethnic minority. This generally means that the leading
business associations will also be dominated by that minority, although
the ethnic majority would probably form business associations as well.

The second is the size of businesses. The vast majority of firms are
relatively small; however, large corporations attract most attention. It
is frequently important to know whether one is referring to large or
small businesses when using the term 'business'. Large firms are much
more prevalent in affluent countries than in developing countries. In
the United States, plants with 50 or more employees account for more
than 80 per cent of total manufacturing employment. In Thailand
they account for 30 per cent of manufacturing employment, and in
Indonesia and Ghana, 15 per cent (McMillan 2002: 175).

The third factor is the source of investment. According to the
United Nations report *Unleashing Entrepreneurship* (2004), 'domestic
resources are much larger than actual or potential external resources.
Domestic private investment averaged 10-12% of GDP in the 1990s,
compared with 7% for domestic public investment and 2-5% for
foreign direct investment (FDI)' (UNDP 2004: 9).

Domestic assets with investment potential (including the potential
value of land) are significantly larger than cumulative FDI or private
portfolio flows. Utilising domestic resources – both financial and
entrepreneurial – is likely to create a more stable, sustainable pattern
of growth.

The fourth factor is gender. In many developing countries, women constitute the majority of micro entrepreneurs in the informal economy, and a significant percentage in the formal sector as well. Many are illiterate, and live in poor rural communities. Establishing their own enterprise is usually the only route to employment and earning an income.

In every society, it is important to identify and think about the entire business sector, and not equate business with only one part of what is usually a multifaceted complex set of individuals, organisations, and interests.

Having drawn all these distinctions, I will continue to use the generic term 'business' in the rest of this book. Wherever possible I try to give this term a more precise meaning, but sometimes there is no choice but to refer very broadly to the business sector as a whole.

THE INTERESTS OF BUSINESS

The interests of business are pertinent to the responsibility debate. However, it is important to distinguish between the interests of individual firms and those of business as a whole.

Firms in a particular sector organise themselves in order to protect or promote their interests against those in other sectors. Small business associations regard large corporations as targets for influence. Importers compete with local manufacturers. Businesses in a certain geographic area seek to protect their interests against those in other areas.

Businesses seek an environment in which they can profitably produce goods and services. Individual firms therefore constantly compete against other firms operating in the same market sector. However, the fact that firms compete against each other must be distinguished from the notion that businesses have competing interests. Business generally has a common interest in a stable environment and an enabling framework of governance. Firms only compete with one another within that framework, ie controlled competition, not competitive anarchy.

Business organisations have rather different concerns from individual firms. Where a national business body may well back freer trade, clothing companies dependent on tariff protection will oppose trade liberalisation. These fault lines exist not only between firms and representative bodies but also between different business associations.

In racially, ethnically, linguistically and religiously diverse societies, these factors will further distinguish business interests. Ethnic preference or prejudice may be applied to individual firms, and may affect their access to markets, capital or contracts. When a group of firms chooses to organise on a representative basis along racial, ethnic, language or religious lines, this introduces new factors. Where the ethnic character of the political elite coincides with business organisation, a preferential relationship is likely to exist. Where it differs, tension may well develop (Bernstein & Berger 1998: 13).

Some firms adopt a long-term view of their business and make decisions on that basis rather than the immediate pressures of the balance sheet. Ultimately, the interests of individual firms lie in their immediate competitive environment, and those of groups of firms in the broader environment in which business activity takes place, which then becomes the domain for collective business organisation.

Business and economic growth

It is often asserted that 'the business of business is business', and the numerous demands on business to do more than that is to misunderstand the nature of business itself. However, a more nuanced approach is required.

The most natural political activity for a firm is to lobby for some form of intervention or special dispensation to further its own interests. This makes sense in the short term, but has two negative consequences. The intervention required by a particular firm (eg tariff protection) is not necessarily good for other firms or the economy as a whole. The end result of this process, with each firm acting in its own self-interest, is that business can end up as a major force for an interventionist, expanded role for the state in the economy. Neither of these consequences is good for national economic growth.

Generally speaking, the collective interest of business in sustained economic growth will differ from state interests in four broad areas:

- the extent of government management of or intervention in the economy;
- the role of industrial policy, and the state's capacity to 'pick winners';
- whether and how to compensate for market and state imperfections; and
- how to achieve social and development objectives.

Besides these four areas, the list will be expanded in many developing countries with at least four more issues: ethnic composition of the business sector; tension between some form of affirmative action and the integrity of purpose of institutions; tension between international competitiveness and redistribution policies; and the selection of national priorities.

These are the issues around which business has to organise collectively, and define its interests.

Business and development

In many ways, the term 'development' has been captured by an anti-business, anti-market world view. Business has historically allowed its activities to be excluded from 'good development', and categorised as 'questionable or bad'. It is essential to remove this moral distinction between the two kinds of development, and demonstrate their interdependence.

A useful distinction can and should be drawn between growth and development. It is possible to have economic growth from which only a few people benefit. Development is the process in which the fruits of economic growth are used to improve the circumstances of large numbers of people.

The market economy is a necessary but not sufficient condition for sustained economic growth and development. The extent of development generated by economic growth depends on both the nature and quality of that growth, and the wisdom and efficacy of the development strategies pursued by a given society, notably its government.

At certain times in a country's history, a trade-off seems inevitable between growth and development. Excessive social expenditure can destroy the growth capacity of an economy. Similarly, a failure to embark timeously on selected social expenditures can have disastrous economic and social consequences. There are large areas of social spending that have virtuous impacts on the growth capacity of a given economy.

The link between growth and development policy is important. If the social and infrastructural elements of development are neglected, this will have economic consequences. If government policies on development 'crowd out' the private sector, this will have negative consequences for growth and national development. In the vast majority of countries, if the state tries to deliver all social services itself, it will inevitably fail, and those services will not be provided to the vast majority of citizens except for a politically well-connected minority. And the likelihood of state intervention growing in other parts of the economy will increase. Moreover, the many opportunities for the private sector to help provide infrastructure and social services will not be explored or even countenanced. All this will affect the growth rate and the inclusive nature of economic development.

If companies want to operate in a growing economy characterised by political and social stability, they need to promote government actions that are in the interests of business and its definition of growth and development. The challenge, then, is threefold:

- business has to develop an approach to national economic growth;
- this approach must be integrated with a business perspective on development; and
- both of these have to be marketed in the political arena, and then effectively implemented by the society in question.

So the collective interests of business dictate the need for a common vision that links growth and development; persuasive public marketing of this business vision; an effective strategy for achieving the vision; and the strategic and tactical skills to enable this politically.

Business and government

The term 'government' seems much simpler than 'business'. However, closer examination soon reveals its complexity. At least three distinctions must be drawn. Government has executive and legislative branches; operates in most countries on a national, regional and local level; there are important differences between politicians and officials, and between career bureaucrats and political appointees.

In democratic political systems, governments exercise the powers of state in a way that upholds the constitution, and keeps them or their party in office. Where politicians hold elected office (in, say, a legislative assembly) and also exercise an executive role in regional or national government, the interests of their electorate will inevitably be modified by the demands of government.

Government experts, technocrats, and bureaucrats may develop distinct interests. They may need to develop expertise and influence that will survive the vicissitudes of party-political elections. In particular, those employed in the executive are likely to derive power from their ability to make state systems work, and their mastery of bureaucratic procedures and politics. The impact of new ideas and new interests on these established avenues of government activity is likely to be of decisive interest to this group.

If it is accepted that business is a social actor, and that it has common interests which supersede those of individual firms, it needs to rethink its relationship with government. In essence, if business wants to influence government, it needs to reach a far better understanding of government as well as business-government relations. It needs to understand that government has very different imperatives to those of business. Under democratic conditions, at any rate, government is accountable in different ways and to different groups than individual businesses.

The relationship between business and government must be underpinned by the recognition of several important realities. When dealing with government, business is engaging with an entity whose legitimacy must be recognised if democratic order is to be preserved, and if business interests are to have any influence over it. Business is one of a number of interest groups in society, and no interest group in a democracy has a legitimate claim to rights and privileges that are not available to the others.

Business therefore needs to engage with government as a common, organised set of interests, and ensure that its views are communicated and heard. This will require effective mechanisms for interaction within the business sector and between business and government.

BUSINESS AND DEVELOPING COUNTRIES

The dominant global discourse on business and its social role routinely implies that large multinationals are a threat to poor countries. Most developing countries have a very different perspective. By contrast, their concerns are: how do we persuade more large companies to invest in our country? Let's look at some key issues from a developing country perspective.

How to think about development

The development narrative has been distorted. It is troubling that some of the richest governments in the world, their official aid agencies and citizens' groups insist on thinking about development in other countries as a process primarily involving international donors, international NGOs, and recipient governments. They mainly see poverty and development as processes largely separate from markets and the normal operations of companies; problems that need to be solved by outsiders; and victims who need help. They frequently fail to relate their own country's history and how they became rich and prosperous to strategies for developing countries. They view developing countries in a different light, somehow requiring approaches that differ from – and in fact fundamentally contradict – those that work in their home societies. This is not a process that delivers.

Development has to be rooted in national governments working with their own citizens, rich and poor, and their own businesses (large, small, domestic and foreign). Development has to be rooted in local and national politics. The key challenge is how to turn countries into effective, competitive environments for enterprise. Business will then generate the resources which smart, competent governments can use to improve the welfare of their citizens. Smart governments know how to *channel* international aid, and use it to maximum domestic advantage. And it is only when state-market relationships are working well, from however modest or imperfect a base, that we start to see processes emerging which actually improve the lives of large numbers of people, and in a sustained way.

In this context, foreign investment by companies can be a turbo-charged vehicle for growth and development. Theodore Moran has argued that developing countries are best served when they adopt 'build up' rather than 'trickle down' approaches to capturing the benefits of foreign direct investment. In his view, 'build up' requires a number of strategies on the part of host country governments:

- sound macroeconomic management, including realistic exchange rates and trade liberalisation;
- provision of reliable infrastructure and dependable commercial and regulatory institutions;
- policies that allow indigenous firms as well as foreign investors equal access to benefits and incentives;
- the creation and ongoing support of a workforce that is at least modestly skilled and trainable; and
- efforts to maximise backward linkages that spill over to small and medium-sized as well as large indigenous firms (2002).

He advises national governments to actively seek numerous investors; provide fair and equal support to SMMEs and large local companies; break down isolated labour markets; mix higher-skilled operations with lower-skilled activities, thus easing the transition of workers to higher-level activities, and increasing pressure on wages; improve the administration of special enterprise zones (often via private operators, including those with international experience); improve national supervision of the treatment of workers; combine vocational education and skills training with programmes that strengthen the connection between foreign investors and local suppliers and generate spill-over benefits for indigenous firms and workers. In addition, sensible governments modernise and privatise infrastructure; reform their commercial institutions, including those that monitor, adjudicate, and enforce national labour statutes; and examine barriers to trade, especially imports (ibid).

On the basis of his comparative research in a number of developing countries, Moran argues that countries which allow only a few large corporations to operate on their soil tend to derive few benefits from foreign or domestic investment and growth. These are countries where companies hold monopoly positions, appointments are made through patronage rather than merit, free association is not allowed, and the hallmarks of more open societies do not come into play to root out abuse and improve training, education, workplace safety, and treatment of workers (ibid).

These issues differ greatly from those that preoccupy the activists and fellow travellers that comprise the CSR movement. Among other things, their focus on foreign rather than domestic firms skews the debate in important ways. Much of the discussion tends to ignore the fact that most business executives are citizens of the country concerned. This will affect how they see national challenges, how they engage with government, and what they are prepared to do, either to shape popular opinion or apply corporate resources.

Business in newly democratic countries

Businesses – whether individual enterprises or groups of enterprises – tend to be self-contained. Individual businesses raise their own capital, design their own production processes, and define and service their own markets. Where political power is exercised feudally, or in an authoritarian context, business organisations will negotiate their social space – their right to do business, and the terms on which they are allowed to do so – with the prevailing political authority. Often this will entail private arrangements between individual companies and government, which often provides government, or some government officials, with specific benefits.

The relationship of a business entity with other social actors in such less developed and undemocratic societies is equally likely to take a certain form. Labour will be recruited under individual contracts drawn up unilaterally by the employer. Businesses are not scrutinised by an independent, critical press, and shareholders tend to be compliant.

Increasing modernisation, especially under democratic or democratising circumstances, will change this. Relations with government are defined by laws and regulations. Besides taxation, companies need to respond to a widening set of public interests. Labour rights, environmental responsibilities, corporate governance, stock exchange rules, and consumer rights begin to impact on both the character and conduct of business.

As this happens, business is inevitably drawn into a public policy marketplace – moving from simple 'deals' with ruling groups, giving them a 'right to trade', to broader social interaction where it has to legitimise itself and defend its economic and other interests in the cross-play of multi-interest politics.

Business becomes part (indeed, a very important part) of civil society. It develops a vital interest in the rule of law and the fair application of contracts. It develops a close interest in fiscal and monetary policy; it can no longer protect its economic interests with a series of private deals with political mandarins, but must instead argue in the public and political marketplace for the adoption of general policies that favour its interests.

In the process of democratisation, other powerful interest groups – organised labour, consumers, environmentalists – gain space and political leverage. To ensure a broad public policy environment in which it is able to survive, business will have to engage, often compete, with these different groups to determine the outcome of policy debates.

Business has often failed to understand its changing position within a democratising social order. It has been slow to define its social and political interests and is defensive, reactive, and inept in promoting them. Business as a corporate citizen is often less than effective (Bernstein & Berger 1998).

THE DILEMMAS OF BUSINESS ACTION

The business sector faces a number of dilemmas when it comes to collective and social action. The first is one of organisation: how can a large number of competing firms effectively come together to promote their common interests?

The second is one of action: how do companies whose skills lie in pragmatic activities – production, marketing goods, investment, etc – develop a sophisticated understanding of the society in which they operate, of their own interests in that society, and the most effective political strategies to promote and protect those interests?

The third dilemma is one of content: what should business actually do and say to promote its interests? What is the right strategy for growth and development in any particular country and situation?

Business, democracy, and economic growth

The critical questions concerning the relationship between business and democracy are the hardest. Is democracy in the interest of business? Does it facilitate or impede growth and development?

Where democracy is sustained the pressures for development become irresistible; a government which is tested at the polls every four to five years has to take improving voters' lives seriously. The relationships between more and less democratic forms of government and economic growth are more complex – the prerequisites for gaining power and managing an economy are often at odds with each other, at least in the short term.

Evidence suggests that development and growth are possible in non-democratic political orders. Whatever one's preferences might be (and mine are for democracy), authoritarian regimes can serve the interests of business and economic growth. They would need to meet the following conditions:

- establish effective control over the country concerned, and maintain a degree of political and social stability for a reasonable period;
- implement intelligent, and effective economic and social policies that benefit large numbers of people;
- avoid a reign of terror involving widespread human rights abuses and possibly bloodshed; and
- keep corruption in the public sector within reasonable limits.

Although these conditions can be met simultaneously, comparative experience suggests this rarely happens. This difficulty is compounded when one insists that all four conditions need to be sustained over time. Sooner or later, the interests of the business sector will dictate that democracy is the better option.

Thus, in countries with authoritarian governments, business has an interest in a successful transition to democracy. This means it needs to clarify and promote its own interests during the transition, as the outcome of such a fundamental social transformation is not guaranteed. In the process, it has to deal with two difficult issues.

Because business is able to adapt to different political orders, and needs to cooperate with the authorities in order to get things done, it is often perceived as identifying with the old regime rather than the new democratic order. In such a situation, ways must be found to legitimise and popularise business and explain its value for a new democracy. Its contribution to economic growth, development, and democratisation needs to be effectively marketed.

Business interests dictate two sets of activity, the one positive, the other defensive. On the positive side, business as a collective must be clear about what kind of transition and future institutions will be best for economic growth. Business must campaign and build alliances, in a very fluid environment, for the transitional mechanisms and policies that will promote growth and development.

On the defensive side, business actors need clear policies and strategies as reference points in a period of uncertainty. It is quite possible for business to share a common desire for a successful transition with other actors but differ from them about the most effective strategies for growth and development, or the nature of a future democratic system.

In a democratising society, a business community that wishes to support growth strategies has to do so distinctively. In a non-democratic political order, business makes private deals with the power elite. In a democratising society, business must argue its case in a public marketplace of ideas.

To do that effectively business must organise differently. In a democratic society, in which public policy is made in open debates in national assemblies or councils, business is most effectively represented by business organisations. Business leaders from large corporations may still exert some influence through informal channels. However, if their views are not also presented in the public policy marketplace by credible, representative business organisations (often supported by independent market-oriented think tanks), they will not be able to influence the national debate.

Business and democratic consolidation

In a democracy, then, especially a newly formed one, business has a distinctive role to play. It has an interest in the consolidation of the new political order, and in ensuring the new government adopts and implements non-populist economic and social policies.

In general, business should promote policies and strategies to encourage rapid economic growth and sustainable development while remaining sensitive to the political and social problems which these policies may cause in the short to medium term. Business should resist policies encouraging state-centred patronage and ensure that the fallacies and dangers of such policies for the country, economic growth, the business sector and the poor are publicised. They must also promote alternative policies on economic as well as broader development issues.

In the process, business should:

- Emphasise the importance of giving citizens new hope. This can be done by selecting feasible priorities for national attention.
- Advocate policies that deal with unemployment in a sustained, large scale manner.
- Help to strengthen civil society, and maximise the contribution of the private sector and markets to service delivery.
- Emphasise international experience in similar situations, thus helping the new government and other social actors to learn from those experiences as quickly and thoroughly as possible.
- Underline the scale of the challenge and the need to achieve sustained, widespread results, rather than merely creating new pockets of privilege.
- Emphasise the need for the new regime to be a competent meritocracy focusing on serving the public and empowering individuals and communities rather than bureaucrats and politicians.

Business and the politics of development

One of the challenges facing large companies operating in developing countries is how to manage their political interactions with host governments and local communities. Companies entering a developing country without a strategy to deal with human rights issues or a weak or corrupt state are asking for trouble. Strategic preparation is required; companies must have the political and public relations expertise needed to deal with the challenges and controversies that will inevitably arise. A company needs a clear vision of its own values and purpose, an effective strategy for communicating this to widely divergent audiences – its own managers and employees, local politicians, other social groupings, local and international media, the governments of their host country and country of origin, local and international NGOs.

Companies should not wait to be attacked, letting their critics define the terms of the debate and responding belatedly and in outmoded ways to well-planned, politically astute campaigns which often serve as fund-raising tools for the attackers. In general, large companies are ill-suited to the quick responses required in international and local 'issue management', and suitable executive resources need to be devoted to these kinds of situations.

For many business leaders, corporate life is so encompassing that it's often hard for them to think outside the envelope and have any sense of how they are perceived, or how the other 99 per cent live in a developing country. In this context managers and executives may be blind to how internal decisions with their own corporate logic will be interpreted outside the company.

Companies need to work with politicians and government officials in order to secure permission to operate. This takes place in the most sophisticated societies; it is even more necessary where rules and procedures are less clear or have not yet been properly developed. Business must look to its own interests, and companies have an interest in stable political environments that foster national, regional and international markets.

One of the principal challenges facing multinational corporations is how to manage their political interactions with host governments. In a 21st-century world, they can do so in two basic ways. The first is to avoid interfering in domestic political issues – but how realistic is this? Can powerful companies really avoid becoming politically entangled in some way, especially when the government in a developing country is weak or unstable or they are one of few organisations in the country with capacity and global links?

The second is to recognise that they have political influence, and then to try to wield this responsibly. Will local management and head office agree on how to respond to local political situations? Will whatever the company decides to do – exert some pressure, speak out on issues – actually have any impact?

Shell's original approach of embedding itself in Nigerian society and remaining on good terms with authoritarian rulers was precisely what opened it up to attack from activists (foreign and local, although a breakdown of who funded the local groups would be interesting). Shell was accused of funding corrupt national rulers who did not spend tax revenue in the areas where the company operated. It has now adopted a new strategy, with two components. First, it has spearheaded a 'publish what you pay' campaign in terms of which large companies publicise how much they pay a given government in taxes. Second, it actively provides 'public' goods and services to the local communities in which it operates – a tricky area which raises important issues of roles and outcomes. What is appropriate for a company to do, when does it let the government off the hook or open itself to further and unrealistic public demands?

It is in the interests of companies to pay far greater attention to the political, social, and cultural situations in host countries. They need to be more cognisant of potential sources of conflict with indigenous societies. By developing a deeper understanding of the social and political context in which they do business, appreciating the intricate nature of problems that may arise, and remaining sceptical about any advice or techniques which purport to provide simple solutions, companies will be less likely to walk blindly into political problems.

Litvin (2003) argues that big companies have tended to focus on what they consider to be their core business functions, namely production and marketing, and regard social and political issues as peripheral. As a result, the latter are often dealt with on a reactive, ad hoc basis, and companies commonly try to solve them simply by hiring public relations firms or lobbyists. Investment in community projects or even national development programmes can sometimes help companies build relationships and gain a deeper understanding of the intricacies of the local situation, but sometimes these activities and their impact are blown out of proportion, or sometimes it is not clear what the best kind of 'responsible' corporate behaviour in a particular situation will be, or that companies will necessarily avoid political friction by getting involved in them.

In general, what is lacking from most companies' efforts in this arena is the kind of long-term, strategic, fact based approach which they would typically apply to other parts of the business (financial planning, analysis of economic trends). In Litvin's view,

> What is needed is a serious attempt by companies to understand objectively the political and social context in which they operate, both at a local and international level, and to pinpoint the complexities, risks and dilemmas that may lurk initially unseen within it (2003).

Lobbying, PR, and statements about the company's social activities may be useful additional techniques, but cannot provide a substitute for a comprehensive strategy.

Following a searching historical and contemporary examination of a number of large corporations operating outside 'the west', Litvin concludes that

> The views of westerners as to which are the correct standards and the more important issues do not always coincide with the views of local people or of host governments, and the experience of companies themselves has shown that solving complex ethically ambiguous issues from afar is not easy (ibid).

CONCLUDING REMARKS

This chapter has highlighted a number of missing themes which need to inform any sensible discussion about business and development.

We should not discuss 'business' in isolation of a broader context that roots companies in national markets and politics.

Economic growth is vital for national development. We now have numerous examples of countries that have operated within imperfect global conditions of trade and worked in partnership with domestic and international businesses to transform the trajectories of their nations for the better.

Development is a phenomenon closely aligned to but different from economic growth, and poverty is far more complicated than the easy sound bites suggest.

One of the key areas of neglect in the responsibility conversation is politics, notably national politics, and how business can organise to influence national policies to promote growth and development.

An important component of this complex dynamic is the issue of attitudes to business itself. So much of the discussion about business is punitive, protectionist, partial, or guilt-ridden that fundamental issues are neglected. This is a major factor holding back liberalisation and economic growth in many developing countries, and should be high up on the agenda of business as well as host governments.

Chapter Nine

WHAT MORE CAN BUSINESS DO?

'There are few things more awesome than the power of a vast company that alights in a small country. The constants of life there – that there are no roads to get about on, that the government is hopeless – melt suddenly away. ... Exxon created its own private air service to link the oil field to the capital; it created its own electricity system with six times as much generating capacity as existed for the rest of the country; it built a road that bisected the oil region.'

Sebastian Mallaby, *The World's Banker* (2004)

HAVING unpacked and criticised the CSR world view, and begun to develop a different framework for thinking about business and society, I will now briefly explore what business can intentionally undertake, and be expected to do, 'outside the factory gate'.

Once again, the current discourse is not very helpful or well developed. The boundaries between marketing, PR, and CSR are not clearly defined nor are the definitions of CSI, philanthropy, public, or corporate affairs. It is often difficult to classify and assess the resources which companies allocate to marketing, building relationships with governments or communities; public relations; charity, welfare and social investment. These difficulties are compounded in the case of global companies.

The field has recently become even more crowded. C K Prahalad's work on 'bottom of the pyramid' activities by large multinationals (2006) is a welcome new addition to the debate. He argues that companies have new opportunities for expanding their markets by looking towards poorer communities in developing countries as potential consumers. His work has influenced the World Business Council for Sustainable Development, which argues that developing new markets requires thinking of the poor as business partners and customers. In the process, companies may have to develop new ways of buying, manufacturing, packaging, marketing, distributing, advertising, and charging for their products (WBCSD 2004).

The work of Michael Porter and Mark Kramer (2006) on linking corporate social activity with company or industry competitiveness is another welcome voice of greater pragmatism and strategy in this arena.

The Centre for Global Development in Washington is a leading think-tank on development issues. It is therefore instructive to assess its recent report entitled *Joining the fight against global poverty: a menu for corporate engagement* (Warden 2007). Based on interviews with 15 companies, it aims to present a framework that will help companies formulate their options. It puts forward a menu of six different approaches, in the following order: standards compliance; charitable giving; resource engagement (ie, directly contributing a company's own goods and services); commercial engagement (running successful businesses); developing entrepreneurship (with an explicit commitment to the poor as the core strategy); and policy advocacy.

It is revealing that this influential organisation endorses the idea of 'global standards' for labour, environment and so on. And it is surely cause for concern that running successful businesses features as only number 4 on the list. It is given the same level of importance as the other items as though the contribution business makes in running successful companies is on an equal plane with philanthropy. Also noteworthy is the attention paid to business relations with NGOs rather than business-state relationships (ibid).

In this chapter an alternative perspective is developed that does not take 'the ordinary activities' of companies for granted. Rather, I argue that we need to place them at the front and centre of any discussion about the relationship between business and society.

Through their normal activities in pursuit of profit, business can make a profound difference to individuals, communities, cities, and countries. And all this arises out of what is generally ignored, neglected, underplayed, or taken for granted in the prevailing conversation about business and 'doing good'.

Besides all this, large companies – particularly multinationals – are rightly committed to playing an intentional, broader social role, and are prepared to commit significant sums of after-tax money to doing so. These are precious resources, both human and financial, that should be used to maximum effect.

How best to do that?

The challenge is to outline a new framework for effective corporate public action and social spend – one that makes greater use of the core strengths and interests of business, recognises the dynamics of markets and the realities in developing countries and poorer communities.

I will briefly focus on some priority areas of 'extracurricular' activity by business, many based on my own experience of working and thinking about business and development in a middle-income developing country, South Africa.

IMPROVING THE BUSINESS ENVIRONMENT

The quality of the environment in which business operates makes an enormous difference to the success of individual firms, and ultimately the economy at large. It affects the competitiveness of cities, regions, and countries, and helps to determine access for new enterprises.

World Bank studies have revealed massive differences in the time and costs involved in starting, registering, or closing down businesses in various countries. This has an enormous impact on existing companies as well as new start-ups. Creating a favourable business environment has an extraordinary impact on economic growth and the expansion of opportunities for those previously excluded.

Regulatory environments also have a major impact on decisions by prospective foreign investors, and therefore on the growth prospects of a particular economy. A key part of improving the environment for business includes lobbying to remove laws, rewrite legislation, and promote the establishment of state Impact Assessment units that monitor new legislation for its regulatory effect. How business does this – individually or collectively – will differ from country to country, but it is a priority area for involvement.

Improving the competitiveness of cities, countries and continents

In 2007, for the first time in history, more people were living in urban than in rural areas. More than half of the gross domestic product of most countries derives from urban-based economic activity, and the figure tends to rise in lock-step with urbanisation. The productivity of cities is therefore central to national growth, development, and welfare. In many countries, though, far too little attention is paid to the effects of national economic and other policies on their cities.

Business has an important role to play in helping cities to become good business platforms. In South Africa, my organisation, the Centre for Development and Enterprise, has put it this way:

> National business leaders need to link urban strategy to their
> macroeconomic vision. ... The success of macroeconomic reform
> will be fundamentally influenced by how effectively our cities
> can compete as arenas for investment. ... In every city, business
> leaders need to strategise about the future of that place, and how
> it affects their interests ... Business leaders have an interest in a
> sound national urban policy, an effective urbanisation strategy, and
> an approach that sees cities as the key arenas for macroeconomic
> growth. Cities must move up the list of priorities for South African
> business (1996b: 31).

There are many examples around the world of business engaging
with local government to change the future direction of an urban
area. They range from Cleveland in the United States, where 'a
benign conspiracy' of the top 50 companies helped turn around a
declining manufacturing city, to Bangalore in India, where a business-
government partnership led by the CEO of Infosys is trying to make
the city a world-class environment for business and citizens.

Another potentially far-reaching example is Business Action for
Africa (BAA), a new international network of businesses and business
organisations coming together in support of three objectives:

- positively influence policies needed for growth and poverty reduction
  by creating a platform for a clear African and international business
  voice;
- promote a more balanced view of Africa by highlighting business
  success stories and promoting balanced reporting; and
- develop and showcase good business practice by facilitating new
  partnerships communicating business actions (BAA 2009).

They have established loose alliances to work together on projects.
One example is an initiative aimed at achieving measurable progress
in customs reform by 'retaining a strong private sector lead while

working in a wider co-operative relationship with governments' and other stakeholders (eg local business associations) in Africa. On the basis of a business-focused study in 20 countries, recommendations were developed that are now being applied in six East African countries. The focus is on the need to fast-track customs services for compliant, low-risk taxpayers and traders, and to support efficiency reforms in customs administration.

According to BAA, its projects demonstrate three important features:

- they see the private sector as an important driver of change, with all their projects benefiting from strong business leadership;
- they combine a core business issue with a core development issue – tackling corruption and enhancing customs administration are both business imperatives and central to Africa's development; and
- their projects are deeply embedded at the national level, driven by national task forces, but with local ownership (ibid).

Partnering governments in national development

Large, wealthy corporations can partner national governments in development, adding significantly to state revenues through local taxation, and contributing to public infrastructure. One company that has demonstrated the scope and potential of this kind of partnership is AngloGold Ashanti, the second largest gold producer in the world, based in South Africa. In 2007, Bobby Godsell, then its CEO, commented on its partnership role:

> To the ten governments who are our partners, we want to demonstrate that the gold we mine in their countries is a resource

blessing, bringing fair benefits to them as well as to other stakeholders. ... Plainly, the benefits of resources can be used by all stakeholders, including governments, well or badly. ... In Africa, governments face major challenges. They face the challenge of becoming financially self-sufficient. They face the challenge of renewing and expanding physical infrastructure. They face major challenges around employment creating economic growth. In all these challenges, gold mining companies like our own can be positive partners. In most of the African countries we operate in, we are now, or recently have been in discussion about both levels and forms of taxation. We absolutely believe we should be paying our fair share of tax. ... The burden of 'invisible' taxes needs to be on the table. If mines have to make major (often complete) contributions to physical infrastructure such as roads, water supply, or energy, this should be recognized in the tax take (2007).

Clearly, this kind of role can only be played by the few very large, wealthy corporations – typically a relatively small number of companies involved in the extraction of valuable resources. However, their role in national development can be far-reaching.

OBTAINING A LICENCE TO OPERATE

A second broad area of engagement concerns the notion that corporations need to secure a 'licence' to operate in a given country, region, or community. Initially, many companies saw this primarily as obtaining a formal licence or agreement with national governments. Increasingly, though, they have realised that, particularly in developing countries, those 'licences' (formal and informal) must be obtained and renewed at the local level as well.

Think of the realities of a very large company – involved in mining or oil – arriving in a dirt-poor area to set up operations. Frequently the place in which gold, platinum, or oil is found and where the company must operate is a remote rural location in a developing country far from the centres of power and national politics; where local government is weak or non-existent; and where civil conflict often takes a violent form, thus presenting the company with a very difficult set of choices.

Who protects company employees from armed political opponents of the state, or criminal gangs? If they call in the police, will they be seen to be taking sides? If they use their own security personnel, how far can they go without infringing the laws of the land (assuming they are clear), or risk being seen to take sides in a civil conflict? A different and often related set of issues concerns the enormous deprivation of surrounding communities and the disparity between the modern corporation and its operations with electricity, running water, supplies, formal houses for managers, tarred roads, and so on. It is in this context that the notion of a licence to operate is useful and important for companies.

All businesses, particularly those in extractive industries, and those with a major impact on the physical and social environment, need to recognise that their right to operate derives not only from the state but also from the communities in which they operate. AngloGold Ashanti has described this as the 'moral licence to mine, a licence that derives from the consent of the people' (Jonah 2005: 41). Godsell has commented on this aspect of CSI:

> A fourth key stakeholder is the community around the mine. …
> We cannot mine if our immediate hosts do not also see benefits
> for themselves in the activities we undertake in their midst. To
> ensure that we enjoy a social licence to operate from these 21
> communities, and a licence which we must constantly renew, we

have developed a strategy to build partnerships with those local communities. ... The product of such partnerships is an agreed set of priorities in terms of social investment. Our hope is to leave communities better off for our presence (2007).

BP is one of the main foreign investors in Colombia, a country with significant issues of violence, human rights abuses, and challenges to the state's ability to maintain security. In 1998, Sir John Browne, then head of BP, commented as follows on BP's activities in that country:

We have made mistakes, but I don't believe they were deliberate, and we have learned from them. One of the things we learned is that we cannot stand aside from the problems of communities in which we work. We cannot try to operate in splendid isolation, and cut ourselves off from local realities behind a security fence (1998).

BUSINESS AND GETTING THINGS DONE

Although more people are acknowledging the unique capacity of business to make things happen, this conversation has a long way to go. Activists grudgingly acknowledge the capacity of business, and then try to exploit it for their own ends. Business may be happy to offer some corporate capacity to deal with 'poverty' without spelling out why companies are good at getting things done, or how best to use market forces to get other parts of the economy to be more effective for more people.

Government breaks down, business steps up

As the residents of devastated towns in Mississippi and Louisiana began returning home in the days after Hurricane Katrina hit the American coast in August 2005, many found their way to Home Depot stores. They were among the first to reopen in the storm's wake, offering rebuilding supplies plus 'even more precious commodities of electricity and normalcy' (*Fortune* 2005a).

This large American retail chain started to mobilise four days before Katrina slammed into the coast. At the company's hurricane centre in Atlanta, Georgia, staff from maintenance, HR, and logistics worked 18-hour days to get ready. A day after the storm, all but ten of the company's 33 stores in Katrina's impact zone were open. 'We take tremendous pride in being among the first responders,' said Home Depot's CEO, Bob Nardelli (quoted in *Fortune* 2005a: 51-2).Wal-Mart began planning for Katrina six days before the hurricane swept through New Orleans. Its Emergency Operations Centre deals with hurricanes all the time. In 2004 it responded to four Florida hurricanes in five weeks. It has studied customer buying patterns in hurricane-prone areas so it stocks up on the essentials people will want to buy. The needs of Wal-Mart store managers are addressed – back-up generators, fuel, dry ice, so if generators fail, frozen food can be kept from thawing for 72 hours. The company's meteorologists predicted the path of the hurricane as it headed east of New Orleans, 12 hours before the National Weather Service issued a similar advisory. As a result Wal-Mart reloaded trucks and hauled hundreds of thousands of cases of essential goods to distribution centres outside the city. It was a big job but still fairly routine for a company with 117 distribution centres around the United States (*Fortune* 2005b).

The point of this story is not to suggest that business is always better than government – or that we should privatise every public service and function. Elected officials have a different, in some respects more difficult job than executives; Home Depot and Wal-Mart had to keep stores open and goods flowing, not evacuate an entire city. That said, these accounts illustrate:

- the size and scale of large multinational companies and the skills and resources at their disposal;
- the capacity of successful companies to deliver exactly what is needed, on time and at a cheaper cost than anyone else;
- the speed with which corporate decisions can be taken and implemented;
- the reality that businesses comprise individuals who care about meeting needs of fellow citizens.

These stories of corporate response illustrate the scale and depth of the debate we should be conducting in every country, especially in less developed regions, about precisely what services and goods market forces and companies can provide. And within what kinds of structures and relationships, to ensure that we benefit from the discipline and innovation of market competition without undermining probity or accountability.

WHY IGNORE MARKETS WHEN THINKING ABOUT DEVELOPMENT AND SOCIAL ISSUES?

Even when the strengths of business are acknowledged, this is usually done unreflectively, and obvious conclusions are not drawn – even by business leaders themselves.

Niall Fitzgerald, chairman of Reuters, and former CEO of Unilever, has reflected that at times of crisis – the Asian Tsunami, Hurricane Katrina, the Pakistan earthquake – the impetus to come to the aid of fellow human beings has seen some 'remarkable feats of corporate leadership and action'.

> CEOs have made available company know-how, systems and resources (machinery and disciplined manpower) as well as products and services. ... Corporate resources are capable of tackling situations beyond the reach of volunteer efforts – and with unmatched speed and focus (Fitzgerald & Cormack 2006: 18).

Hans Eenhoorn, a former vice-president of Unilever and member of the Millennium Task Force on Hunger, says:

> Business has a vital role to play not least in its ability to contribute expertise, such as problem-solving and project planning, and to share business methods and know-how such as cost reduction techniques and large-scale logistics (2004).

According to Eenhoorn, spending time in the world's worst hunger spots challenges one's thinking about how best to tackle seemingly intractable problems (ibid).

What is puzzling and simultaneously intriguing is why neither of these business leaders draws the obvious conclusion. Businesses have the skills they do because of the fiercely competitive, innovative world in which they survive. Multinationals succeed in the marketplace because of the processes and performance measures they have introduced in order to compete, and make profits.

Why do most businessmen not think through the role of markets and enterprise for combating poverty? Why don't they make the connection between the many inefficiencies of the donor world – the lack of competition or effective accountability in many cases – and the world of competitive markets and ongoing public scrutiny?

How do we get the best of business practices into fighting deprivation and disadvantage without introducing markets and competition? How do we close down inefficient generally unaccountable organisations? If a company is inefficient or corrupt it will soon go out of business, but this is not the case with international NGOs or aid organisations.

When it comes to poverty or social issues, business leaders tend not to think about market forces, entrepreneurs, and the role they can play. Their response is generally a philanthropic rather than an entrepreneurial one.

Entrepreneurs and education

Easterly recounts the story of two young Delhi entrepreneurs who started a private computer school in the early 1980s. Their National Institute of Information Technology (NIIT) was an instant success, and they struggled to keep up with demand. Their breakthrough idea was to franchise new schools. Franchisees were local professionals who carried NIIT ideas, methods, and techniques throughout the country, even to smaller towns. NIIT protected its brand name by standardising classrooms, teacher training, and advertising as well as by performing frequent audits and setting rigorous exams. The company grew into a giant, with a stock market capitalisation of two billion dollars (2006: 356).

The odds are that many if not most business leaders send their children to private schools. Why don't they consider the role that enterprise could play in providing private education for the children of the poor?

James Tooley has done ground-breaking research in developing countries on the role of private entrepreneurs in providing schooling in poor communities that are at least as good and often better than public schools (Tooley 2006). Private schools today serve some of the poorest children in the world. The majority of these schools are run as businesses, not philanthropic initiatives, and created largely by local entrepreneurs. There is scope for 'edupreneurs' to help provide and improve schooling for poorer communities in many countries.

A greater recognition of the innovative role that the private sector and markets can play in providing quality education to poorer learners is an essential new dimension of the debate about delivery, state capacity and the role of the private sector. The freedom of choice and pursuit of excellence that a private education offers is not appropriate only for the children of business executives and cabinet ministers.

Markets, business and land reform

In most countries, land reform is seen as the purview of the state. In 2001 South African business leaders – prompted by the Zimbabwean situation, and following discussions with the government – commissioned my organisation to examine land reform in South Africa. We discovered that the approach being taken to land issues was far too narrow, failing to take into account some important realities, among them the role of markets and business.

South Africa has a robust rural land market; more than 5 per cent of commercial agricultural land is offered for sale every year. Between 1997 and 2000, the value of land transferred from whites to blacks in commercial transactions was five times higher than the value of land transferred by the state under its land reform programme; and land transfers to blacks have occurred much faster when the government has not been involved. It is possible that the market is transferring as much or more land between whites and blacks than state land reform (CDE 2005b, 2008). Nonetheless, this form of redistribution is not taken into account when the state or other agencies report on progress towards meeting the government's land redistribution goals.

Private sector organisations, including large agribusinesses and co-operatives, have become increasingly involved in land and agricultural reform, and have achieved meaningful results through a wide range of initiatives (especially in sugar and timber). Emerging black farmers are supported through the transfer of expertise, producer agreements, and financing (ibid).

MORE BUFFET, LESS SENTIMENT

'CSR and partnerships are often drops in the bucket nibbling at the edges of major public problems. They are not the road out. The road out is a functioning government, a good court system, and economic opportunity for growth. The path is not hard to name, but it's hard to implement.'

Adam Greene, US Center for International Business (CSRI 2004)

Corporations can use their resources in any way they wish, within the bounds of the law. Therefore, corporate funds used for public purposes are a special resource, and we need to think about them in these terms. Societies should not take corporate largesse for granted.

Corporate social spend can assume various forms. However, I want to focus on the social spend described as corporate social investment, and how this could be used to maximum effect. In general, this is a universe of free-standing projects supporting individuals, good ideas, NGOs and their programmes, individual schools, and various other initiatives. Too often, it's a world of good intentions and minimal evaluation; where inputs matter a great deal more than outputs, and much well-intentioned spending has disappointing results.

It's important not to confuse money, words, or good intentions with a successful development outcome. Harvard business professor Rosabeth Moss Kanter has commented as follows on CSI projects in the United States:

> Traditional solutions to America's recalcitrant social ills amount to little more than Band Aids. Consider the condition of public education. Despite an estimated 200,000 business partnerships with public schools, fundamental aspects of public education have barely changed in decades. And performance is still weak (Kanter 1999).

This is the case in South Africa as well. Two major studies by my organisation of private sector funding for maths and science schooling projects has led to the following conclusions:

- This is the single largest area of private sector funding in the country.
- The scale of money involved is impressive, especially bearing in mind that it mainly comes from some 20 or so of the country's largest companies.
- The amount of money involved is minuscule compared to the public education budget of R140,4 billion in the spending plans of provinces and national government for 2008/09 (South African National Treasury 2009).
- Corporations fund hundreds of individual projects that generally

have no relationship to each other, and there is little mutual learning in the sector.

- South Africa's performance in maths and science schooling is dismal, and increases in private sector expenditure on education projects seem to have had little impact on maths and science results in the system as a whole (CDE 2005a, 2007).

One of the country's leading education experts has concluded that the vast majority of South African schools (75 per cent) are so weakened by a mix of educational backlogs, socioeconomic pressures, a lack of support from the Department of Education, and limited capacity that they are effectively beyond the reach of external interventions, no matter how well-intentioned or even well-conceived these initiatives may be. He has concluded that 'add-on' programmes will only make a difference once conditions in schools have been improved by meaningful system-wide reforms rather than small projects funded by the private sector (CDE 2007: 40-1).

In the light of realities such as these, it would be valuable for companies, probably in all countries, to think about a much more strategic approach to their social expenditure. This will require clarity about the appropriate roles of state and private interventions, and applying the same tough criteria in respect of targets and outcomes as those used for their commercial activities.

A STRATEGIC APPROACH TO MAXIMISING CSI

The discussion by activists on what business should do outside 'the factory gate' frequently sounds as though this is the most important business contribution to society; or as if what business does in this arena will affect the future of a country or 'global poverty'. In fact in any society corporate social investment – however generous, however large the business sector – is a very small amount of money seen in terms of national budgets and national needs. It is 'a drop in the ocean', but if used right it can make an important and catalytic contribution.

Against this background, companies could seek to maximise the effects of their social investment in at least the following ways:

Risk capital

One of the biggest problems facing all societies, especially developing countries, is that of development at scale: how to match limited resources to very large, even overwhelming needs. In this context, social investment is best used as risk capital, or money for social innovation. Companies should fund experiments that involve new ways of doing things. These could cover numerous areas, including:

- how to involve private enterprise in the provision of social services and infrastructure in poor communities;
- how to improve the quality of education in a country or region; and
- how to produce low-cost housing using a combination of 'sweat equity', private companies, and state resources.

First prize would be to develop a pilot project, undertake its design, monitoring and evaluation in collaboration with government, and secure an agreement that if the experiment works the state will take it to scale.

Enterprise promotion

The second arena in which companies are well suited to play important catalytic roles is that of enterprise promotion. Outsourcing certain functions to employees turned entrepreneurs or other local entrepreneurs can turn into a useful source of cost saving as well as a way of empowering previously disadvantaged citizens or employees. SABMiller has done this in South Africa – turning company drivers into entrepreneurs and supporting small farmers who can produce barley for beer (CDE 2004).

Promote excellence and company values

The third area in which company resources could be well spent also arises from company values. It concerns excellence – individual and institutional. This has both local and national implications. In trying to deal with poor service delivery in developing countries many interventions attempt to spread available resources equally across the national terrain, frequently resulting in bringing good performers down to the lowest common denominator. In fact, it is far better to identify centres of excellence, and try to bring more and more institutions and people into this circle of achievement and delivery. After all, that is how markets operate; successful companies demonstrate what works, and others follow. A third viable, creative area of funding for CSI, then, is to invest in excellence, whether by individuals or institutions, through bursaries and grants.

Companies becoming involved in this arena often fund bursaries for students in disciplines relating to their immediate fields of activity or interest – for example, engineering companies send engineering students to university. However, companies and foundations established by entrepreneurs should also think more broadly. For example, all companies, and the societies in which they operate, need well-trained economists interested in promoting successful market economies; or effective public servants who understand markets and the role of enterprise. Similarly, companies should not simply fund tertiary educational institutions without considering what is taught at those institutions, and their attitudes to private enterprise.

Market-based ideas and think-tanks

A fourth valuable arena for corporate support concerns policy relevant information and ideas. Information and analysis are in short supply in most developing countries. Thus business support for market-oriented research and analysis is important. Identifying sound policies based on international good practice and comparative analysis is another good tool. Public policy think-tanks that function as independent voices supporting market-based approaches to national development are essential. Think-tanks built on market values can be very useful interlocutors with governments – city and national – on national priorities for competitiveness in a tough global environment, effective education and training strategies so vital for economic growth; migration policies that enable countries to compete in global markets for skills and investment; and effective urban and urbanisation strategies to manage cities as competitive places in which to do business. Effective independent think-tanks can become national resources – funded by companies in their own interests, but in the national interest as well.

Strategic business alliances

This leads us to another major area of social intervention. Business attracts strong leaders, who tend to be competitive and individualistic. Moreover, business sectors in all countries are diverse, and individual companies have different interests. Even when companies have common concerns, they do not readily adopt common approaches or develop common strategic understandings. Sometimes that is a useful social resource – different companies supporting vastly different social experiments. Sometimes, societies and donors learn what *does* work and energy and resources start to flow to the better alternative. However, corporate public impact can be considerably enhanced if strategic alliances can be brought into being on selected issues.

BUSINESS, APARTHEID, AND THE ABOLITION OF INFLUX CONTROL

In 1976 South African business came together to form the Urban Foundation. Speaking at the founding conference in November 1976, H F Oppenheimer, head of South Africa's largest corporation, Anglo American, stated: 'We in South Africa are going through a very critical time. Business people have a very important role to play and it is in order to organise business people that this conference has been arranged.' This organisation was to perform

---

a remarkable and unique role over the next fifteen years.

Originally set up 'to improve the quality of life in urban black communities', the Foundation's role grew far beyond this initial idea. By the end of the 1980s the organisation was the country's leading independent development agent, demonstrating through practical projects innovative ways of tackling development challenges that would face a government committed to housing, educating and servicing all the country's citizens. The organisation also led the business sector in opposition to apartheid laws.

The foundation educated and persuaded business leaders about the harmful consequences of influx control on the economy and all South Africans; mobilised the international and domestic research evidence and arguments to counter government thinking on the necessity of retaining controls over black movement to the cities; mobilised business resources and influence to persuade government and its supporters that influx control must go; publicly lobbied and galvanised others to join in this campaign; and then having obtained government support in principle for the abolition of this key pillar of the apartheid system, ensured that legislation came to parliament as quickly as possible and that it carried through the intentions of abolition (not partial reform) in all respects.

Through the support of key business leaders and their companies the Foundation could play a leadership role with respect to ideas, development programmes and policies. It was a bridgehead in the white establishment for a new SA not based on race; a place where professionals and activists could think creatively about the development needs of a new SA and how to deal with those burgeoning needs (Bernstein 1998: 191-2).

Companies can use their relatively limited resources to influence government policy and expenditure. This is perfectly acceptable behaviour in democracies, where other interests try and do the same.

CSI is very limited when you look at a country's development needs. But money isn't everything, and often it is how you spend it that really counts. Well-targeted interventions – experiments, policy interventions, institutional innovation, people – can have disproportionate impact. Business leadership, influence and action can make a profound difference to a country, a city or an issue.

The public and private sectors are very different spheres, and should not be confused. Companies encourage inflated expectations and set themselves up as 'scapegoats' if they do not define the boundaries of their social activities very clearly. This is difficult in developing countries where governments are weak and where institutions and delivery mechanisms are strained and generally inadequate.

GLOBAL INITIATIVES AND PARTNERSHIPS

Thinking about CSI in one country is hard enough; thinking about it on a global scale is even more challenging. Even the most generous corporate budgets are minuscule in the context of global social challenges.

When trying to understand the growing enthusiasm for private sector involvement in global initiatives to deal with poverty or governance gaps, it is revealing to look at changing patterns in financial flows from the developed to the developing world. Consider the following: in 1970 about 70 per cent of financial flows from the United States to emerging markets were public, and 30 per cent private. Today, only about 20 per cent of financial flows are public and about 80 per cent are private. About half of private financial flows (40 per cent in total) consist of private sector flows, and the other half of personal remittances, donations by religious organisations, scholarships, and NGO grants (CSRI 2004).

Many people involved in Official Development Assistance (ODA) have realised that the reigning system since World War Two has been superseded. Ending domination by the public sector and a few NGOs, most American investments in developing countries now come from private sources. USAID, through its Global Development Alliance, researched these issues in the early 2000s. According to Holly Wise, director of the secretariat of USAID's global development alliance:

> In this new global operating environment, we recognised that official development assistance (ODA) had become a 'minority shareholder' in determining our mark on the world, and we needed to think about development in a different way. We had to get smart about how to reorient ourselves to engage with a variety of private players. … We established the Global Development Alliance, which aims to expand the impact of our own foreign assistance efforts – and those of other agencies and governments involved in international development – by mobilising the ideas, efforts and resources of nongovernmental organisations, foundations and private business. To date, we have leveraged $2 billion worth of private resources to meet this goal (CSRI 2004: 53).

It is clear that the landscape of global aid and corporate social investment is changing, and that 'global partnerships' or multi-stakeholder and sector initiatives represent its new terrain, covering every conceivable subject in which companies are doing business: from fishing to forestry, agriculture to electronics, local government to water (WEF 2005).

These global campaigns and initiatives vary considerably, making it difficult to summarise or generalise. Thus the one on water might have very senior corporate leadership and involve a major effort to do something significant on scale about water constraints. At the same time an initiative on some other topic could have all the hallmarks of the difficulties discussed in the earlier chapter on 'sweatshops'. It is immediately striking that many activities involve outsiders looking at developing societies and deciding what they think would be a good way to develop these places. The missing actors are frequently governments of developing countries and other vital interests such as trade unions; and I would suspect the organisations involved, so-called 'civil society', are heavily biased towards a few organisations that are based in rich countries or, if they do come from developing countries, are frequently funded by sources outside their own country. Each initiative would have to be investigated and assessed in its own right.

What is the model of change here?

What is clear is that most global initiatives or partnerships involve very different kinds of activities. There are some initiatives which stand apart from conventional CSR. Take the Extractive Industries Transparency Initiative (EITI). Its aim is to make the embezzlement of revenues generated by extractive projects more difficult and through greater transparency to stimulate wider dialogue within developing countries about public expenditure priorities. Partners in this initiative include some governments, the World Bank, oil, gas and mining companies and civil society organisations.

On the face of it, this seems like an excellent intervention. It puts pressure on governments and the predatory elites that often run them to explain what they are doing with tax money and how is it being utilised. It could help to empower local players to put pressure on governments. And in doing this, it might help to curb corruption. For large companies invested in these societies it means they can differentiate themselves from corrupt governments in the eyes of the host country population as well as to a range of international audiences. In principle then this is a positive intervention that promotes greater transparency in governance and empowers local communities, and could have beneficial results. How many countries and companies will sign up, how effectively they will reveal what they are supposed to reveal, and what impact this will have in practice remains to be seen.

A second area in which global partnerships seem worthwhile concerns the health sector. A report from the London School of Economics and Political Science found that between 2000 and 2004, public private partnerships invested $112 million to stimulate research on ten neglected diseases, including malaria, tuberculosis and leprosy. As a result more than 60 new drug research projects are under way, with the potential for half a dozen new drugs being registered by 2010 (Brainard 2005: 25). The challenge is how to marry the phenomenal capacity of competitive pharmaceutical companies' research and development capability with the market for poor country diseases that cannot sustain this level of research. Some innovative ideas on how to 'mimic' market incentives for private companies, through offering guaranteed purchase commitments for successfully tested vaccines and disease treatments are being developed. This is a promising approach to harnessing the power of companies within a simulated market.

The African Comprehensive HIV/AIDS Partnership launched by Merck in collaboration with the Bill and Melinda Gates Foundation and the government of Botswana represents unprecedented expenditure of private resources – $50 million from each donor – and a high degree of cooperation with a developing country government.

This extraordinary marriage of private resources with government activities is promising. The people of Botswana are fortunate that their country has been chosen as the site for this massive private investment in public health. And its government has clearly done all it can to encourage the project. What is not clear is whether it is meant to be a pilot to test and evaluate the impact of such a large outside intervention as well as the efficacy of the different programmes to deal with various aspects of the disease, its treatment, and prevention. Can this intervention be replicated elsewhere? And is that the intention of this initiative?

Many people want to change the world. How you do it, is the interesting and important challenge. I know that in one developing country – South Africa – people often talk a lot about partnerships as a way of avoiding or confronting harder issues. Sometimes the service or development to be undertaken would be far better handled by the market and well managed privatisation than a partnership. Sometimes a different government with different policies is what is required and without a radical change in policy and the effectiveness of officials, no partnerships will work at all. So 'partnerships' need to be interrogated carefully and resources allocated as strategically in these relationships as in any other area of corporate expenditure.

CONCLUDING REMARKS

Max Weber made an important distinction which is valuable in concluding this discussion. In his famous lecture on 'Politics as a vocation', he distinguished between two types of ethics, roughly translated as an 'ethic of attitude' and an 'ethic of responsibility'. The first holds that what matters morally is the attitude of the actor; if that attitude is morally pure then the actions following from it are morally valid. In some respects this approach can be likened to 'the end justifies the means'. An ethic of responsibility, on the other hand, is to calculate the appropriateness of available means to desired ends, to look at the probabilities of success, to attempt to foresee both intended and unintended consequences in a world of uncertainty, relativity and compromise. It is easy to be seduced into a 'politics of moral purity that disdains the calculus of means, costs and consequences' (Berger 1969: 145).

Anyone wishing to intervene in society, and especially in poorer countries where people have so little, needs to think hard about these two kinds of ethics.

Many people when confronted with the stark facts about poverty and the terrible conditions under which people live in many parts of the world want to do something about it – and, given the perceived urgency, almost anything will do. However, these efforts often have little or no impact on poor people's lives, and sometimes make them worse. 'The poor' are not an undifferentiated mass – there are many and varied reasons why individuals and families are and remain poor. Unpacking these is a vital starting point, and an essential prelude to designing a successful intervention.

Many people also have the impulse to fix poverty where they find it – in a rural area, for example – when frequently the best solution for most people would be to encourage them to move to urban areas where they would have a stronger political voice and far greater economic, educational, and social opportunities.

Many people also want to work on the symptoms of poverty – malnutrition, informal housing, lack of water – rather than identifying political or structural processes in a particular community or country that are holding people back. And then deciding what interventions will really help to lift most people out of poverty on a sustained basis.

And while this idea may not be too popular with business critics or the global poverty industry, it is often more effective to first create a growing and politically independent middle class than to deal immediately with mass poverty.

Business leaders need to think hard before adopting other people's agendas for social intervention. They should define their own local, national or global agendas, and on their own terms. Business knows a lot more about development and sustainability than many so-called development experts or NGO activists. Companies have an interest in defining their own social roles, and communicating those roles and their many contributions to social progress as effectively as possible. Business should not accept responsibilities that other institutions have failed to fulfil.

Once this is done, business can go forward and identify ways in which it *can* make a major difference to development – ways which will be more closely aligned to their core activities and skills, as well as social and economic realities in the developing societies in which they operate.

In this chapter I have briefly set out some thoughts concerning how companies might think about the additional activities they could get involved with outside 'the factory gate'. This is a complex arena, and one that is characterised by a great deal more emotion and marketing than analysis and strategy. The key is to marry business interests with social involvement and to build on business strengths rather than pretend to be experts in topics far removed from company activities. Most important is to focus on results far more than has generally been the case in this arena.

PART THREE

The battle of ideas matters

Chapter Ten

THE CASE FOR BUSINESS

'I have been impressed time and again by the schizophrenic character of many businesses. They are capable of being extremely far-sighted and clearheaded in matters that are internal to their business. They are incredibly short-sighted and muddle-headed in matters that are outside their business, but affect the possible survival of business in general.'

Milton Friedman, 'The social responsibility of business is to increase its profits'(1970)

IT IS a strange irony that, as capitalism finally triumphed against its communist nemesis, business was increasingly on the defensive. Instead of being universally celebrated, companies almost immediately came under intensified scrutiny and attack.

This frequently involved critics saying they accepted the reality of market economics, but coupling this with a desire to change companies and profit-making processes into something else. Discomfort with the turbulence of trade and competition was often conjoined with a failure to understand and appreciate the nature of markets and business, as well as the enabling role of states and democratic politics.

This new desire to 'tame' the capitalist process and its key agents, companies (especially large multinationals), took the form of a range of attacks and proscriptions that has fed into and helped to create what I have called the CSR movement. In almost all respects this movement is built upon the idea that the everyday activities of companies are harmful to society, and that they either engage in destructive activities in their own and other countries around the globe, or, at best, in their relentless search for profits, contribute little or nothing to building 'the good society'.

This set of ideas is misguided, and out of touch with reality. The processes that encourage enterprises and individuals to seek profit actually have hugely positive effects on societies.

KEY FINDINGS ON BUSINESS AND SOCIETY

The critics call on companies to 'put people before profits'.
The opposite turns out to be the better route for individuals
and societies.

By seeking out opportunities for profit, businesses contribute to social and economic development. In a competitive context, companies are forced to innovate, and find new markets and new ways of utilising resources. If successful, they provide enormous benefits to investors, managers, workers, suppliers, customers, shareholders, and the communities and countries in which they operate.

The effects of the search for profits and the broadly beneficial outcomes of these activities can be contrasted with companies that try to put other priorities above profits and soon go out of business.

Successful companies do not profit at our expense. Greed differs from a rational calculation of self-interest, and selfishness should be distinguished from self-interested activities in the economic arena. Profit is not a four-letter word.

The attack on individual companies has expanded to an attack on globalisation. The grounds for the assault on companies operating in multiple markets and countries do not stand up to scrutiny. Countries benefit when they participate in global economic processes, not when they are excluded from them.

Countries that have participated in the global economy – even under prevailing, sometimes unfair, rules of global grade – have used this to encourage domestic economic growth and gain phenomenal improvements in living standards. They have left less market-oriented, less business-friendly countries struggling in the dust. Instead of focusing on how to change or influence bad governments, corporate critics spend their time trying to dictate how companies should behave in those countries, which plays a far smaller role in achieving large-scale positive outcomes. The ideas, assumptions, and world view that underpin the anti-globalisation movement reveal a profound animosity to business, trade, and markets that is not justified by the facts.

The critics of business and proponents of CSR have been deeply influenced by these negative ideas about globalisation and antagonism towards multinational corporations. They ignore or underplay the role of governments in shaping markets and the economic prospects of millions of people; underplay the role of technology in disruptive processes of change; overemphasise the ability of business to determine events; and victimise people living in developing countries who are making the best choices available to them under difficult circumstances.

The demand that multinationals should change their character or the nature of their operations in order to become 'socially responsible' is based on faulty assumptions. The best form of social discipline for companies is to have more of them, competing fiercely for market share under reasonable rules laid down by effective states.

Calls on business to 'put a human face on globalisation' make little sense, and are actually dangerous. Globalisation *has* a human face. It consists of hundreds of millions of people who are finally getting opportunities to work, get off the land, move away from the lowest survival levels, and start thinking about new options and opportunities. It consists of hundreds of millions of consumers who can now acquire the goods they need and want at affordable prices in both developed and developing countries. It can be seen in the entrepreneurs, big and small, who are taking advantage of new opportunities to create wealth.

Companies are not more important or more powerful than states, and are not the key actors creating 'the global economic space'. The arguments activists put forward about large companies are simply wrong. Companies are not taking over the world. Global competition does not prevent governments from taxing, spending, regulating or declaring war. Western and other democracies are not at risk from expanded trade and economic integration. Globalisation, far from harming the poor, offers many of them unprecedented opportunities.

The current conversation about business and its social impact is distorted and one-sided. It ignores the fact that millions of shareholders benefit from the operations of successful companies, and that governments are largely funded by taxes paid by successful companies. Critics portray businesses as rapacious organisations which exploit the societies in which they operate, and must therefore be made to 'give something back'. On the contrary, it is their core activities, driven by profit, that benefit those societies most.

The notion of 'corporate social responsibility' and its many variations, such as the 'triple bottom line', is not only built on faulty ideas about profits, markets, business, and globalisation, but is itself inherently flawed.

To whom should a company be responsible – its current employees, consumers, or shareholders, or its potential future ones? And for what exactly? The notion of what is socially responsible behaviour is inevitably political and controversial. The fact that companies should take account of and respond to many aspects of their environment, from energy issues to the presence of Al Qaeda, does not mean they are responsible for them, or accountable to them. The wide scope of

CSR, whose remit stretches from corporate governance to genetically modified food, makes the conversation even more unhelpful.

The wide-ranging impact of companies via their core business activities provides a different starting place for the conversation about business and its role in society.

The debate about 'responsible' corporations takes for granted the everyday activities of companies and their contribution to society. This makes it possible to focus so much attention on what else a company must do to contribute to the social good. However, the ordinary activities of companies and their broader impact can change people's lives for the better. They create possibilities for individual progress, and provide the wealth for societies to afford collective projects from building bridges to going to the moon. They are centres of excellence, and arenas for individual talent and training. They provide opportunities for consumers to acquire goods previously so expensive that only kings and queens or corrupt kleptomaniac dictators could afford them. They deliver on 'the promise of democracy'.

Companies also have many indirect impacts on the communities and societies in which they function, and, in many different, often invisible ways, redefine the possible for entire countries, and create their future. 'Doing business' has many unintended, mainly positive consequences.

In the course of their everyday functions in the marketplace, individual companies have unexpected effects on society. These hidden effects are profound, far-reaching, and not generally the subject of boardroom decisions. These are the unintended consequences of everyday business activity – the social, political, personal, and economic effects of regular company activities and their impacts.

Large multinational modern companies are 'transmission belts' for modernity, and motors of national development. In their search for talent, companies break down previously irrational barriers preventing individuals from participating in economic opportunity. If managed

well by the governments concerned, their activities can change the
course of national development, and the prospects of millions of people.
They inadvertently help to strengthen the rule of law and other vital
institutions; and promote the organisations and ideas that fuel civil
society. In their very existence separate from the state, they provide
an important sphere of autonomy and an alternative to state-directed
control and dominance of all aspects of social life. In authoritarian
societies they can form 'zones of liberation' and alternatives to the
prevailing ways of doing things. Modern work practices require and
encourage new forms of individualism and human rights, and more
consensual approaches to getting things done. Companies are centres
of excellence, promoters of radical new ideas that cannot be stopped
after hours, and incubators of people who create the technological and
organisational future.

*Business – through its normal, everyday, business activities – has an
unintended, and in many respects revolutionary, impact on people and
places.*

Business qua business is therefore a constant agent of social change.
Far from the notion that companies help to maintain the status quo
in societies with repressive regimes, or that all their activities are
essentially destructive, companies inadvertently act as 'stalking horses
for democracy, human rights, greater freedom and modernisation'
(Bernstein & Berger 1998: 6).

The current conversation about business is fundamentally flawed.

Rather than celebrating the existence of profitable companies,
their detractors take them for granted. They underplay the positive
contribution of profitable companies and ignore the less visible but
nonetheless remarkable positive aspects of normal company activities.
From these flawed vantage points, corporate critics want to impose on
companies a broad range of new responsibilities.

Many of these demands are not necessarily in the best interests of society or 'the poor'. Some demands, perhaps many, are actually harmful. Critics often want companies to usurp the role of governments, and the new regulations and restrictions they want to impose would function to undermine the risk-taking, 'future-creating' role of companies and their capacity to innovate in unexpected, unpredictable ways.

The current debate tends to be dominated by international advocacy NGOs, sometimes in alliance with first-world trade unions, large multinationals, and, increasingly, large multilateral institutions. This is replayed in the dominant western media which are most closely attuned to these actors, and can access them easily. What is significant is how many interests do not form part of this conversation.

The missing voices include those of developing country governments; the economic, trade, and finance ministries in developed countries; workers and their organisations in many developing countries; companies in developing countries; and the vast numbers of smaller companies around the globe. This is in fact a one-sided conversation, reflecting the interests, current preoccupations, and tactical choices of the dominant interests in rich countries.

No one can represent 'global civil society', and international advocacy NGOs represent no one other than themselves.

There are many different kinds of NGOs, from service organisations to religious ones. Our concern here is with international advocacy organisations. While many of these new players on the global scene are sharply critical of corporations, they have their own major flaws.

Although they claim to speak on behalf of 'society', 'the people', 'the poor', and 'the environment', they represent only themselves. As someone with considerable experience of international trade debates has argued: 'It's far from clear why the WTO should answer to Greenpeace, which is scarcely accountable to 2,5 million members, rather than to the Indian parliament, which is elected by 600 million voters' (Legrain 2002: 204). And yet the same favoured handful of international organisations are invited to participate in discussions at multilateral organisations concerned with global development and the role of corporations; or to participate with multinational companies in projects or initiatives concerned with globalisation and developing countries.

Advocacy organisations have an interest in perpetuating a 'business against society' perspective on corporate activity, and depicting themselves as society's selfless guardians. Many of their campaigns are conducted in alliance with western trade unions or affiliated organisations. These latter organisations, worried about competition and job losses (and therefore declining membership), are finding that the international solidarity of the working class does not extend to workers in poorer countries, who see a low-paid job as a fantastic improvement of their life chances.

There are considerable vested interests in the business of 'taming' the corporate beast, and some of the most entrenched interests in society are to be found outside the flimsy barricades of corporations.

Most of these international campaigning NGOs and other critics of business, markets, and globalisation have locked themselves into an unreasonably pessimistic view of the state of the planet.

Arguments attacking companies are put forward as though the last 50 years have not happened. There is a remarkable pessimism about poverty and prospects for progress that essentially denies that, over the past 50 years, hundreds of millions of people have moved out of poverty more quickly than ever before. International inequalities are overstated, and evidence of progress is denied or underplayed.

In the current guilt-charged atmosphere, many big businesses have decided to accept the premises of their critics and engage on the role of business almost entirely on their opponents' terrain.

Governments, politicians, regulators, media, academics, and other commentators now view the relations between business and society almost exclusively through the prism of whether corporations are being socially responsible.

In accepting the notion of 'corporate social responsibility' – as though companies are naturally socially irresponsible, and also have greater social obligations than other types of institutions – business has adopted the language and assumptions of its attackers.

Many former activists now work at the highest levels in companies, helping them to 'change' , 'reform', and 'become responsible'. They are now driving the activist agenda from within those companies, and helping them to engage with their more radical brethren. Many of these people are committed proponents of very broad definitions of CSR, and their jobs depend on deepening their influence within companies as much as dealing with outside pressures.

'Sleeping with the enemy' has been a bad strategic decision by large companies, perhaps buying themselves some short-term peace with the activists at the price of longer-term, more important negatives.

By accepting the premises of the attack, and bringing activists into their companies, corporate executives have lent respectability to ideas and assaults on corporate behaviour which bodes ill for the future. In doing so, they have allowed their critics to shape the debate about business and society. This has helped to put businesses on the defensive, seemingly accepting the assumption that business in general has something to answer for, even before the critics get to each corporation's specific sins, which they will in time.

As a result, the conversation is focused on issues important to the activists rather than those vital to companies or to developing country populations or governments.

The Millennium Development Goals should not be a business project. Business should put forward its own agenda for development and growth.

Although the MDGs include many worthy goals, they represent an approach to development and a set of priorities that do not foreground the interests of companies and states which want increased economic growth as the foundation for development. The MDG focus – welfarist rather than growth-oriented – differs considerably from the route chosen by the most successful of the less rich countries such as China, India, Chile, Singapore, Vietnam, and Botswana. Given the limited capacity of most developing countries, a vital issue of governance is the choice of priorities. Should they focus on redistribution or on markets? Should they concentrate on dealing with the symptoms of poverty, or on tackling the causes of systemic disadvantage and exclusion?

The business interest is clear. The motor of sustained development is economic growth, and higher growth requires countries to improve the business environment. The MDGs do not mention many of the most important challenges facing countries trying to become good places in which to do business, and attract the investment they need to prosper: economic infrastructure, getting rid of regulations that hamper competitive enterprise, making themselves effective arenas in which to attract foreign direct investment, dealing with skills shortages, creating a solid middle class and social stability.

The business agenda centres on creating a better climate for enterprise and investment that, in time, can help a country to develop a self-sustaining growth path and a better chance of dealing with poverty. To work on the priorities for growth and competitiveness and simultaneously attempt to achieve all the components of the MDG package is impossible for most developing countries even to contemplate, let alone achieve.

Business leaders and companies should not unthinkingly sign on to the MDGs and the approach to development they embody. (Nor should developing country governments.) A business agenda for development would differ greatly from that promoted by the 'poverty wallahs', who see capitalism as something to be tamed rather than embraced, and profit-making as a cause of poverty rather than the solution. To make poverty history requires more than a shopping list of indicators to be improved. It requires a strategy for inclusive development driven by developing countries themselves, and finding their own path out of poverty, which is the only way any country has ever done it.

CSR exponents – outside and inside corporations – are committed to global standards with respect to labour and other social issues. However, like some other campaigns initiated in the industrialised world, this is misplaced, has protectionist consequences, and runs counter to the interests of developing countries.

The presumption that all countries must develop the standards, tastes, and preferences of activist groups in rich countries is outrageous. People who work for foreign companies or their subcontractors are a tiny minority at the apex of the labour markets in poor countries. If one was really concerned about mass poverty in those countries, or their overall development, this is the last place to start a long-term process of change.

Citizens of poorer countries are better off without outside activist interference in the 'standards' by which their countries should develop.

The 'global standards' campaign includes moves to rein in the financial sector. Companies should not aim to appease the activists in rich countries. The stakes are too high. Developing country governments and companies with influence over the IFC should not allow the Equator Principles to stand.

The Equator Principles, promoted by the IFC and signed by more than 40 of the world's largest banks, are intended to prevent projects in poor countries that do not comply with stringent environmental standards. They present a series of hurdles which companies have to surmount when seeking project finance.

The South African example of a middle-income developing

country adopting the rich world's latest and best environmental impact analysis standards is instructive. After a trial period, they have been acknowledged by the country's politicians from the president down, to have delayed development for the poor, held back housing programmes, and made the speedy delivery of a better life for South Africans harder and more expensive. The discussion of these issues in the western world does not reflect the reality that countries make trade-offs when deciding on development projects and strategies, and decide to follow certain courses of action even if these have some negative consequences. Many campaigning NGOs are actually opposed to growth and modernisation, no matter how 'sensitively' this is undertaken.

The endless calls on business to 'do more', promote development, and get involved in social issues often mistake energy for achievement, and assume that as long as business is doing something, showing good intentions, and feeling guilty about its core money-making activities, this will start a self-sustaining process of long-term community or country development. This is not the case.

Important elements are missing from the dialogue between international NGOs and corporations about 'global poverty', and the role of business in alleviating it. These include the vital role of markets in economic and social arenas, and the essential role of the state in creating the context for growth and development. This is a world where multinational corporations matter more than any other kinds of enterprise (such as domestic companies or smaller enterprises), and are seen as worthy of more attention than almost any other participant in the development process, including governments.

In this artificial discussion, companies and what they can or should do takes place a remove away from issues of economic survival of the corporation; small, unconnected projects are talked about as if they could make a numerically meaningful impact on 'global poverty'; and good intentions matter a great deal more than outcomes.

Most curiously, the conversation has little to offer on the politics of national or global development. As a result, far too little attention is paid to trade-offs and the inevitable process of compromise, bargaining, and deals that characterise development in any country. National interests and priorities are far more important than many of the initiatives being demanded from companies in isolation of these dynamics.

It is assumed that nation states have a diminishing role in national, regional and global development; and that the outcomes of social interventions are predictable. Poverty is regarded as a more important organising principle or point of departure for thinking about social change and development than the drivers of economic growth and prosperity. Successful companies are taken for granted; it is simply assumed that companies have considerable, almost unlimited, resources to devote to social issues. And the factors resulting in successful corporations are assumed to bear little relationship to profits, competition, and the dynamics of capitalism. If one starts the conversation about business and development with a set of negative presumptions and faulty ideas about business activity, development, and how to combat poverty, one ends up with more and more rules about how business should engage with the developing world. On the other hand, if one starts with a positive approach to business, and an appreciation of the risk-taking nature and precariousness of companies as institutions, one thinks about creating and nurturing environments in which competitive enterprise can flourish, and help build the social capital that makes nations great.

There are things that companies can and should do 'beyond the factory gate'. It is in their long-term interests to do so, and should be handled in a far more strategic way than is generally the case.

Companies have an interest in improving local, regional, and national business environments. They have an interest in actions that encourage and consolidate their 'licence to operate' in countries and communities. Business leaders should appreciate and advocate the role of markets and competition in development and social policy. A much more strategic approach to the use of business resources (people, money and influence) for domestic and international policy change and large-scale interventions is required.

This is a complex arena, characterised less by analysis than advocacy. The key is to marry business interests with social involvement and to build on business strengths rather than pretend to be experts in arenas far removed from company activities. Most important is to focus on results far more than has generally been the case in this arena.

Business leaders and business organisations need to think hard before signing up to other people's agendas. They should define their own community, national or global agendas, and on their own terms.

The main contribution of business to development and the 'road out of poverty' is doing business – operating successful companies that pay taxes, employ and train people, and promote economic growth. Every discussion about business and society needs to start here, and recognise its full meaning and impact before moving on to the 'other' things business should, could, or might do.

Current schools of thought about business and its social role are not adequate for the challenges facing companies and business leaders today.

The CSR approach is fundamentally flawed, often but not always more gesture than reality, more a critique of business than a serious and useful contribution to development, and frequently has dangerous consequences for all societies but especially for developing countries. The game being played by western-based companies and international NGOs from rich countries has a short shelf life.

Activists are increasingly calling for the legally enforced regulation of business activities, and are being joined by some large and visible corporations which want their competitors to abide by the same rules the activists are imposing on them. How this will play out in an increasingly global arena in which huge new corporations are emerging from developing countries, hungry for market share and less burdened by the pressures afflicting western business people, remains to be seen. It is unlikely that they will agree to significant constraints on their operations, or the imposition of global standards. It is far more likely that they will reject western-defined notions of 'corporate responsibility', and adopt attitudes more suited to developing country contexts. This will have implications for the current CSR market leaders in the corporate world.

The approach characterised by the slogan 'the business of business is business' is too narrow, and has too many gaps to be helpful to either business leaders or society at large. Continual repetition of this fundamentalist attitude is not useful to companies or governments operating in developing regions, where the threat of an overbearing state is equalled, and perhaps overshadowed, by the reality of no state or a very weak state. It is too often interpreted very narrowly to imply that companies can and should operate in isolation of the societies in which they are embedded.

The notion that corporates should 'do no harm' is also not helpful beyond a certain point, as it ignores the 'creative destruction' at the very heart of capitalism. What is required is a new, more positive approach that starts from a comprehensive description and acknowledgement of the many important ways in which profit-making activity ensures enormous contributions to social progress. A set of ideas to inform such an approach will be put forward in the final chapter.

QUESTIONS YOU'VE WANTED TO ASK THROUGHOUT THE BOOK

In order to avoid any misunderstandings, I will pose and answer a few questions critics may want to ask arising from this analysis.

Can companies do no wrong?

Individual companies can do abhorrent things, and their actions can have negative impacts.

A company could sell a product that has been shown to be harmful to consumers. In apartheid South Africa a company continued to sell skin lighteners to black South Africans after it was found that this product could cause skin cancer. Such companies should be taken to court, and if found guilty they should be severely punished.

A company could enter a poor country, acquire a licence to operate from the ruling dictator or his family, and pay 'royalties' in return, thus strengthening a corrupt government and perhaps an oppressive minority. I would favour legislation in the company's home country that criminalises this kind of corruption as if it had happened there and exposure of the company concerned in the media.

Government should intensify their efforts to combat all fraud and corruption, and laws to this effect should be enforced far more strictly.

Are some companies better than others?

Absolutely.

Opposition to the prevailing notion of CSR does not mean that all companies are equivalent. Companies are run by individuals, and like individuals anywhere, business people operate according to their values and ideas.

Notions of how companies should behave also change. What might have been acceptable in an earlier era is no longer acceptable today. Companies are part of societies, and evolve in line with social mores.

Should companies worry about people and poverty?

Yes.

Ultimately, business is about people – employees, consumers, service providers, and investors. Companies should be concerned about poverty, especially when it affects large percentages of the population. Large-scale poverty may lead to social instability, thus affecting the business environment as well as property rights. Companies need consumers, and have an interest in the largest possible domestic and regional market, which is clearly constrained by poverty. Companies need healthy, well-trained, and highly skilled workers and managers. Corporate interests vary from country to country, and in different business sectors. Global companies have an interest in declining numbers of poor people for all the same reasons as in domestic economies, but also because this demonstrates the empowering and beneficial impact of increased global economic integration.

Are you saying that sweatshops are to be welcomed, and that conditions in them are no problem?

So-called sweatshops are most definitely to be welcomed and encouraged in a developing country or economically backward region.

They represent the first stepping stones into the modern economy for many unskilled people who have no other or far worse options. I cannot think of many countries that have taken off economically which did not start their industrial revolutions with anything but awful (by modern standards) conditions in its mines and factories or on its farms. How else does a country with few other comparative advantages get started?

Are the conditions in these 'sweatshops' a problem? Of course they are. Are they the worst conditions in that particular country?

No. They are the best working conditions on offer to many people, and the workers in them are often the best paid in the country. This is not forced labour.

How does a country move towards better conditions in its workplaces?

The evidence shows that conditions start to improve as labour markets tighten. In other words, as more and more 'sweatshops' and other industrial and modern work opportunities open up, through the expansion of the foreign and domestic business sector. As economic growth expands and starts to take off, democratising pressures also emerge – trade unions, exposure of conditions in the emerging media, and so on. There is nothing inevitable about this, but it's the only sustainable way forward at scale, and we now have enough examples of countries where this is exactly what happened.

Is business getting all the benefits of globalisation?

Of course not.

All sorts of people are benefiting from globalisation. 'Fat cat capitalists' might benefit from globalisation; workers whose pensions are invested in large multinationals might also benefit; and consumers certainly benefit from cheaper goods, but the biggest beneficiaries are workers and their families in poor countries. For example, in Honduras the average clothing worker earns \$13,10 a day, while nearly half the population lives on less than \$2 a day (Entine 2006: 62).

Economic growth and increased international trade has positive results. It generates jobs, taxes, training, and new opportunities for people who have never had them before, and this is all helping national economic development. Hundreds of millions of people in China, India, Vietnam, Malaysia, Chile, Brazil, South Africa, Mauritius, Lesotho, Ghana, former communist countries, and many other places have – partly through globalisation – found opportunities for work and enterprise creation that has helped them to move out of poverty. In all these countries, business and consumers benefit. In industrialised countries we know that inflation has been lowered by increased global trade, and new jobs have been created to meet the needs of large emerging markets.

There are of course losers in the new internationalisation of trade: uncompetitive companies, and those mainly unskilled or less skilled people in richer countries whose jobs have been swept away by the twin forces of technological change (the major factor) and migration of jobs to more competitive places. Countries and cities have to become more and more attractive places in which to do business, as new places, previously off the 'economic' map of possibility, emerge as arenas for enterprise. On the globalisation ledger there are far more winners than losers.

Are all NGOs a bad idea?

Absolutely not.

I am in favour of groups of citizens and individuals exercising their democratic rights to organise around any issue they like, whether it's a domestic or an international issue. Within a society voluntary groups of citizens play enormously important roles in raising issues of concern or looking after people whose needs have been neglected.

The organisations with whom I have real difficulties are those international organisations, mainly based in rich industrialised countries, who claim to represent and know what is good for millions of people in other countries. They may mean well, but I don't like their tactics – they sensationalise issues, generalise from ad hoc examples, and attack companies without putting the situation in context. They are generally biased against corporate activity.

I don't like many of their recommendations, which range from legally enforced global standards to pressurising companies to withdraw from countries altogether without any cost-benefit analysis of either of these courses of action.

Of course they have a right to exist, but I advocate turning a much more critical eye on such organisations, their activities, their mandates, and their interests.

Are you saying that business doesn't and shouldn't care if a society is democratic or not?

No.

I strongly prefer democracy, but this is not always possible. Some exciting business possibilities are found in undemocratic societies. Companies can directly benefit the citizens of those societies by creating employment, have a democratising and empowering impact, and contribute to national economic growth, which often helps to propel a society along a more democratic path.

One of the great strengths of business is its ability to operate under almost any political regime. The durability of economic enterprise – often requiring considerable steadiness of nerve in the midst of turbulence – has resulted in one of democratic South Africa's greatest assets. That country emerged from decades of authoritarian rule with an energetic, reasonably competitive business sector, which puts it ahead of many other developing societies. This steadiness under pressure and ability to risk capital and resources amidst uncertainty is a positive feature of business.

So what should business do in non-democratic societies?

It's important not to generalise.

Each country needs to be looked at individually, and its particular situation assessed. Companies need to look at their interests, and what might be of concern in a specific political situation. A mining company with a 30-40 year investment horizon is obviously in a different situation from a consumer goods company or a textile design business.

In general, companies should invest in less than ideal political situations if they believe they can make money, will not be nationalised – ie, property rights are reasonably secure – and are able to behave in a way consistent with their core business values. Difficult choices will have to be made. Companies operating in less than ideal environments should think through how they are going to cope with a number of difficult issues. In an orderly society subject to the rule of law, issues seem clear-cut, and it is relatively easy to respond to challenges in line with certain principles. In the far less certain, often chaotic, environments in many developing countries, the right way to protect assets and staff and have productive relationships with local communities and national governments, might not be that clear.

Once a company enters a non-democratic society, further difficult issues will arise. Circumstances within countries change. A company operating in China today is one rather small set of interests in a vast state. In twenty years' time, when more, hopefully independent Chinese-owned companies with interests similar to those in western societies might have appeared, the leverage of the business community as a whole might be significantly increased in perhaps a city like Shanghai if not the whole country. And then strategic issues will arise about how to achieve and maintain stability (through democracy, or the retention of one-party rule), and what role individual companies and business leaders might be able to play in such a process.

Sometimes companies exaggerate the limitations on what they can do. Today, many companies which were active in apartheid South Africa would say that they could not speak out about injustice or why apartheid was bad for the country, because of what the government might have done to their business interests. However, some business leaders and companies did speak out more than others, and did not suffer significantly. This is something that can only be closely assessed in a particular country.

On balance, then, I prefer companies to invest in countries where they believe they have viable business opportunities. Calls for disinvestment are often simplistic and misguided. For example, what would be achieved by disinvesting from a country such as Sudan? What would happen to corporate assets, workers, and their families? If no one else will buy the company, will state ownership help the people of Sudan? Or if Chinese enterprises (mostly state-owned) buy the company – as happened when Talisman left Sudan – will that help Sudan?

Companies that do invest in non-democratic countries, or find themselves in a country in which democratic rule is overthrown, need a good political game plan, and the capacity to understand fast-changing dynamics. They will need an excellent communications strategy for both domestic and foreign audiences, and strategic initiatives for handling the complexities of 'licence to operate' politics, both locally and nationally.

Did South African companies do enough to oppose apartheid?

No.

For those, like myself and others, who argued for business leaders to play a larger, more strategic role in changing apartheid South Africa, this had to be done within the context of hard realities. How could the sector perform its economic functions and simultaneously contribute significantly to the process of political change?

The role of business in apartheid South Africa was complex and mixed. Most companies adapted to the prevailing politics, and it was only in the 1980s when the immediate interests of many corporations were threatened, that some business leaders began to speak out more loudly against apartheid, and companies began to act in ways that directly opposed or undermined apartheid policies. Prior to that, business would by and large indicate their opposition to government policies as these affected economic and workplace issues, and then get back to business.

And yet this is only part of the story. From the late 1970s a number of companies funded and supported a large number of NGOs – small community groups, educational projects, health, welfare and other service organisations, research institutes – which played a role in opposing, or providing an alternative to apartheid, and provided bursaries to thousands of black South Africans. They played a meaningful, important role beyond the 'factory gate', which was strongly criticised by other businesses.

Most South African companies were slow to see what their real interests were in a difficult political situation, and did not do enough to oppose apartheid. But then, how many South Africans did? And how would we define enough in any case?

The story of South African business is revealing in respect of what we have called 'invisible corporate citizenship' – that is, companies' indirect, unintended impact on the society. As discussed previously, business moved ahead of other sectors in paving the way towards a non-racial society.

When one raises questions about business and its social role and responsibilities, it is important to be realistic. It is not reasonable to ask more of business leaders than we do of other organisations or individuals. Moreover, issues like these need to be placed in a broader context. Very few South Africans gave up everything to fight against apartheid. Under very difficult circumstances, most black South Africans did not join the ANC or other nationalist opposition movements before or after they were banned. Most people carried on with their lives as best they could. In this context, how do we assess or judge the business sector?

Like the majority of South Africans, business people could have done much more to oppose apartheid. There were sins of omission and commission that need to be examined, and lessons learnt. It is not good enough to apologise profusely and then go back to business as usual, or establish a relationship with the new government which is as uncritical as that with the previous one. The success of democracy and non-racialism will depend on all South Africans – particularly those with more power than others – actively working to build a different society. Business has a vital role to play in this process.

A different set of issues arises when one considers the interests and responsibilities of companies in helping to change societies from within. Here again, circumstances will differ. One of the key variables is the strength of domestic business interests, and how foreign and domestic companies can work together. In apartheid South Africa, it was vital for business leaders and organisations to speak out against racial discrimination. Some did, many didn't. Some companies provided leadership and resources to help change society. Many did not. A few companies correctly identified their longer-term interests, supported non-racial opposition to apartheid, and built relationships with opposition groups, but the vast majority were timid and did too little.

Should companies be free to do anything they want? Should anyone monitor business?

Companies should operate within the law.

Consumers and any other group have the right to monitor the activities of business, and to publicise any genuine wrongdoing by a particular company. Of course, business also has the right to monitor them as well. The most important way of 'disciplining' business or getting the most out of business for society is to ensure that a country has a truly competitive environment, so that companies have to compete with other companies offering the same product. Globalisation increases the potential number of competitors. South Africans recently discovered that the major bread companies were colluding with each other to agree on the price of bread. The country's competition commission rightly imposed a very large fine on the largest company concerned.

A completely different example can be found in Europe. Should western democracies allow their oil and other companies to help build Russian expertise and technical capacity? Russia has already indicated that it intends to use its resources as instruments in international politics. Should companies be allowed to become stakeholders in the Russian economy, thus helping to strengthen a country which could soon 'blackmail' Europe over gas supplies? This is obviously a difficult question, one best handled as part of the domestic politics and public debate in western democracies, as it might be vital for European security. In other words, this issue should not be left to corporations alone, but should rightly be dealt with by governments, parliaments, and all the other processes democratic societies have developed for taking difficult decisions.

Your analysis of CSR might be right, but does this really matter to business?

Yes, it matters a great deal.

How societies think about profit-making and companies is crucial. I am less concerned about the impact of the CSR movement on companies themselves, as nearly all companies will respond vigorously to increased competition, act to protect their interests, and once again act like real businesses. Money and resources will have been wasted on a number of diversionary, unhelpful, and even dangerous initiatives. However, 'living within the lie', where profit-making is seen as something bad, will have negative consequences for business, government, and society.

The precautionary principle inherent in so much of the attacks on business entails real risks for social progress. If corporate leaders are not clear about the benefits of their companies and the importance of markets and companies for social welfare, they become part of the problem. Too many politicians take successful enterprise for granted, and think that adding more regulations or additional accountability measures will have no impact on companies' core business and bottom lines. This is dangerous for the process of innovation and risk-taking at the heart of capitalism.

Reuters chairman Niall Fitzgerald has argued:

> If companies did not exist, and you wanted a means for delivering innovation, you would have to create them. In competitive markets, the ability to innovate … is central to the survival of the company. Innovation involves new sciences and technologies, access to raw materials and in some cases finite resources. It may involve new ways of working and patterns of organization. These are often contentious areas that are within the law but breaking new ground. For the company to succeed in delivering innovation, the confidence and trust of society in the principles and values guiding corporate leadership is essential (Fitzgerald & Cormack 2006: 8).

The critics' desire to insert a 'precautionary principle' into almost every aspect of business life is a dangerous idea that could hamper, perhaps even cripple, the risk-taking experimental nature of enterprise – the key source of its vitality. As Michael Porter and Mark Kramer have noted:

> If governments, NGOs and other participants in civil society weaken the ability of business to operate productively, they may win battles, but will lose the war, as corporate and regional competitiveness fade, wages stagnate, jobs disappear and the wealth that pays taxes and supports non-profit contributions evaporates (2006: 7).

As the economic crisis that began in 2008 has illustrated, globalisation is not an irreversible process and the battle of ideas in this arena continues. Another era of economic stagnation and protectionist retreat behind national borders would hurt everyone, especially those with the least resources to survive a downturn. In this context, it is foolish and contrary to their own best interests for business leaders to repeat, support, or promulgate the faulty ideas inherent in the critique of globalisation, especially false notions about companies. Corporate acquiescence to activist demands in the discussion of global labour, environmental, and other standards will feed into protectionist politics in rich countries, which will be bad for developing countries. Business needs to strengthen the forces in rich countries arguing against protectionism, not support those interests raising obstacles to investment and new jobs in developing countries.

The consequences of protectionism in rich countries will be serious for developing economies. As the OECD puts it:

> Protectionism in the North in the form of export subsidies price support mechanisms and other trade distorting domestic support measures, tends to destroy markets in the South as they lead to overproduction and drive down world prices to levels where farmers cannot compete. … Many industrialized countries impose high tariff barriers against agricultural imports protecting their

farmers from more competitive producers in Asia, Africa and South America. More troubling, tariffs are even higher for processed food, discouraging developing countries from upgrading their food industry (International Chamber of Commerce 2004: 9-10).

Instead of focusing on the key development challenges that hold back economic growth – increasing national competitiveness, and creating a better environment in which to do business – too many companies spend too much attention on welfarist approaches to development. Many companies are fiddling around with numerically insignificant projects or supporting collectivist or failed approaches to development such as the MDGs, an undue focus on aid, or other international fads.

The almost universal acceptance of the premises and main arguments of the 'responsibility' school of thought contributes to the anti-business tone of much public discussion. In accepting that companies have a case to answer, and one that is uniquely onerous (what other sector of society has to specifically define its social responsibility?), business advocates of CSR or those who accept many of its assumptions contribute to undermine the legitimacy of business activity.

Advocates of CSR downgrade the primary role of business, and undermine the claim of profit-oriented enterprise to legitimacy and recognition. They push the debate about business and society to focus on 'what else' business can or should do rather than on its core functions and activities. In the process they divert attention away from important challenges companies need to deal with, and core business issues are neglected: weaknesses in the way in which companies are governed; how innovation and risk-taking in the financial sector need to be managed and regulated; the incentives for remuneration in the financial sector; and how executives are remunerated and made accountable for their failures.

CONCLUDING REMARKS

The case for business is a persuasive one. It's just a pity that so few voices are prepared to make it, unambiguously, powerfully, and without apology.

The misconceptions inherent in the attacks on business and the CSR perspective are not trivial. They could have major negative consequences reaching far beyond individual societies and particular companies.

Let us now turn to what business should do about all of this – how, in fact, business leaders can 'stand up for business and the global economy', and promote their own agenda.

Chapter Eleven

BEYOND APPEASEMENT —
THE REAL BUSINESS AGENDA

*'In the arena of public opinion and public policy, tigers in
competition have appeared before the public as lambs,
bleating in appeasement.'*

Michael Novak, *On Corporate Governance* (1997b)

THERE IS no persuasive alternative to an enterprise-driven, market-based approach to economic growth. And yet, in countries in which capitalist endeavour has produced the highest standards of living in human history, business has been placed on the defensive. David Henderson has argued persuasively that business is complicit in its own prosecution:

> … Many large corporations that have come out for CSR whether directly or through organisations which they have created and continue to finance, have lent support to ideas and beliefs that are dubious or false. On behalf of business, they have been ready to endorse uncritically, ill defined and questionable objectives; to confess imaginary sins; to admit to non-existent privileges and illusory gains from globalization that require justification in the eyes of 'society'; to identify the demands of NGOs with 'society's expectations' and treat them as beyond question; to accept over-dramatized and misleading interpretations of recent world economic trends and their implications for business; and in some cases to condemn outright the economic system of which private business forms an integral part (2001: 58).

In this chapter, I want to point the way towards a different agenda. First, however, it is necessary to examine why and how business has allowed this situation to develop.

BUSINESS AND ITS STRATEGIC WEAKNESSES

It is important to frankly and realistically assess some of the issues and constraints affecting business as a social actor.

Business sells its critics the rope with which it is hanged

In the first half of the 20th century, Joseph Schumpeter produced his brilliant, modern analysis of capitalism. It was he who turned Karl Marx's 'hateful gangs of parasitic capitalists' into innovative, beneficent entrepreneurs. In 1943 he argued that 'the public mind has by now so thoroughly grown out of humour with (business), as to make condemnation of capitalism and all its works almost a requirement of the etiquette of discussion' (McCraw 2007: 351).

Schumpeter's words could apply to many dinner parties in the capitals of the world's richest countries today, and are the common currency of pulpit and academia. In the face of the sentiments they express, most corporate executives have wobbled and failed to defend not only specific activities but the very rationale of corporate existence. I have found few speeches by a current corporate executive that is an unapologetic argument for profit-making and capitalism.

This lack of conviction has bred appeasement. Some 2 000, at most 3 000, of the largest companies in the world now act as the cheerleaders for 'responsible' companies. Many executives seem so defensive about the value of capitalism, business and corporations that we have moved beyond them selling their enemies the means by which they will be hanged (viz Hayek); they are now more likely to give it to them as a grant.

Companies often encourage more pressures on themselves

The boundaries of 'social responsibility' are imprecise. Even senior executives find it difficult to define the limits to social engagement. Two examples are illustrative.

In December 2007 a large business grouping called the Global Business Coalition on HIV/AIDS, Tuberculosis and Malaria placed an advertisement in the *Financial Times* to inform the public what they were doing to help combat HIV/AIDS. What was curious was that there was no mention at all about how corporate expenditure and effort should be seen in the context of a wider response. Not one word about the responsibilities of national governments in responding to the epidemic.

By failing to situate the generous business response in the context of appropriate roles and responsibilities for all actors – especially governments and individuals – this ill-thought-through intervention was a clear example of business contributing to the pressures on it to 'always do more', and 'shoulder more than its fair share'.

In 2003 the CEO of Nestlé, Peter Brabeck-Letmathe, while making due obeisance to engaging in 'responsible business', applied himself to the tricky task of defining the boundaries of this engagement. He argued that there were three broad categories of 'boundary' that

companies should apply:
- basic non-negotiables (obey the law and stay in business);
- complex non-negotiables (manage risk and minimise harm); and
- negotiables (create positive solutions beyond what is required by law, risk management and the protection of short-term value) (Davies & Nelson 2003: 7).

Despite its contorted formulation, this is probably one of the better definitions. However, the implications for managers in, say, Indonesia or other developing countries far from sedate Switzerland are less than clear. This lack of clarity is likely to multiply rather than curtail business responsibilities.

Business has failed to appreciate the full extent of the forces working to undermine its legitimacy

Business operates in an environment in which most other major actors do not appreciate its merits.

Many politicians and senior government officials do not appreciate the hard work involved in starting and maintaining successful companies. They do not respect business or its achievements; take businesses for granted; frequently see them as entities to be controlled, taxed, made more accountable, or at best encouraged to do what governments want them to do. Many journalists (outside the financial media) do not appreciate the difficulties of running a successful business. Many also assume that business is inherently immoral, and pursue stories of individual miscreants which confirm this perception. The 'gotcha' mentality of the media and the pursuit of sensationalism in order to sell newspapers do not contribute to a supportive environment. The lack of business heroes in novels or on

TV and movie screens also helps to perpetuate the generally negative image of commercial endeavour. The irony is that, in Hollywood, these negative images of business are being created and perpetuated by some of the largest companies in the world.

The roots of anti-business sentiment start early. In 2008 *Newsweek*'s Stefan Theil examined the way in which German and French school textbooks deal with business – with startling results. According to a major French textbook studied for university entrance exams, economic growth leads to overwork, stress, nervous depression, cardiovascular disease, even cancer. It tells students that entrepreneurs are linked with the technology bubble, the Nasdaq crash, and massive redundancies. Another French textbook describes capitalism as 'brutal', 'savage', and 'American' (Theil 2008).

German textbooks depict company managers as idle, cigar-smoking plutocrats, and link them to child labour, Internet fraud, mobile phone addiction, alcoholism, and redundancies. Germany's rich entrepreneurial history is all but ignored. Another text explains that China and India are successful because they practise state ownership; conversely, it says the freest markets exist in sub-Saharan Africa, thus implying that unrestrained capitalism has disastrous consequences. Theil concludes that:

> ... the surprise is the intensity of the anti-market bias. Students learn that companies destroy jobs, while government policy creates them. Globalization is destructive if not catastrophic. Business is a zero-sum game. If this is the belief system within which most students develop intellectually, is it any wonder that French and German reformers are so easily shouted down? (ibid).

A business strategy that concentrates almost all its energy on trying to reach accommodation with campaigning NGOs and their supporters in government is far too narrowly focused.

The individualistic nature of businesses is a strategic weakness

The term business describes a category of behaviour, not a collective set of actors. By its nature many business people are individualistic, highly competitive, and egotistic. Collective action is difficult and frequently boils down to the lowest common denominator.

Numerous companies have been isolated and 'smeared' by activist groups. Entire industries have been attacked and branded in negative ways – from Big Pharma through the oil and mining companies to the 'insurance giants'. Nonetheless, the most common response by most companies has been to quietly wait and hope that they will not be next. When they are, they are frequently totally unprepared for the campaign against them.

One recent example of this is Wal-Mart. This giant corporation seemed taken aback as attacks on it started to mount in 2004 and 2005. Why the world's largest corporation thought it would be immune to criticism (by activist NGOs in alliance with disgruntled unions) is unfortunately a typical reaction by corporate leaders. Wal-Mart eventually established a 'War Room', filled with operatives (strategists, spin doctors, etc) from the Clinton presidency, to respond to these attacks, but only did so in late 2005.

Wal-Mart's commissioned research on the company's beneficial impact on American inflation appeared only in late 2005. A documentary movie in its defence appeared only when opponents had already released their documentary attacking the company. Why did the company not prepare a multifaceted strategy much earlier on?

One would have thought that large corporations would prepare in advance for an inevitable attack. That large companies would talk to each other about what could be done by individual companies to deal with these attacks, and what might be done collectively by business leaders and organisations to seize the high ground and not wait to be picked off, one by one.

Business has failed to put together a compelling account of its positive impact ...

At no stage has business (individual companies or organisations) tried to pull together a persuasive case in its own defence. A few documents defending globalisation have emanated from business organisations and the OECD, but little else is readily available.

Few companies have done the detailed work of itemising and assessing the positive ramifications of their normal business activity or their sector and its impact on society. This is not a call for a taxonomic listing of dry facts but an imaginative campaign telling the full, complex story of a company's direct and indirect impact on a country, region or continent.

Business should document the full economic and developmental impact of corporate activity, and explain why this is the only approach to sustained development. Doing this properly requires some PR imagination as well as unimpeachable research.

Big companies have tended to focus their attention on core business functions, while regarding social and political issues as peripheral. They need to make greater efforts to understand the political and social context in which they operate and how to engage successfully.

As India, China, Brazil, Indonesia, and other emerging markets start to play a growing role in the global economy, their governments, companies, workers, unions and consumers will become increasingly important. They will be far more important allies for business in the longer term than self-appointed western organisations with no real standing in and understanding of those countries.

At the height of the anti-globalisation protests why did no company or business organisation bring Indian trade union leaders to Washington or Seattle to speak for globalisation and against global standards? Or small business organisations or farmers from developing countries to explain the implications of increased standards and regulations for their activities? Why are western companies not talking to the governments of India, Brazil, Mexico, and other emerging economies about these issues and how best to stop minority interests in industrialised countries imposing protectionist standards, thus holding back growth in poorer countries?

To devise effective communication and other political strategies for companies or groups of companies or sectors of industry requires the right help. Instead of hiring former activists to drive a company's social activities or responsibility agenda, why not hire professional communications experts, risk managers, and crisis management 'hawks' who support enterprise and are eager to defend it (Nichols 2002). Where are the political scientists, economists and sociologists hired to think about a pro-business strategy for an industry, or company? Where are the academics encouraged to write textbooks on business and its contribution to national development in different countries? Where are the competitions to encourage filmmakers to produce documentaries and films that reflect a more balanced picture of business?

... and those businesses that try inevitably slip back into defensive mode

When trawling through speeches by business leaders and documents produced by business organisations, one very infrequently comes across attempts to boldly explain the role of business in human progress. A good example is the World Business Council for Sustainable Development publication entitled *The Role of Business in Tomorrow's Society* (2006). Under the heading 'Business does good by doing business', the report opens by making the case for the positive impact of business in unambiguous terms:

> Any successful company will both create shareholder value and operate responsibly. ... Most companies benefit society simply by doing business. We meet customers' needs for goods and services. We create jobs. We pay wages and salaries. We provide for employees and families through pensions and health plans. We innovate to create products that contribute to human progress. We pay taxes that fund public services and infrastructure. We create work for millions of suppliers, many of them small- and medium-sized companies. Our search for competitive advantage leads to efficiency, and thus to reduced consumption of resources, less pollution, and higher quality products. The purpose of any business that seeks to be sustainable has to be more than generating short-term shareholder value. ... This includes building trust among communities and maintaining a healthy environment in which to do business. All of these benefits are created in the normal course of responding to the market (WBCSD 2006).

However, the reader's excitement generated by this positive start soon dissipates. Throughout the rest of the report, the lessons of this insight appear to be lost. Rather than arguing for the expansion of business to enhance its beneficial effects, the report deals with all the other things business must do in order to be 'responsible', including the introduction of CSR programmes, and the curbing of business activities in the name of 'social responsibility'. This is typical of speeches by many business leaders.

Concluding remarks

There is no objective reason why business should be on the defensive about its social role. There is no need for business to wait for hostile forces to amass support for anti-market views, and then react in a defensive way.

What is required is an awareness of common business interests; an understanding of the positive role that business does play in society, both inadvertent and deliberate; an appreciation of the diverse forces encouraging a negative attitude to companies; the development of institutional mechanisms for defining and agreeing on common interests, and effective strategies for promoting them.

What would such a positive, politically astute, and globally relevant business strategy look like?

THE REAL AGENDA FOR BUSINESS

'It's time for the CEOs of big companies to recast the Friedman versus corporate social responsibility debate and recapture the intellectual and moral high ground from their critics ...'

Ian Davis, *The Economist* (2005)

Find new allies

One of the issues business leaders worry about is that if they do start to play a more active public role, they and their companies will be highly visible, and make the business sector in general a more prominent target for their critics. This is a valid concern in some respects. However, the idea that 'going along to get along' will work is an illusion. And companies are being criticised all the time in any case. If more companies become more assertive about the value of what they are doing, this will make it harder to isolate individual corporations.

In addition, companies can fund other voices and institutions to defend business activity, and corporate leaders have more allies than may be immediately apparent. The strategic trick is to mobilise them effectively.

Forge alliances with interests in developing countries

One of the new opportunities in the global economy is that business leaders who are willing and ready to defend market processes and the expansion of business activities can now seek to form alliances with interests in developing countries – seldom present or heard in the current conversation.

Multinational business leaders should establish a (politically astute) working alliance with the governments of developing countries, their business communities, trade unions, and other market-based interests in those societies. Democratic developing countries such as India, Brazil, South Africa, and Mexico are good places to start, especially as they themselves provide the base for the emergence of new multinational companies.

What would such an alliance do? First and foremost, it should establish an energetic, effective policy and advocacy presence in world centres such as London, Washington, New York, Geneva, and Brussels. These offices should be mandated to ensure that the interests of developing country nations in expanded economic growth, greater globalisation, more trade (and on fairer terms) are represented in important forums.

In order to be effective and really have a powerful influence over the terms of the debate about business, globalisation, and development, the necessary materials (books, reports, documentaries on business and society, globalisation and the positive role of multinationals) need to be produced. They should be widely distributed and used to counter unrepresentative, mainly first world groups and other interests from propagating ideas and policies harmful to developing countries, without vocal and effective opposition.

Involve economic ministries in the debate

In both industrialised and developing countries, ministries dealing with various aspects of the economy are rarely involved in many of these 'responsibility' issues; these include ministries and departments responsible for the treasury, taxation, trade and industry, and key sectors of the economy. They could also include the Reserve Bank or the international advisory councils a number of presidents have established to help them formulate economic policy. The politicians and officials involved in these institutions need to be exposed to the issues, and the pressures and interests working against the expansion of markets and business activity.

Business should look for allies in domestic politics as well

Each country will be different, but many diverse groups in society have an interest in or will benefit from greater economic growth and more opportunities for companies to start up and prosper. These include smaller businesses, aspirant entrepreneurs, workers, urban governments, national ministries charged with growth and development concerns. On selected issues, coalitions and alliances can be established.

Develop and argue the case for business, markets, and globalisation

In order to muster the most effective case for business, markets, and international trade, a dossier of reports needs to be produced to substantiate and demonstrate the enormously powerful and positive role of competitive enterprise in the global economy.

Companies should produce authoritative reports on the social impact of their everyday business activities, whether nationally, regionally and globally. Very few companies have produced anything like this. The few reports that do exist have often been hastily produced in response to an attack of some kind or they are so dry that no one would read them. They usually cover only some aspects of the direct impact of corporate activity – taxes paid, employees trained, health care provided, pensions paid, local governments supported. Even less has been written about what I have called 'invisible corporate citizenship' – the profoundly important indirect consequences of corporate activities.

The tone of the report should not be defensive. It should make readers feel that their country or continent is lucky to have such a company operating in its borders. This would immediate place the discussion on a different footing – we are already doing all these things, now what else do you think we might be able to fit in? Such reports would also help to influence governments about to impose fresh restrictions on businesses or hesitant about allowing large foreign companies into their economy.

Amidst the plethora of positive impacts of company activity there will also be potential or actual negative effects as well. For example, changes in sourcing and rapid reconfiguring of supply chains can leave small suppliers with no market for their products, and affect employment. Companies and their boards should fully understand the impact of their activities, and act to minimise any negative impacts and maximise their positive spin-offs. They should also put forward constructive proposals for how local, regional or national governments can work with companies to minimise these negatives.

A compelling document should be written on the role of companies in global and national prosperity. This should provide the foundation for a new, forthright, positive approach to business. It needs to be packed with surprising, interesting stories of how corporate activity has created wealth and helped to build nations, cities, regions, and empowered and enriched their citizens. Building on both the direct and indirect impact of everyday business activity as well as the many other contributions that companies have already and can make, a persuasive document can be produced on how companies – big and small, formal, informal, public and private – have helped to transform lives and modernise societies.

Each one of these reports should be used to start changing the terms of the conversation about business and society. They need to be written by experts, and produced by the right processes. They need to reflect the concerns of companies in both developed and developing countries and the process should not be dominated by experts in developed countries.

Develop clear positions on business and development issues

Critics of business and globalisation demand that business should 'fill the gap in global governance', or deal with large-scale challenges of disease or disadvantage that are being ignored or neglected by developing country governments. Their ideas are often entirely unrealistic, far removed from a legitimate business agenda (reforming global institutions, for instance), or simply implacably opposed to markets and business. Instead, the global and national conversation about business and development should be placed on a sounder, more realistic footing. This should start with some compelling additional documents that will form the basis for a wider strategy. These should include:

A document dealing with a market-based approach to growth, development, and poverty reduction in developing countries. It is striking how often business leaders ignore the role of markets outside strictly economic arenas. This report should set out the positive role of markets and private enterprise in development, concentrating mainly on profit-making activities but also including 'extramural' contributions by individual companies or groups of companies. Its first and one of its most important target groups would be business leaders themselves.

A competitiveness charter or agenda. This should be a set of priorities that constitute the essential ingredients in making countries competitive arenas for investment, expansion of business and long term growth – the only way to reduce poverty and ensure sustained development. These should deal with world-class telecommunications, infrastructure, administrative competence, safety and security of people and property, export logistics, urban management, border controls, port development, education, training, and so on. Rather than the MDGs, a set of competitiveness goals that will help countries produce wealth, encourage enterprise and through these means reduce poverty. This should not only deal with country competitiveness but how to make national economies more competitive themselves.

Guidelines for doing business in developing countries, and how governments can make the most of foreign investment. It would be useful for multinational companies and developing country governments to develop some guidelines for corporate behaviour in terms of the difficult issues they confront in many countries. The guidelines should be voluntary and need to emerge out of discussion among domestic and international companies as well as national governments. They should deal with technology transfer (the Chinese or Costa Rican experience could be a useful example), intellectual and property rights, political, security, social, human rights, and environmental issues. They need to be realistic and appropriate to developing countries. If they are too complex, too bureaucratic or too demanding, they will merely raise the costs of doing business and therefore stifle investment. They should not attempt to impose western standards in developing countries.

What about corporate social investment? This precious after-tax money needs to be spent wisely. *A 'drop in the ocean' when it comes to dealing with social issues at scale, this resource needs to be leveraged to ensure maximum impact.* Instead of adopting an agenda written by their critics, or delegating this function to juniors, business leaders should pay far more attention to identifying and thinking through corporate priorities in this arena. A strategic approach is required that focuses far more on business interests and how best to influence the national and international policy and institutional environment to be supportive of enterprise.

All the relevant facts and insights about the appropriate role of business in the matrix of development should be placed – strategically, imaginatively – in global and national arenas of discussion. Business should involve itself fully in the debate about how to develop countries, regions, or communities in a market-supporting way that is cognisant of national and developmental realities and sustainable in the long term.

DON'T WAIT TO BE ATTACKED;
SEIZE THE HIGH GROUND

M any of the preceding recommendations are attempts to 'seize the high ground' on a range of issues. There are two additional areas in which pre-emptive work by business could be beneficial.

The first are areas of corporate weakness. Companies are not perfect, and market dynamics may give rise to negative trends in business practice. As a result, business leaders should think about publishing an authoritative report on corporate governance, dealing with issues such as executive remuneration, executive accountability, and political lobbying. It should frankly examine the thorny ethical issues facing corporations in these and other areas, and recommend changes. This would demonstrate that companies are willing and able to respond to public concern where this is warranted. In the process, business can play a larger role in shaping national and international discussions of these topics. In this way business leaders move ahead of the game, not reacting defensively but forcing others to be practical and, rather than slinging mud, actually making reasonable suggestions.

A document on *How to seize the high ground in the event of a corporate attack* would also be useful. More is now known about the organisations that launch and coordinate attacks on large companies, and the best ways of responding to different kinds of 'brand-jacking'. Has any company commissioned serious analytical and political work assessing, say, the Nike campaign, the Nestlé campaign, or the Wal-Mart campaign? I have been unable to find anything like this in the public domain. Perhaps some canny business leaders have such a report in their bottom drawers, but I am sceptical.

Such a manual should contain advice on 'turning the tables', and how to raise a series of questions about organisational governance, ethics, transparency, and accountability as they affect NGOs, unions and other institutions. Why should companies be the only 'responsible' social players? What about other voluntary organisations? Using the current mechanisms that regulate and deal with malfeasance in the corporate sector, a range of useful and probing questions could be inserted into the public debate about NGOs, government departments, multilateral institutions, and how exactly they use and account for public money. Comparing the rules that govern business with those affecting other parts of society would be instructive in itself.

CHANGE PERCEPTIONS OF AND ATTITUDES TO BUSINESS

Other steps must be taken to strengthen the voice of pro-market advocates in the international arena, and to ensure that a more balanced and fair representation of business starts to emerge. Companies can start to use their resources in their own interests in the world of public policy; reformers in governments can be enrolled to assist as well. Money speaks, and it's time to provide incentives for pro-market voices to emerge and be strengthened.

Business should commission an authoritative study of what is being taught about business in schools in various world regions. The results of this study should be examined and new textbooks lobbied for, written, and distributed.

In 1973 David Packard, chairman of Hewlett-Packard, argued that business should continue supporting higher education but should no longer give universities unrestricted grants that gave them complete control over how the funds were used. He asked whether universities should serve as 'havens for radicals' who wanted to destroy the free enterprise system, and whether students should be taught that American corporations were evil and deserved to be brought under government control. He believed this was happening at far too many institutions, and that unrestricted corporate dollars underwrote much of the problem (Miller 2006: 37). Without threatening academic freedom in any way, corporate funding could be used to encourage research on topics that support the market system and a positive (or at minimum balanced and fair) view of business; establish centres of specialisation and excellence on companies and markets, and the impact they have on national development; and create academic chairs for professors working on topics relevant to corporate concerns in this arena.

Business should also encourage the voices of pro-market individuals and institutions to be heard in the print and electronic media as well as on the Internet.

American corporations, foundations, and individual donors have helped to establish influential pro-market centres and think-tanks in the USA. Very little has been done to encourage such centres in developing countries. The Atlas Foundation is doing a valiant job but most of its free market think-tanks around the world are tiny operations. A much more concerted effort to support market-based thinking on development issues is required, and here again corporate support could make an enormous difference. Business has hitherto tended to leave this to others. An examination of most large American foundations indicates that many of them do not like business and will not fund market friendly initiatives or think-tanks. The reason why Henry Ford II resigned from the board of trustees of the Ford Foundation in the 1970s would still hold for many business-funded foundations today. As would the comment of John Knowles of the Rockefeller Foundation who suggested in response to the Henry Ford letter that organisations such as his own did not need to concern themselves with strengthening capitalism because corporations would do it on their own (ibid: 189).

WHY HENRY FORD II QUIT THE FORD FOUNDATION

In 1977 Henry Ford II announced that he was resigning from the board of trustees of the Ford Foundation, America's largest foundation at that time, with an endowment of $2,3 billion. Ford had been a trustee since 1943, and his departure meant that for the first time the foundation would not have a member of the family on its board. The foundation's commitment to left-wing politics compelled him to quit. In a four-page letter of resignation, he stated that:

'... the foundation exists and thrives on the fruits of our economic system. The dividends of competitive enterprise make it all possible. A significant proportion of the abundance created by US business enables the foundation and like institutions to carry on their work. In effect the foundation is a creature of capitalism. ... It is hard to discern recognition of this fact in anything the foundation does. It is even more difficult to find an understanding of this in many of the institutions, particularly the universities, that are the beneficiaries of the foundation's grant programs.

'... the system that makes the foundation possible very probably is worth preserving. Perhaps it is time for the trustees and staff to examine the question of our obligations to our economic system and to consider how the foundation as one of the system's most prominent offspring might act most wisely to strengthen and improve its progenitor' (Miller 2006: 188-9).

Individual companies and the representative business organisations they fund need to think hard about how to change the way in which business is portrayed and talked about in the key institutions of our societies. They need to focus on how to strengthen voices that support market economics and the role of companies in the countries in which they operate, as well as any international processes in which they are involved. They also need to think about encouraging market-based approaches to national policy-making and development strategy for developing countries or neglected communities. They need to dovetail their strategies and expenditure with the global thrust to change the terms of the entire debate.

THE SELLING OF IDEAS AND THE DEFENCE OF BUSINESS AND MARKETS MUST BE TAKEN AS SERIOUSLY AS PRODUCT MARKETING

A professional, well-funded campaign – set of campaigns really – should be mounted to put across the facts, arguments and ideas that will emerge from the series of reports suggested above. They should be aimed at disrupting the terms of what is now a well-established discourse so as to highlight the positive benefits of enterprise and markets. To do this will require serious consideration of how to communicate these ideas and how to insert all these reports into which audiences, in which order and at what time. This is not a job for amateurs.

Influential corporate leaders across the globe need to be mobilised to use and support these reports and the ideas they espouse, and developing country governments, and other interests must be enrolled to help spread them.

It seems redundant to suggest that business leaders – who manage very large marketing campaigns for their products – need to think afresh about how to communicate in imaginative ways, but when it comes to standing up for business this needs to be the case. The marketing of ideas like these has not traditionally been a corporate activity, and will require new expertise and political understanding. This will need to be married to the more traditional skills of corporate marketing departments. So a key part of the entire set of ideas rests on the development of a professional, well-pitched, multifaceted and phased global marketing campaign that resonates with different audiences in different countries.

Reports alone are not enough

Corporate resources should be devoted to conferences and speaking tours by prominent experts and corporate leaders. For example, the World Economic Forum in Davos and subsequent regional forums around the world should be used as powerful platforms to stand up for business, markets, and globalisation – unapologetically. Business should demand that these new alliances and perspectives be put on the table at meetings of multilateral organisations. Corporations should work with the potential 'alliance' partners identified earlier and others in promoting these facts and ideas on business and development in creative ways.

There is an important link between the activities I am proposing at the global level and those that should be undertaken by individual companies. In time, they will start to reinforce each other.

Individual companies should ensure that responsibility for their business and society activities are assigned to senior executives, perhaps even the CEO, and regularly discussed at board meetings. This broad field needs to include all the issues we have been discussing, from how to present the contribution of the company to national and global development in the most positive way, through analysing the current political environment affecting that product and industry, to knowing what pressures are developing around the company in question.

Professional communication that plays its part in the 'battle of ideas' about business is important. The De Beers diamond company has run an excellent advertisement in South Africa depicting three African women with greying hair, sitting solidly in their chairs. The caption states: 'Meet the shareholders of our company. ... Not quite who you had in mind.' This is a clever way of shaking up traditional concepts of who owns De Beers. It also touches on a vital issue that companies have largely neglected when trying to communicate their value to society. The millions of shareholders in the largest companies stretch far and deep into society. Why don't companies make more of this when they are attacked for putting 'profits before people'?

In essence, companies need to find ways of ensuring that (the very many aspects of) the creative dimension of 'creative destruction' is communicated in much more effective ways.

In the battle of ideas about business as a positive force in countries, companies need as many ambassadors as possible. Often the first place to start is by ensuring that company employees, managers and executives are all fully informed about the company, its direct and indirect social impact, and how to engage with the many questions about its role in an unfriendly or untrusting external environment. After all, they (and their families) are members of society too. Beyond the company itself, members of wider networks with which the company interacts should also be informed about its social impact, and 'enrolled' as informal envoys for business. This would include suppliers, contractors, subcontractors, consultants, shareholders, and retirees.

Don't fund your enemies ...

William Simon, former secretary of the United States Treasury, put this well when he said: 'Capitalism has no duty to subsidise its enemies' (Poole 1982).

Most business leaders are mystified when one raises this issue. The business supported World Wildlife Fund sounds like an organisation no one could oppose – but then one discovers that it was part of the anti-globalisation protests in Seattle in 1999. So companies and business leaders need to know who their enemies are, and ensure that they are not being funded somewhere in the corporation. This requires an understanding of the politics and funding linkages and interconnections between organisations on the left.

Companies should not provide support for enemies of the market and business; nor should they legitimise their views, or their claims to represent 'poor people', 'civil society' or 'the environment'.

Companies need to think carefully about participating in UN or other multilateral institutions or initiatives that give undue influence to unrepresentative NGOs, or place a few corporate executives in positions where they supposedly 'represent' business. One has to understand that, for many activists, politics and public policy issues are a full-time career, whereas for chief executives this is not the case. One has to take the politics of international NGO survival and their need for sensational campaigns very seriously indeed.

... but identify and support your friends

Companies and business organisations need to identify and support 'market-friendly' voices in the global and national policy arenas.

Business needs to help ensure that these voices are heard much more loudly than hitherto in international and national institutions and forums. Companies can ensure that they have the funds they need to maximise their contribution to a hopefully growing orchestra of pro-market institutions speaking up for business and its positive role in society.

Don't play alone. A more sophisticated approach to 'selling' the positive role of companies in society does not mean that companies or business leaders should do this on their own. Business should enlist other interests in issue-based coalitions, and strengthen pro-market forces, institutions and individuals. Often there are prominent people in politics or government who support pro-market policies and ideas, but they need to be fortified. Pro-market think-tanks can play a vital role in developing the application of market thinking to national policy issues, for example, providing cabinet ministers with information and arguments in their internal debates about policy options. The business sector in a given country should think strategically about how all the 'arrows in their quiver' can be used to influence the general business environment, or particular policy issue. In the global arena, some developing country governments and some trade unions will be useful allies in resisting the imposition of rich country standards that would threaten existing and potential jobs in their countries.

I have put forward eight different strategic thrusts that could start to tip the balance in the battle of ideas about business and society. How would this play out in a country and perhaps a regional context?

THE REAL BUSINESS AGENDA

Find new allies

- Form an alliance with developing country governments and other interests in developing countries

- Form alliances with economic ministries in rich and poorer countries
- Identify interests who have a stake in more business activity (eg small enterprise, trade unions seeking more jobs and more members) and more liberalisation in each country

Stand up for business, markets and globalisation

Develop individual company reports and three authoritative, globally oriented reports that demonstrate:

- The impact of everyday business activity of large individual companies in the many sectors and countries in which they operate
- The collective global impact of large multinational companies in their everyday business activities – direct and indirect consequences of profit seeking activity – which help make the world a better place
- The role of markets, states and companies in global and national prosperity
- The case for increased globalisation and the positive role of multinational and other companies in this process; including the argument against protectionism and the harm it does and will cause in both rich and developing countries

Develop clear positions about business, development and poverty

Produce four persuasive reports dealing with:

- A market-based approach to growth, development and the significant reduction of poverty for developing countries, including the positive role of markets and enterprise in development (involving large multinationals and smaller companies)
- Key targets or priorities in achieving increased national

competitiveness (eg education, infrastructure) and liberalisation of trade and an improved environment in which to do business; perhaps a competitiveness charter or MDGs for competitiveness

▫ Guidelines for doing business in developing countries; and how governments can make the most of foreign direct investment

▫ A strategic approach to corporate social investment that relates to business interests in achieving a licence to operate, clarity on how best to leverage private money and influence government policy and expenditure, promoting market based approaches to national delivery and development challenges

Don't wait to be attacked; seize the high ground

▫ Get ahead of the game on corporate governance issues such as executive accountability, remuneration and so on

▫ Think through how to deal with corporate attacks (as a business sector and as individual companies)

▫ Insist on other organisations becoming as accountable and as transparent as business (NGOs, government departments etc)

Change society's perceptions and attitudes to business

▫ Ensure that markets, business, capitalism and globalisation are getting fair treatment in school textbooks

▫ Stop providing corporate money for universities without thinking through their approach to business and how best to promote pro-market voices without in any way infringing on academic freedom

▫ Provide incentives for market-oriented films, TV series, novels, documentaries, journalism etc

- Establish and support market-oriented think-tanks on public policy and national and global development issues

Take the selling of ideas and the defence of business as seriously as product marketing

- Make this an executive accountability and item of board agenda discussion
- Run professional communication and 'change the terms of debate' campaigns
- Ensure that the frontline of company managers, employees, contractors and others are informed about the company's positive impact of doing business

Don't fund your enemies

- Make sure you know who is opposed to the market economy and how they operate
- Do not fund them or parent foundations or bodies who might in turn fund them
- Do not provide them with legitimacy or credibility or in any way promote their claims to represent anyone other than themselves

Know your friends, support and strengthen them

- Know who your potential allies might be, and aim to increase their strength and number
- Ensure that they are represented at national and international discussions on development, globalisation and the role of business.
- Don't play alone. Use all the organisations you fund and support to promote the positive role of business in many different ways.

THE NATIONAL BUSINESS AGENDA

Different countries have different needs and priorities. The prevailing politics around business and its social role will also differ considerably.

The first requirement is a strategic overview of a country's economic and political prospects. Within that framework one needs to develop a *national business agenda,* whose main elements will vary from country to country, depending on their levels of political and economic development as well as their particular cultural and historical trajectories. However, whatever priorities emerge from this strategic overview should be pursued in a broadly similar way, whatever the national context.

The national business agenda in any country will need to be coupled with effective implementing institutions based on effective business organisations.

Business and its allies should strive to change general perceptions of and attitudes to business and its social role through strategic initiatives involving education and the media.

Companies and business organisations should be clear on appropriate roles and relationships involving the state – national, regional and local – and markets. Companies active in developing countries should think about establishing specialist organisations to help governments become more effective in certain areas – such as combating crime, or education and training – that are vital for business. They should also think about how to introduce information and new ideas about business and national development into public debates.

Companies need to think hard about their role in policy reform and social change, and reflect on business successes and failures in influencing policy, in that country and globally. Business leaders need to develop strategies for how to engage in public debate and influence the terms of that debate, as well as how to handle interaction 'behind the scenes' with government, and how best to marry the two. The delicate balance between 'the helping hand' of companies and the need to talk truth to power needs careful thought and management. And where corporate malfeasance is discovered, business leaders and organisations need to speak out quickly and clearly, spelling out the desired approach by companies. For example, when companies are found guilty of anti-competitive behaviour it is important that corporate leaders do not keep quiet, thus giving the appearance that they only speak out when it is government policy or actions that need fixing.

CONCLUDING REMARKS

There is a global battle of ideas about business and its role in society. In this theatre, many business leaders have been less than effective. Instead of using their influence and resources to argue the case for business, they have been defensive, inept, and allowed others to determine the terms of debate.

They have hoped that if they keep their heads down they will be left alone. When that hasn't worked, they have adopted the language and many of the ideas of their opponents, and accepted a wide range of extraneous responsibilities as though what they do every day is harmful and needs recompense.

The battle for capitalism is ongoing and the contest over globalisation is entering a difficult period. If the largest companies in the world and the organisations they fund will not stand up for global markets, then who will? Or will they wait until the wolf is at the door?

Sociologist Peter Berger argues that capitalism as an institutional arrangement has lacked plausible myths – that market economies do not generate the ideas and images which inspire people to undertake acts of commitment and sacrifice. By contrast, socialism (or the left more generally) has been blessed with myth-generating potency. It has all the best slogans, T-shirts, and songs! He concludes that 'capitalism has a built-in incapacity to generate legitimations of itself, and it is particularly deprived of mythic potency; consequently it depends upon the legitimating effects of its sheer facticity, or upon association with other, non-economic legitimating symbols' (1986: 208).

In this context, business leaders need to stand up for the market economy. They need to participate, vigorously and confidently, in the battle of ideas about business and 'the good society'. They have a direct interest in this and in reshaping the framework within which the conversation about corporate citizenship and the role of companies in contributing to the public good is conducted.

The debate about corporate power and responsibility is vital because it bears on the role of market dynamics in the world economy and individual nations, the place of business organisations within the market, the relationship of both the market and business organisations with politics, the nature of development and modernisation, the best route out of poverty, and the relationship of all of this with the global community.

We need a new framework and a different, more positive, language for describing the contribution of business to social progress. A different lens is required to bring into focus the contribution of large multinational corporations in developing countries, which, in turn, illustrates the broader role of business in all societies; and to think about the rights and responsibilities of corporations in the 21st century.

Business leaders and their advisers need to build a more compelling, positive, and exciting set of ideas within which to locate companies as a part of the civil world. This means they need to stand up for business, stand up for globalisation, and stand up for markets and market-based approaches to dealing with poverty and development.

Only when we have such a framework will it be possible to correctly situate business misdeeds as aberrations rather than symptoms of the evil nature of corporations. What is vital is to explore the development problematic and place business, markets, civil society, and state actors within this frame; ensuring that the discussion affirms rather than undermines markets; and is developmentally sensible and economically rational.

I will allow myself a bit of hyperbole here: We must find a poetic (mytho-poetic, if you will) language to talk about capitalism and about business.

Capitalism has produced an ongoing revolution that has transformed the human condition, overwhelmingly for the better. Millions of people have been lifted from dehumanising poverty to a decent life, and this process is continuing today in one country after another. This revolution, while it does not automatically lead to democracy, creates strong democratising pressures. Simply put, the freedom of the marketplace is strongly related to the freedom of the ballot box – and thus to the expansion of human liberties and human rights – and what poetry there is to that! As for business itself, it is the locale of high drama – innovation, risk-taking, and epic struggles in the course of what Schumpeter called the 'creative destruction' of capitalism. Poetry indeed!

Why has this poetry not been reflected in the writing and teaching of contemporary cultural elites? These elites emerge from an anti-capitalist, anti-business tradition since its inception in the bohemian intelligentsia of the early 19th century. In a curious way, this intelligentsia apes the attitudes of the old aristocracy – anti-bourgeois, looking down at the grubby activities of people 'in trade'.

It is time to break with this tradition. Business people are not likely to be poets or for that matter intellectuals of any sort, just as the latter would make lousy business people. In the meantime, though, they can stand up for what they do, and do this in the genre that is congenial to them – in prose. The facts are on their side.

LIST OF REFERENCES

AngloGold Ashanti.

—2006a. *Annual Report 2006*. http://www.anglogoldashanti.com

—2006b. *Report to Society 2006*. http://www.anglogoldashanti.com

BankTrack. Online. About BankTrack. http://www.banktrack.org/show/pages/about_banktrack

Basker, Emek. 2005. Selling a cheap mousetrap: Wal-Mart's effect on retail prices. *Journal of Urban Economics,* 58 (2). September.

Baue, William. 2004. Are the Equator Principles sincere or spin? *Sustainability Investment News: Social Funds.* 4 June.

Beattie, Alan. 2004. World Bank chiefs reject proposal to quit oil and coal finance. *Financial Times.* 3 February.

Beaumont, Val. Executive Director, Innovative Medicines South Africa. Personal communication with author.

Berger, Peter L.

—1969. *A Rumour of Angels: Modern Society and the Rediscovery of the Supernatural.* United Kingdom: Penguin Books.

—1986. *The Capitalist Revolution: Fifty Propositions about Prosperity, Equality and Liberty.* New York: Basic Books.

Bernstein, Ann and Peter L Berger, (eds). 1998. *Business and Democracy: Cohabitation or Contradiction?* London: Cassell Academic.

Bernstein, Ann.

—1998. South Africa: normative conflicts, social cohesion and mediating institutions. In Peter L Berger (ed), *The Limits of Social Cohesion: Conflict and Mediation in Pluralist Societies.* Boulder, Colorado: Westview Press.

—2005. Learning from 'edu-preneurs'. *Business Day*. 23 November.

Bhagwati, Jagdish.

—2004a. *In Defence of Globalization*. Oxford: Oxford University Press.

—2004b. *Do MNCs Hurt Poor Countries?* American Enterprise Institute. June.

Bluestone, Barry and Bennett Harrison. 1982. *The Deindustrialization of America: Plant Closings, Community Abandonment, and the Dismantling of Basic Industry*. New York: Basic Books.

Brainard, Lael.

—2005. *Investing in Knowledge for Development: The Role of Science and Technology in the Fight against Global Poverty*. Washington DC: Brookings Institution.

—2006. *Transforming the Development Landscape: The Role of the Private Sector*. Washington DC: Brookings Institution Press.

Brooke, James. 2000. Canada's anti-corporate crusader. *The New York Times*. 3 April.

Brown, Justin. 2007. Mining laws to be cut to win investors: SA lags resource economies on investment. *Business Report*. 7 February.

Browne, Harry. 2001. Who makes life better for you? *World Daily Net*. 29 May. http://www.wnd.com/news/article.asp?ARTICLE_ID=23001

Browne, John.

—1998. *International Relations: The New Agenda for Business*. The 1998 Elliot Lecture, St Anthony's College, Oxford. 4 June.

—2004. Powers and Responsibilities – The Role of Corporations in Human Progress. Taplin Environmental Lecture, Princeton Environmental Institute. 4 October. http://www.bp.com/generic article.do?categoryId=98&contentId=7001429

Business Action for Africa. Online. Introduction. http://www. businessactionforafrica.org/about_eng_whatisBAA.htm

Business for Social Responsibility, USA. The Wider Picture. *RasGas Magazine*. Issue 20, Autumn 2007. http://www.rasgas.com/files/articles/RG20_English_30.31.pdf

Business Roundtable. 2000. *Corporate Social Responsibility in China: Practices by US Companies*. February.

Centre for Development and Enterprise (CDE).

—1996a. *Business and Democracy: Cohabitation or contradiction?* Development and Democracy: The role of business series, Number 10. May. Johannesburg.

—1996b. *Cities and the Global Economy: New Challenges for South Africa*. The Big Cities Series, No 3. October. Johannesburg.

—2002. *Johannesburg: Africa's World City*. CDE Research: Policy in the Making, No 11. October. Johannesburg.

—2004. *Key to Growth: Supporting South Africa's Emerging Entrepreneurs*. CDE Research: Policy in the Making, No 12. June. Johannesburg.

—2005a. *Private Schooling for the Poor?* CDE In Depth, Issue 3. November.

—2005b. *Land Reform in South Africa: A 21st Century Perspective*. CDE Research, No 14. June. Johannesburg.

—2005c. *Why Globalisation Works*. New Frontiers, Issue 3, February: Johannesburg.

—2007. *Doubling for Growth: Addressing the Maths and Science Challenge in South Africa's Schools*. CDE Research No 15: Johannesburg.

—2008. *Farmers' Voices: Practical Perspectives on Land Reform and Agricultural Development*. CDE Round Table No 9. February. Johannesburg.

Chandler, Alfred D. Jr. 1992. Managerial enterprise and competitive capabilities. *Business History*. 34 (1). January.

Christensen, J. 2004. Asking the do-gooders to prove they do good. *The New York Times*. 3 January.

Clay, Jason. 2005. *Exploring the Links between International Business and Poverty Reduction: A Case Study of Unilever in Indonesia.* An Oxfam GB, Novib (Oxfam Netherlands), Unilever and Unilever Indonesia joint research project. Eynsham, UK: Information Press.

Commission for Africa. 2004. Overview of evidence. Secretariat paper presented to the first meeting of the Commission on 4 May. http://www.commissionforafrica.org/english/about/meetings/first/trends_and_evidence.pdf

Corporate Social Responsibility Initiative (CSRI). 2004. *Leadership, Accountability and Partnership: Critical Trends and Issues in Corporate Social Responsibility.* Cambridge, MA: John F Kennedy School of Government, Harvard University. Report of the Launch Event: 4 March.

Davies, Robert and Jane Nelson. 2003. *The Buck Stops Where? Managing the Boundaries of Business Engagement in Global Development Challenges.* IBLF Policy Paper No 2. International Business Leaders Forum.

Davis, Ian. 2005. The biggest contract. *The Economist.* 28 May.

Deneys Reitz Attorneys. 2007/08. *Doing Business in South Africa 2007-08.* http://www.deneysreitz.co.za/images/news/Doing_Business_in_SA_2007.pdf

Dhanarajan, Sumi. 2005. Managing ethical standards: when rhetoric meets reality. *Development in Practice,* 15 (3&4). June. Oxfam Organisation: Routledge Press.

Diamondfacts.org. Website of the World Diamond Council (WDC). Diamondfact #19. http://diamondfacts.org/facts/fact_19.html

—Economic impact: generating revenues. http://www.diamondfacts.org/difference/economic_impact.html

—Educational improvements. http://www.diamondfacts.org/difference/educational_improvements.html

—Testimonial by Thomas Tlou. http://diamondfacts.org/pdfs/media/perspectives/opinion_pieces_testimonials/Tlou.pdf

Donaldson, Thomas. 2005. Defining the value of doing good

business. *Financial Times.* 2 June.

Driessen, Paul. 2003. *Eco-Imperialism: Green Power, Black Death.* Washington DC: Free Enterprise Press.

Drucker, Peter Ferdinand. 1954. *The Practice of Management.* Ann Arbor, Michigan: University of Michigan.

Easterly, William R.

—2001. *The Elusive Quest for Growth: Economists' adventures and misadventures in the tropics.* Cumberland: MIT Press.

—2006. *The White Man's Burden: Why the West's efforts to aid the rest have done so much ill and so little good.* New York: The Penguin Press.

—2007. Africa's poverty trap. *Wall Street Journal.* 23 March.

Ebell, Myron. 2004. Illarionov explains Russian position on Kyoto Protocol. *Cooler Heads Digest*, VIII (3). 13 February. Washington DC: Competitive Enterprise Institute.

Eenhoorn, Hans. 2004. *Millennium Development Goals: The Contribution of Responsible Business to Sustainable Development.* Commonwealth Business Council Conference, Royal Institute of International Affairs. 15 July. http://www.unilever.com/Images/Millennium%20Development%20Goals_tcm13-5517.pdf

Eisenberg, P. 2000. Why charities think they can regulate themselves. *Chronicle of Philanthropy.* 4 May.

Engineering News. 2006. EIAs: government's scapegoat. 3 November.

Entine, Jon. 2006. Globalisation trumps microfinance evangelism. *Ethical Corporation Magazine.* December.

Ethical Corporation Institute. 2007. *Corporate Responsibility, Maturing Innovation: A Sector-by-sector Guide to Voluntary Initiatives.* Special Report. March.

European Commission. Online. Corporate social responsibility. http://ec.europa.eu/enterprise/csr/index_en.htm

Fitzgerald, Niall and Mandy Cormack. 2006. *The Role of Business in Society: An Agenda for Action.* John F Kennedy School of Government, Harvard University; The Conference Board; The

International Business Leaders Forum. http://www.iblf.org/docs/ CGIRoleofBusiness.pdf

Fitzgerald, Niall. 2003. *CSR: Rebuilding Trust in Business – A Perspective on Corporate Responsibility in the 21st Century.* Distinguished Speaker Series. Unilever and The London Business School. October.

Florini, Ann. 2003. Capitalism and its critics. Transcripts of an IMF Book Forum, 9 September. Washington DC: International Monetary Fund. http://www.imf.org/external/np/tr/2003/ tr030909a.htm

Fortune.

—2005a. A meditation on risk: the lessons of the storm. *Fortune Magazine,* 152 (7). 3 October.

—2005b. The only lifeline was the Wal-Mart. *Fortune Magazine,* 152 (7). 3 October.

Friedman, Milton. 1970. The social responsibility of business is to increase its profits. *The New York Times Magazine.* 13 September.

Friedman, Tom L. 2006. *The World is Flat: The Globalised World in the Twenty-First Century.* London: Penguin Books.

Geneen, Harold. 2001. Corporate Social Responsibility can do wonders for your brand. *Financial Times.* 5 October.

Giraud, Lucie and Corrie Shanahan. 2006. *IFC Adopts New Environmental and Social Standards.* Washington DC: The International Finance Corporation.

Glewwe, Paul. 2000. Are foreign owned businesses in Vietnam really sweatshops? *Minnesota Agricultural Economist,* 701. Summer.

Global Business Coalition on HIV/AIDS, Tuberculosis and Malaria. 2007. Business as usual is not enough, Advertisement in the *Financial Times.* 1-2 December.

Godsell, Bobby and A Fourie. 2007. Matters of the heart for private SA. *Business Day.* 9 July.

Godsell, Bobby. 2007. AngloGold Ashanti in Africa. Address to the Indaba African Mining Conference, Johannesburg, South Africa.

6 February.

Godsell, Robert Michael. 2006. Unpublished manuscript. Johannesburg.

Gore, Al and David Blood. 2006. For people and planet. *San Francisco Chronicle.* 4 April.

Gray, Rob, Jan Bebbington and David Collison. 2006. NGOs, civil society and accountability: making the people accountable to capital. *Accounting, Auditing & Accountability Journal,* 19 (3), 319-48.

Gross, Daniel. 2005. Don't look now ... here comes inflation. *Slate Magazine.* 5 October.

Hayek, Friedrich A. 1945. The use of knowledge in society. *The American Review,* 35 (4). September.

Heineman, Ben W Jr. 2005. Are you a good corporate citizen? *Wall Street Journal.* 28 June.

Henderson, David.

—2001. *Misguided Virtue: False Notions of Corporate Social Responsibility.* United Kingdom: The Institute of Economic Affairs.

—2004. *The Role of Business in the Modern World: Progress, Pressures and Prospects for the Market Economy.* Washington DC: Competitive Enterprise Institute.

Hewko, John. 2002. *Foreign Direct Investment: Does the Rule of Law Matter?* Carnegie Paper no 26. Democracy and Rule of Law Program, Carnegie Endowment for International Peace. April. http://www.carnegieendowment.org/publications/index.cfm?fa= view&id=952&prog=zgp&proj=zdrl,zted

Hilton, Steve and Giles Gibbons. 2005. *Good Business: Your World Needs You.* New York: Texere Publishing. http://www.unilever. com/Images/A%20Perspective%20on%20Corporate%20 Social%20Responsibility%20in%20the%2021st%20Century_ tcm13-5520.pdf

IDC. 2007. *White Paper: The Economic Impact of IT, Software, and the Microsoft ecosystem on the global economy.* October. Microsoft. http://www.microsoft.com/presspass/presskits/globalimpact/default.mspx

Ignatius, David. 2005. Corporate green. *Washington Post.* 11 May.

Institute of Business Ethics. Online. Frequently asked questions. http://www.s145828053.websitehome.co.uk/faq.htm

International Chamber of Commerce (ICC). 2004. *Standing up for the global economy: key facts, figures and arguments in support of globalisation.* http://www.iccwbo.org/home/statements_rules/statements/2004/Globalization%20paper%2004.pdf

International Finance Corporation (IFC).

—2000. *Paths out of Poverty: The Role of Private Enterprise in Developing Countries.* Washington DC: IFC Press.

—2007. Who benefits from the IFC's projects: profiles by industry. Development Effectiveness Unit. http://www.ifc.org/ifcext/devresultsinvestments.nsf/AttachmentsByTitle/IFC_DE_Stakeholders_by_Industry_Final1.pdf/$FILE/IFC_DE_Stakeholders_by_Industry_Final1.pdf

—2009a. Environmental and social standards. http://www.ifc.org/ifcext/sustainability.nsf/Content/EnvSocStandards

—2009b. IFC exclusion list. http://www.ifc.org/ifcext/disclosure.nsf/Content/IFCExclusionList

International Institute of Tropical Agriculture. 2002. *Child Labour in the Cocoa Sector of West Africa: A Synthesis of Findings in Cameroon, Cote d'Ivoire, Ghana and Nigeria.* August.

International Monetary Fund (IMF). 2003. Capitalism and its critics. Transcript of an IMF Book Forum. 9 September. http://www.imf.org/external/np/tr/2003/tr030909a.htm

International Rivers. Online. About International Rivers. http://internationalrivers.org/en/about-international-rivers

Jonah, Sam. 2005. Regenerating Africa. *Optima,* 51 (2). June. Johannesburg: Anglo American.

Kanter, Rosabeth Moss. 1999. From spare change to real change: the social sector as beta site for business innovation. *Harvard Business Review.* May- June.

Kelkar, Vijay. 2005. *India's Economic Future: Moving beyond State Capitalism.* 26 October. http://www.kelkar.net/images/ Moving%20Beyond%20State%20Capitalism%20-%20 Presentation.pdf

Khosla, Vinod. 2004. Speech delivered at the Global Business and Global Poverty Conference, 19 May, Stanford Graduate School of Business.

Kirby, Neil and Laura Sauer. 2006. *South Africa: New Environmental Law Regulation.* Werksman Incorporated.

Klein, Naomi. 2000. *No Logo: Taking Aim at the Brand Bullies.* USA: MacMillan Press.

Klein, Naomi. 2008. *The Shock Doctrine.* New York: Metropolitan Books.

Knight, Robin. 2000. Gaining street cred. *Time Magazine, Europe.* 157 (3). 22 January.

Kristof, Nicholas D. 2006. In praise of the maligned sweatshop. *The New York Times.* 6 June.

Krugman, Paul. 1997. In praise of cheap labour: bad jobs at bad wages are better than no jobs at all. *Slate Magazine.* 21 March.

Kyle, Beth and John Gerard Ruggie. 2005. *Corporate Social Responsibility as Risk Management: A Model for Multinationals.* Working Paper No 10, Corporate Social Responsibility Initiative. Cambridge, Massachusetts: John F Kennedy School of Government, Harvard University.

Lal, Deepak. 2005. The threat to economic liberty from international organisations. *Cato Journal*, 25 (3). Cato Institute.

Lambert, Richard. 2006. Speech to the Social Market Foundation, 5 September, in London, United Kingdom.

Legrain, Philip. 2002. *Open World: The Truth about Globalization.* New York: Abacus.

Leith, Sam. 2000. No Logo: Naomi Klein. *The Guardian.* 23 January.

382

Lewis, Charles Paul. 2005. *How the East was Won: The Impact of Multinational Companies on Eastern Europe and the Former Soviet Union.* New York: Palgrave MacMillan.

Lichtenstein, Nelson (ed). 2006. *Wal-Mart: The Face of Twenty-First-Century Capitalism.* New York: The New Press.

Lim, Linda. 2000. *My factory visits in Southeast Asia and UM code and monitoring.* Gerald R Ford School of Public Policy, University of Michigan. http://www.fordschool.umich.edu/rsie/acit/Documents/LimNotes00.pdf

Litvin, Daniel. 2003. *Empires of Profit: Commerce, Conquest and Corporate Responsibility.* New York: Texere Press.

MacKay, Graham. 2005. The critical importance of the hard business case. *Financial Times.* 14 September.

MacLeod, Fiona. 2006. Mbeki joins assault on green laws. *Mail & Guardian.* 7 August.

Mallaby, Sebastian.

—2004. *The World's Banker: A Story of Failed States, Financial Crises, and the Wealth and Poverty of Nations.* New York: The Penguin Press.

—2005. Progressive Wal-Mart. Really. *Washington Post.* 28 November.

Manheim, Jarol B.

—2001. *The Death of a Thousand Cuts: Corporate Campaigns and the Attack on the Corporation.* Mahwah, New Jersey: Lawrence Erlbaum Associates.

—2004. *Biz-War and the Out-of-Power Elite: The Progressive-Left Attack on the Corporation.* Mahwah, New Jersey: Lawrence Erlbaum Associates.

McCloskey, Deirdre N. 2006. *The Bourgeois Virtues: Ethics for an Age of Commerce.* Chicago: University of Chicago Press.

McCraw, Thomas K. 2007. *Prophet of Innovation: Joseph Schumpeter and Creative Destruction.* Cambridge, Massachusetts: The Belknap Press, Harvard University Press.

McCully, Patrick. 2001. The use of a trilateral network: an activist's perspective on the formation of the World Commission on Dams. *American University International Law Review,* 16 (6).

McMillan, John. 2002. *Reinventing the Bazaar: A Natural History of Markets.* New York: W W Norton.

Medved, Michael. 1992. *Hollywood vs America: Popular Culture and the War on Traditional Values.* New York: Harper Collins.

Meredith, Robyn. 2007. *The Elephant and the Dragon: The Rise of India and China and What It Means for All of Us.* New York: W W Norton.

Micklethwait, John and Adrian Wooldridge. 2005. *The Company: A Short History of a Revolutionary Idea.* London: Random House Publishing Group.

Miller, John J. 2006. *A Gift of Freedom: How the John M Olin Foundation Changed America.* Lanham, Maryland: Encounter Books.

Milloy, Steven J. 2007. *Unsustainable environmentalism.* Competitive Enterprise Institute. 17 February. http://cei.org/gencon/019,05789.cfm.

Mitra, Amit. 2003. Secretary-General of the Federation of Indian Chambers of Commerce and Industry. Personal communication.

Moore, Mike. 2003. *A World Without Walls: Freedom, Development, Free Trade and Global Governance.* Cambridge: Cambridge University Press.

Moran, Mary, Anne-Laure Ropars, Javier Guzman, Jose Diaz and Christopher Garrison. 2005. *The New Landscape of Neglected Disease Drug Development.* Pharmaceutical R&D Policy Project, The London School of Economics and Political Science.

Moran, Theodore H. 2002. *Beyond Sweatshops: Foreign Direct Investment and Globalization in Developing Countries.* Washington DC: Brookings Institution Press.

Muller, Jerry Z. 2003. *The Mind and the Market: Capitalism in Western Thought.* New York: Anchor Books.

Murray, Sarah. 2004. Developing countries: social issues gain importance. *Financial Times.* 29 November.

Narayan, Deepa with Raj Patel, Kai Schafft, Anne Rademacher and Sarah Koch-Schulte. 1999. *Can Anyone Hear Us? Voices from 47 Countries.* New York: World Bank, Oxford University Press.

Narayan, Deepa. 1999. *Voices of the Poor: A 23-Country Study for the WDR 2000/01 on Poverty.* Washington DC: World Bank.

Nelson, Jane. 2006. *Leveraging the Development Impact of Business in the Fight against Global Poverty.* Working Paper No 22. Corporate Social Responsibility Initiative, John F Kennedy School of Government, Harvard University. http://www.hks.harvard.edu/ m-rcbg/CSRI/publications/workingpaper_22_nelson.pdf

Nichols, Nick. 2002. *Rules for Corporate Warriors: How to Fight and Survive Attack Group Shakedowns.* United States of America: Free Enterprise Press.

Noland, Marcus and J Brooks Spencer. 2006. *The Stuff of Legends: Diamonds and Development in Southern Africa.* Johannesburg: Business Leadership South Africa.

Norberg, Johan.

—2003a. *Why corporations shouldn't be socially responsible: a critical examination of CSR.* Keynote address at the conference 'Managing on the Edge', organised by the Dutch National Research Network on Corporate Social Responsibility, University of Nijmegen, The Netherlands, 25 September.

—2003b. *In Defence of Global Capitalism.* Washington, DC: Cato Institute.

—2004. Three cheers for global capitalism. *The American Enterprise.* 1 April.

Novak, Michael.

—1996a. *The Future of the Corporation.* Washington, DC: The American Enterprise Institute Press.

—1996b. *Business as a Calling: Work and the Examined Life.* New York: The Free Press.

—1997a. *The Fire of Invention: Civil Society and the Future of the*

Corporation. New York: Rowman & Littlefield.

—1997b. *On Corporate Governance: The Corporation as It Ought to Be*. Washington, DC: American Enterprise Institute.

O'Dowd, Michael C. 1996. *The O'Dowd Thesis and the Triumph of Democratic Capitalism*. Plano, Texas: The Free Market Foundation.

openDemocracy. 2003. *Masters of the Universe?* openDemocracy roundtable discussion with Martin Wolf, Sophia Tickell, Malini Mehra and Tom Burke. 10 April. http://www.opendemocracy.net/theme_7-corporations/article_1141.jsp

Oppenheimer, Nicky. 2007. *Why Africa Will Succeed*. Speech delivered to the Royal United Services Institute for Defence and Strategic Studies (RUSI), 31 May, London. *New African*. July. http://www.africasia.com/newafrican/na.php?ID=1386&back_month=071

Peking University, Tsinghua University, and University of South Carolina. 2000. *Economic Impact of the Coca-Cola System on China*. August. Columbia, South Carolina: Moore School of Business, University of South Carolina. http://mooreschool.sc.edu/export/sites/default/moore/research/presentstudy/Coca-Cola/China/china.full.aug.pdf

Pharmaceutical Research and Manufacturers of America (PhRMA). 2007. Press release. Washington DC. 12 February.

Phillips, Michael M and Mitchell Pacelle. 2003. Banks accept environment rules: Citicorp, Barclays, others to shun projects that harm environment and livelihoods. *The Wall Street Journal*. 4 June.

Pollan, Michael. 2007. *The Omnivore's Dilemma: A Natural History of Four Meals*. New York: Penguin Press.

Poole, William T. 1982. The *Environmental Complex: Part III*. Washington DC: The Heritage Foundation. June.

Porter, Michael E and Mark R Kramer. 2006. Strategy and society: the link between competitive advantage and corporate social responsibility. *Harvard Business Review.* December.

Prahalad, C. K. 2006. *The Fortune at the Bottom of the Pyramid: Eradicating Poverty Through Profits.* Philadelphia: Wharton School Publishing.

Reason. 2005. Rethinking the social responsibility of business: a *Reason* debate featuring Milton Friedman, Whole Foods' John Mackay, and Cypress Semiconductor's J T Rodgers. October. www.reason.com/news/show/32239.html

Romer, Paul M. 1992. Two strategies for economic development: using ideas and producing ideas. In *Proceedings of the World Bank Annual Conference on Development Economics.* Washington DC: World Bank.

Ruggie, John G.

—2004a. Creating Public Value: Everybody's Business. Speech presented to the Herrhausen Society, 15 March, Frankfurt, Germany.

—2004b. TINA and global responsibility. *The Globalist* (online). 6 September. http://www.theglobalist.com/StoryId. aspx?StoryId=4054

SABMiller. 2007. *Annual Report 2007.* http://www.sabmiller.com/files/reports/ar2007/index.html

Sachs, Jeffery.

—2005a. *The End of Poverty: Economic Possibilities for our Time.* New York: Penguin Press.

—2005b. What I did on my summer vacation. *Esquire.* 1 December.

Santoro, Michael A and Thomas M Gorrie (eds). 2005. *Ethics and the Pharmaceutical Industry.* New York: Cambridge University Press.

Santoro, Michael A. 2000. *Profits and Principles: Global Capitalism and Human Rights in China.* Ithaca, New York: Cornell University Press.

Schoenberger, Karl. 2000. *Levi's Children: Coming to Terms with Human Rights in the Global Marketplace.* New York: Grove Press.

Sobel, Russell S and Andrea M Dean. 2008. Has Wal-Mart buried

Mom and Pop? The impact of Wal-Mart on self-employment and small establishments in the United States. *Economic Inquiry*, 46(4). October. http://www.be.wvu.edu/div/econ/work/pdf_files/06-05.pdf

South African National Government. 1998. *National Environmental Management Act. Acts Online*. http://www.acts.co.za/ntl_enviro_man/index.htm

South African National Treasury. 2009. Budget Speech by the Minister of Finance, Trevor Manuel. 11 February. http://www.info.gov.za/speeches/2009/09021114561001.htm

Sternberg, Elaine. 2000. *Just Business: Business Ethics in Action*. Oxford: Oxford University Press.

SUDEO International Business Consultants. 2007. *Research Report for the Infrastructure Inputs Sector Strategy*. Commissioned by The Presidency, Republic of South Africa. 21 May.

Talisman Energy Inc. 2000. *Corporate Social Responsibility Report 2000: Sudan Operations*.

Taurel, Sidney. 2005. The campaign against innovation. In Michael A Santoro and Thomas M Gorrie (eds), *Ethics and the Pharmaceutical Industry*. New York: Cambridge University Press.

Taylor, Peter Shawn. 2004. Dirty Gold…? *National Post* (Canada). 5 August.

The Economist.

—2002. Corporate social responsibility: lots of it about. 12 December.

—2004. Two-faced capitalism. 24 January.

—2005a. The good company. 20 January.

—2005b. Profit and the public good: a survey of corporate social responsibility. 25 January.

—2006a. Voting with your trolley. Special Report: Food Politics. 9 December.

—2006b. Business and Society: The search for talent. 5 October.

—2007a. Global poverty. 5 July.

—2007b. Poverty: taking stock – the world is winning its fight, mostly. 6 July.

The Equator Principles. Online. The Equator Principles: A financial industry benchmark for determining, assessing and managing social & environmental risk in project financing. http://www.equator-principles.com/principles.shtml

Theil, Stefan. 2008. Europe's school books demonise enterprise. *Financial Times*. 8 January.

Tooley, James. 2006. *Educating Amaretch: Private Schools for the Poor and the New Frontier for Investors*. International Finance Corporation. http://www.ifc.org/ifcext/economics.nsf/AttachmentsByTitle/educating_amaretch_gold_essay.pdf/$FILE/educating_amaretch_gold_essay.pdf

UN Millennium Project.

—2004. *Millennium Development Goals Needs Assessment: Methodology. September*. http://www.unmillenniumproject.org/documents/MDG-needs-assessment-methodology-Nov7-04.pdf

—2005a. *Investing in Development: A Practical Plan to Achieve the Millennium Development Goals. Final Report*. http://www.unmillenniumproject.org/reports/index.htm

—2005b. *Investing in Development: A Practical Plan to Achieve the Millennium Development Goals. Overview*. http://www.unmillenniumproject.org/reports/index.htm

—2006. *Interdependence of Investment Clusters: Country Processes*. http://www.unmillenniumproject.org/reports/country_proc4.htm

Unilever. 2007. *Environment: we love it, we take care of it*. Unilever Online. http://www.unilever.com.br/Images/MeioAmbiente-ingles_tcm95-95565.pdf

United Nations (UN). 2006. *The Millennium Development Goals Report 2006*. New York: United Nations. http://mdgs.un.org/unsd/mdg/Resources/Static/Products/Progress2006/MDGReport2006.pdf

United Nations Conference on Trade and Development

(UNCTAD). 2008. *The growth of 'South-South' trade: it's not just the geography but the content that matters.* Press release, Geneva, 2 April.

United Nations Development Programme (UNDP). 2004. *Unleashing Entrepreneurship: Making Business Work for the Poor.* Report of the Commission on the Private Sector and Development. http://www.undp.org/cpsd/report/index.html

United States Government Accountability Office. 2005. *Globalization: Numerous Federal Activities Complement US Business's Global Corporate Social Responsibility Efforts.* 8 August. http://www.gao.gov/products/GAO-05-744

US Small Business Administration. 2008. Frequently Asked Questions. http://www.sba.gov/advo/stats/sbfaq.pdf

Vedder, Richard and Wendell Cox. 2006. *The Wal-Mart Revolution: How Big-Box Stores Benefit Consumers, Workers, And The Economy.* Washington, DC: The American Enterprise Institution Press.

Vodafone. 2005. *Africa: The Impact of Mobile Phones.* The Vodafone Policy Paper Series, No 2. March. http://info.worldbank.org/etools/docs/library/152872/Vodafone%20Survey.pdf

Vogel, David. 2005. *The Market for Virtue: The Potential and Limits of Corporate Social Responsibility.* Washington, DC: Brookings Institution Press.

Warden, Staci. 2007. *Joining the Fight against Global Poverty: A Menu for Corporate Engagement.* Washington DC: Centre for Global Development.

Webb, Mariaan. 2007. Van Schalkwyk dismisses appeals against new coal-fired power station. *Engineering News.* 4 May.

Webb, Tobias. 2006. UN global compact: financial markets the next big target. *Ethical Corporation Magazine.* June.

Wikipedia. Online. Non-governmental organisations. http://en.wikipedia.org/wiki/Non-governmental_organization#cite_note-0

Wolf, Martin.

—2004. *Corporate Responsibility*. New Zealand Business Roundtable. December. http://www.nzbr.org.nz/documents/publications/publications-2004/corporate_responsibility.pdf

—2005. *Why Globalization Works*. New Haven: Yale University Press.

World Bank.

—2002. *Global Economic Prospects 2002: Making Trade Work for the World's Poor*. Washington DC. http://www.worldbank.org/

—2003a. *Water Resources Sector Strategy: Strategic Directions for World Bank Engagement*. Washington DC.

—2003b. *Striking a Better Balance: The Extractive Industries Review*. http://www.worldbank.org/

—2005. *Doing Business in 2005: Removing Obstacles to Growth*. http://rru.worldbank.org/Documents/DoingBusiness/DB-2005-Overview.pdf

World Business Council for Sustainable Development (WBCSD).

—2004. *Doing Business with the Poor: A Field Guide*. Geneva. March. http://www.wbcsd.org/web/publications/sl-field-guide.pdf

—2006. *From Challenge to Opportunity: The Role of Business in Tomorrow's Society*. Geneva. February. http://www.wbcsd.org/DocRoot/CZ2dt8wQCfZKX2S0wxMP/tomorrows-leaders.pdf

World Commission on Dams. 2000. *Dams and Development: A New Framework for Development*. London: Earthscan.

World Economic Forum (WEF). 2005. *Partnering for Success: Business Perspectives on Multi-stakeholder Partnerships*. Geneva. http://www.weforum.org/pdf/ppp.pdf

World Wildlife Fund, UK (WWF-UK) and Freshwater Action Network. 2003. *Proceedings of 'World Commission on Dams – two years on: a seminar for UK stakeholders'*. 24 January.

Yawitch, Joanne. 2007. *Proposed Amendments to the National Environment Management Act (NEMA), 1998*. Department of Environmental Affairs and Tourism. October.

Zedillo, Ernesto. 2005. A trade fiction. *Forbes Magazine*. 19 September.

SELECTED INDEX